Developing Scholars

Developing Scholars

Race, Politics, and the Pursuit
of Higher Education

DOMINGO MOREL

OXFORD
UNIVERSITY PRESS

OXFORD
UNIVERSITY PRESS

Oxford University Press is a department of the University of Oxford. It furthers the University's objective of excellence in research, scholarship, and education by publishing worldwide. Oxford is a registered trade mark of Oxford University Press in the UK and certain other countries.

Published in the United States of America by Oxford University Press
198 Madison Avenue, New York, NY 10016, United States of America.

Library of Congress Cataloging-in-Publication Data
Names: Morel, Domingo, author.
Title: Developing scholars : race, politics, and the pursuit of higher education / Domingo Morel.
Description: First Edition. | New York : Oxford University Press, [2023] | Includes bibliographical references and index.
Identifiers: LCCN 2022053500 (print) | LCCN 2022053501 (ebook) | ISBN 9780197637005 (Paperback) | ISBN 9780197636992 (Hardback) | ISBN 9780197637036 | ISBN 9780197637029 (epub)
Subjects: LCSH: Affirmative action programs in education—United States. | Affirmative action programs in education—Government policy—United States. | Protest movements—United States—History—20th century. | Social movements—United States—History—20th century. | Educational equalization—United States. | Education and state—United States. | Discrimination in education—United States.
Classification: LCC LC213.52 .M66 2023 (print) | LCC LC213.52 (ebook) | DDC 379.2/60973—dc23/eng/20221206
LC record available at https://lccn.loc.gov/2022053500
LC ebook record available at https://lccn.loc.gov/2022053501

DOI: 10.1093/oso/9780197636992.001.0001

9 8 7 6 5 4 3 2 1

Paperback printed by Marquis, Canada
Hardback printed by Bridgeport National Bindery, Inc., United States of America

To Pedro

And to the 43 students who were part of the first summer program for "disadvantaged youth" at the University of Rhode Island in 1968.

CONTENTS

TABLES

Introduction

Graduation Day

On Sunday, May 17, 1998, the *Providence Journal* ran a front-page feature on Matthew Buchanan. Like many local newspapers across the country in the month of May, the *Providence Journal* featured Matthew as part of their college graduation coverage. Matt, as his family and friends call him, who on that day graduated with a bachelor's degree from the University of Rhode Island, was an unlikely graduate of the state's flagship university.

Born in 1976 in Providence, Rhode Island, Matt is the youngest child of Joan and Joseph Buchanan. "Joe Buck," as his father is known, has been a long-time community activist in Providence who has advocated for tenants' rights, voting rights, and city employment for African Americans, among many other issues. The family grew up in poverty and lived in the Roger Williams Housing Project in Providence. In the 1980s, the projects, like many urban communities throughout the United States, were ravaged by crack cocaine. Matt's family was deeply affected by the crack epidemic of the 1980s.

On December 22, 1986, when Matt was 10 years old, an altercation between his father and several men outside the projects nearly took Matt's life. That evening, Matt and his older brother were in their bunk beds when gunfire began to spread into their bedroom in the second-floor apartment. Just moments earlier, Matt's father had had an argument with

Developing Scholars. Domingo Morel, Oxford University Press. © Oxford University Press 2023.
DOI: 10.1093/oso/9780197636992.003.0001

several men who were smoking crack outside their building and told them to leave. The men returned and started shooting at the Buchanan apartment. The *Providence Journal* article stated that Matt

> remembers his father padding into the bedroom shouting, "Get down! Get down!"
>
> He remembers his big brother rolling off the bottom bunk and scooting from the room. And he remembers dropping from the top bunk then collapsing onto the bottom bed clutching his gut. The gunfire stopped. The cold of a mid-December night poured through the shattered window of the bedroom where a 10-year-old boy lay wounded. Buchanan's mother, Joan, knelt over him. "Are you all right," she asked. He whispered, "I have a stomachache." Mrs. Buchanan hugged her boy, and her hand felt the warmth of his blood. "Get help!" she said. "Hurry up!"
>
> Now, 11 years later, Matt Buchanan still carries a piece of that bullet in his gut.[1]

Matt survived the life-threatening bullet wound. Then, in 1993, as he was getting ready to start his senior year in high school, tragedy struck again. As the *Providence Journal* wrote:

> On a Friday night in September, 1993, Buchanan's 18-year-old cousin Douglas Buchanan went to a party. There were 50 or 60 people there with a DJ and music. Shortly before midnight, Douglas had a brief argument with another teen. The harsh words never even turned to punches before the other guy pulled a pistol and shot Douglas through the eye. He was dead before the ambulance arrived.

Douglas Buchanan, who was less than a year older and like a brother to Matt, was killed. Matt was supposed to be at the party with his cousin that evening. He recalls his cousin's death taking a bigger emotional toll on him than his own shooting. At age 18, he understood the significance of his cousin's death, the violence that surrounded him, and the grief his family felt in ways he was unable to understand at age 10, when he was shot.

Despite the many challenges, and the near loss of his life, Matt graduated from high school and went on to college where he earned a bachelor's degree in human development and family studies from the University of Rhode Island in 1998. Although several barriers would prevent him from earning an undergraduate degree in education, the degree he was interested in pursuing, years later he would earn a master's degree in education. After working in various positions in several schools in Providence, including teaching, advising, and assistant principalship, in the fall of 2019 he became principal of Hope High School in Providence.

Matt's educational and professional achievements, despite the personal and familial tragedies and the anguish that poverty and racism inflicted on him and his community, are a testament to his perseverance. However, what the *Providence Journal* did not mention in the article was that Matt was able to attend the University of Rhode Island because of the support of a college access program called Talent Development (TD).

TALENT DEVELOPMENT PROGRAM

On a fall day in 1993, two recruiters, Leo DiMaio and Frank Forleo, visited Central High School, where Matt Buchanan was a senior, to speak to an auditorium full of seniors about the TD Program. DiMaio and Forleo told the audience of students that although the idea of attending the University of Rhode Island was not considered a reality for many of the students in the auditorium—an auditorium where nearly 100 percent of the students were Black and Latino, poor, and would be first in their families to go to college—the program would offer an opportunity to gain admission even if they did not meet the regular admission requirements.

They were direct with the students by acknowledging that the university's admission requirements, a high B average in a college-prep curriculum, and an average Scholastic Aptitude Test (SAT) score between 1000 and 1100, was out of reach to many students in the auditorium.

Indeed, the average SAT score for a senior graduating from Central High School in 1994 was closer to 800, making them ineligible for admission to the University.[2] Despite this, DiMaio and Forleo said that the program was created to give an opportunity to students who did not meet these requirements, and that is why they were at Central High School that day, as they would be at other urban high schools in Rhode Island that fall. The recruiters said that the program would not only help students get into the University, but they would also provide financial assistance to ensure that students had the financial aid they needed to graduate from the university. Moreover, they said the program would provide academic support and advising to make sure students were taking the right classes to graduate in addition to receiving the emotional support that they would need as they made their journeys through college as first-generation college students.

That recruitment visit convinced Matt that he could attend the University of Rhode Island and Rene Bailey, a Black teacher who mentored him and many other students at Central High School, encouraged him to apply. With the help of Gerald Williams and Brian Scott, two counselors at Central High School, Matt applied to the program. Early in 1994 he learned that he was accepted to the Talent Development Program at the University of Rhode Island. That spring, he joined the rest of the TD incoming class in attending preparatory classes one evening a week. Then, on Sunday, June 19, 1994, two days after his high school graduation, Matt Buchanan began to attend college at the University of Rhode Island.

RACE, POLITICS, AND THE PURSUIT
OF HIGHER EDUCATION

Although Matt had to overcome significant challenges to attend and graduate from college, the program that helped Matt also had to overcome significant challenges. The program was created in 1968, at a moment of social and political upheaval in the United States, as an effort to address enduring racial and economic inequalities. However, despite its success in providing opportunities to students who were not considered "college ready," only a few years after its creation, the program faced threats to its survival. Disinvestment in state support for public higher education and attacks on affirmative action, among other issues, created the political climate for withdrawal of support for the program.

In the face of this ominous political climate, what helps explain the survival of the TD Program? How was the program able to overcome the political challenges that threatened its existence and allowed it to provide Matthew Buchanan and thousands of other students an opportunity to attend and graduate from the University decades after it was created?

In trying to understand the survival of the TD program, other questions emerge. Why was the program created in the first place, and how? What was the underlying philosophy that motivated the creation of a college access program for students of color who did not meet admissions requirements to a university? Since the program was designed specifically to provide opportunities to students of underrepresented groups, how is the program part of a broader history of affirmative action policies in the United States?

In answering these questions, the analysis of the TD Program provides a lens that reveals questions and puzzles, not just about the TD Program but about race and higher education, and American politics, more broadly. As this book will show, the program was created in the 1960s in response to demands by the Black community in Providence. But the program was not unique. Between 1966 and 1968, 14 states created similar programs, which served thousands of students of color, mostly African American. Moreover, we learn that the programs were driven by a radical vision of college access. The community activists who helped create these programs believed that by providing academic, financial, and emotional support to students, regardless of their past academic record, these students could become successful college students.

Their advocacy challenged conventions of merit and deservedness in the college admissions process. Additionally, they challenged conventional views of affirmative action policies, which focused on "selecting" or "identifying" high-achieving students of color to attend elite institutions of higher education. Instead, they argued for a *community-centered* approach to affirmative action, which focused on a logic of *developing scholars*, who can be supported at their local public institutions of higher education. As a result, we come to understand about alternative visions of affirmative action and higher education possibilities that have received less attention in the scholarship.

The book will also show that the urban uprisings of the 1960s did play a role in helping create the political conditions to create these college access programs. Community activists relied on the uprisings, and the threat of future uprisings, to convince policymakers to expand college access opportunities to Black students and other students of color. By showing how violent protest helped create the political conditions for policymakers to adhere to Black political demands, the book helps expand our understanding of the role of protest, and violent protest, in the process of policymaking.

Through an examination of the TD Program, we are also able to learn about the political factors that emerged to threaten these programs and public support for higher education in general. Between the 1970s and 1990s, state support for higher education decreased, which led to shrinking university budgets. Universities, facing budget cuts, decided to cut support for programs. In the 1980s, federal support for higher education, particularly for low-income students, also decreased. At the same time, legal and political challenges to affirmative action led universities to pull back on race-based admissions policies and programs. As a result, some programs became smaller while others were eliminated.

Despite these political challenges throughout the 1970s and 1980s, the TD Program was able to withstand them and provide an opportunity to students like Matthew Buchanan and others in the 1990s and beyond. In the chapters that follow, I will show that the program was able to grow because it has operated as a political organization that has relied on political relationships within the University and at the state level to respond to university and statewide challenges to the program over time.

Equally as important, when the program faced existential threats, like similar programs encountered in the 1970s and then again in the 1990s, TD students mobilized to defend the program by taking over university buildings and demanding the expansion of the program. In this respect, the organization has operated as an ongoing social movement that activates multiple approaches, including protest, in response to threats. By demonstrating how the program has been able to survive these political challenges through the use of protest, the book also contributes to our understanding of not only how policies are enacted but how they are maintained. Building on scholarship by political scientists like Jamila Michener, Mallory SoRelle, and Chloe Thurston (2020), who argue for a deviation from the elite-centered, "top-down" approach to understanding policy processes, this book shows how nonelite actors at the local level help sustain policies through protest.[3]

Finally, although the program has been able to respond to direct and indirect threats over time, an examination of the TD Program also reveals one major challenge that has proven elusive and difficult to overcome. Over time, TD students have found it increasingly difficult to graduate with degrees in education, business, nursing, and engineering. These professions have historically provided a path to the middle class. Indeed, research has shown that the growing difficulty to enter these professions is not unique to TD students. The gap between Whites and Black and Latino students who graduate in these majors has expanded over time.[4]

Scholars have attributed gaps in the selection of college majors to a number of factors including expanded opportunities to choose majors that were previously unattainable to students of color. However, this book argues that the "choice of major" is a myth for many students of color. As later chapters will show, most public colleges and universities in the United States have implemented *secondary admissions* criteria to enter at least one of the selected majors like education, business, nursing, and engineering. These secondary admissions criteria require students to have higher grade point averages (GPAs), and in some instances, standardized test scores, than needed for regular admissions to the university. Additionally, increased accreditation and certification requirements to enter certain professional fields have also contributed to the increasing competitiveness of selected majors.

Whereas explanations for existing racial gaps in majors and professions have focused on individual choices made by students, this book shows that the emergence of secondary admissions processes were a systematic response to the expansion of college access opportunities in the 1960s, particularly for students of color. Building on the policy retrenchment scholarship by political scientists Eric Schickler (2001) and Jacob Hacker (2004), I argue that these hidden forms of restriction are a form of "layering" that emerged to circumvent the political success of the movement to expand college access to marginalized groups.[5] Relying on an original database of GPA requirements for selected college majors (business, education, engineering, and nursing) at state colleges and universities in the United States, this study shows that the strongest predictor of increased GPA requirements for the selected majors was increasing enrollment of students of color and women at an institution, the same groups that benefited from the expansion of college access in the 1960s.

The changing requirements to enter specific majors has had a negative effect on students of color in these fields of study. For students entering universities with the support of special college access programs, the changing requirements are even more problematic. The purpose of the programs—to provide access to students who lack the GPA and SAT scores to enter the university but with support can *develop* into scholars and professionals—has been undermined by these secondary admissions, certification, and licensing requirements.

I argue that these barriers, which are largely invisible, represent a form of what Max Weber and other sociologists have referred to as "social closure," the concept that organizations adopt restrictive policies to cut off access to new competitors. Following the expansion of college access opportunities for students of color in the 1960s, professional organizations like teacher credentialing organizations, the American Bar Association, the American Medical Association, and others worked with state legislatures and university faculty to adopt increasingly competitive admissions and licensing requirements that have amounted to social closure for students of color. The private foundations, professional organizations, and accrediting organizations, which work in conjunction with state governments to establish and modify standards for entrance into majors and the professions, act as *credential cartels,* I argue, to restrict access to the professions.

The emergence of policies that restrict access to specific careers raises questions concerning higher education, the political and economic factors that shape it, and its ability to serve as a mechanism to address inequality. Although many believe that higher education provides the best pathway to upward mobility and addresses concerns with inequality in the United States, the findings in this book suggest that under existing conditions, higher education is incapable of serving as a vehicle for upward mobility. Visible and enduring barriers like concerns with college admissions, decreasing state and federal funding for higher education, increasing tuition, and student loan debt all pose significant challenges for higher education's ability to serve as a vehicle for upward mobility. However, as this book argues, there are less visible barriers that equally challenge higher education's promise of expanding economic opportunity to historically marginalized populations, particularly students of color. Lack of access to majors and to the professions, the underexamined aspect of "college access," is also undermining higher education.

In the pages that follow, I argue that addressing inequality through higher education will require the type of radical vision of college access and investment in higher education that the advocates of the special college access programs fought for in the 1960s. However, that is not enough. Addressing inequality through higher education will also require a political movement to dismantle the secondary admissions requirements and credential cartels that emerged in the 1970s, following the expansion of college access opportunities for historically marginalized populations. Furthermore, I argue that the political mobilization has to be extended to transform the economy, which for the last four decades has focused on privatization and dismantling public institutions, to one that is capable of creating pathways to upward mobility and meaningfully addressing inequality.

Through the study of the TD Program and other special college access programs of the 1960s, and the logic of *developing scholars* that the programs promoted, we can learn about the political dynamics that severely constrain the capacity to address inequality through education. At the same time, by examining the programs of the 1960s, their radical vision and their political struggles, we are also able to better understand the promise of higher education as a vehicle to creating a more equal society. It is this radical imagination of a more equal society that allowed Matt Buchanan to enter and graduate from his own state institution of higher education, which historically had been out of reach to him, and many other poor, students of color, including myself.

I, too, am a graduate of the University of Rhode Island. I am also a graduate of Central High School in Providence. I was in the Central High School auditorium with Matt in the fall of 1993 when Leo DiMaio and Frank Forleo, the recruiters from the TD Program, came to talk to us about attending college. Like Matt, I am a college graduate because of the TD Program.

Our families raised us in economic poverty. By the time we entered our senior year in high school, and the college application process began, we did not have the SAT scores or GPAs that met admissions standards to our state university. Yet, with the support of the TD Program, we gained admission and graduated from the University of Rhode Island (see Figure I.1). Our experience mirrors that of countless students of color across the United States, whose intelligence, "talent," and potential are not recognized by traditional metrics and who therefore do not merit certain life chances.

I am not only a TD graduate, but I also worked for the program. After graduating from the University of Rhode Island, I worked at Rhode Island College where I recruited and admitted students for the Preparatory Enrollment Program, a program similar to TD. After four years in the admissions office, I returned to the TD Program as an advisor, where I worked for seven years before leaving to pursue a PhD in political science at Brown University.

My experience as a student, recruiter, and advisor helps inform the questions I seek to answer in this book. I am aware that there will be questions raised about my ability to objectively conduct this study

Figure I.1 Matthew Buchanan and Domingo Morel, University of Rhode Island graduation (1998).

because I, as a beneficiary of the program, will inherently be biased about the program. I reject this premise. In fact, my insights as a student and staff member motivated the puzzles and questions examined in this book. The questions motivated by these insights led to hypotheses that required original data collection to test, in addition to conducting interviews and researching archival data. I discuss these data methods in greater detail in the following chapter. Equally as important, over my 11-year experience in higher education, I spoke to thousands of students at high schools and community organizations and have advised hundreds of students, all of which has helped influence the questions I examine throughout this book.

The findings, I argue, present novel insights into the politics of college access, the political and economic ramifications of expansion of college access, and, ultimately, our ability to address inequality through higher education. This interrogation and the results published in this volume are no less robust, informative, and important because I am beneficiary of a program created to provide opportunities that did not exist for people like me. Indeed, the more than 20-year period of analysis that has gone into the writing of this book, as a student, recruiter, advisor, and academic, is a rejection of the view in social science that adequate analysis requires separation between the analyst and the "variables" of study. We, the "variables" who have been dismissed and marginalized, have life and agency, and an ability to self-analyze and produce knowledge for us and others.

#### PART I

Social Movements for College Access

Rebellion and College for All

Community-Centered Affirmative Action

and the Role of Violent Protest in Policy

Formation and Policy Maintenance

Why did states create special college access programs for students of color in the 1960s? Since there is debate among scholars about the role of urban uprisings in the creation of college access opportunities, did the urban rebellions of the 1960s play a role in the creation of these programs, and if so, how? Moreover, since these programs were designed specifically for students of color, how are they part of the broader history of affirmative action policy in the United States? Finally, since many of the initiatives that led to greater college access for historically excluded groups in the 1960s—including affirmative action, student financial aid, and state support for higher education—have been significantly diminished, what political factors help explain the survival of a college access program for students of color?

Part I of this book (chapters 1–4) focuses on these questions and begins by examining the politics that led to the creation of special college access programs for students of color. To understand why these programs were created, we have to turn our attention to understanding the evolution of higher education in the United States, the expansion for higher education

Developing Scholars. Domingo Morel, Oxford University Press. © Oxford University Press 2023.
DOI: 10.1093/oso/9780197636992.003.0002

opportunities after World War II, and the Civil Rights movement of the 1950s and 1960s.

EXPANDING HIGHER EDUCATION IN THE UNITED STATES

In the early 20th century, government investment in colleges and universities and college attendance among young Americans was not expansive. However, beginning in the 1930s, the federal government began to increase investment in higher education. During the New Deal, the federal government relied on support from institutions of higher education to promote agriculture policies, public works, and civic training.[1]

Then after World War II, efforts to expand access to higher education and investments in financial aid to assist low-income Americans expanded rapidly. The most significant effort to increase college access came in the form of the Servicemen's Readjustment Act of 1944, more commonly known as the G.I. Bill. Between 1940 and 1960, the number of Americans who attended college more than doubled from 1.5 million to 3.6 million.[2] This was due largely in part to federal support, mainly the G.I. Bill. The expansion of higher education was part of the most significant and successful expansion of the middle class in American history.[3]

And yet, while many were enjoying the opportunities of college access, many more were excluded. Women and people of color were not part of the vast expansion of the post-World War II college access efforts. Although college enrollment rates increased significantly during the post-World War II period, "women's presence as a proportion of college students declined significantly during the postwar era."[4] Deondra Rose writes that "in hope of creating space for returning veterans, some schools implemented quotas for women and nonveterans. Schools that would have welcomed women during the war now routinely rejected them."[5] Similarly, Black Americans were not major beneficiaries of the college expansion of the postwar period. Colleges and universities used racist policies to exclude Black students from entering their universities.[6]

By the 1960s, a growing Civil Rights and Women's Rights movements demanded federal action on expanding college access opportunities to women and people of color. The federal antipoverty programs of the 1960s included several policies designed to address concerns with college access among historically marginalized populations.[7] The Economic Opportunity Act of 1964 created several initiatives, including the Federal Work Study Program and the Upward Bound Program, which provided financial assistance and college preparation services to low-income and underserved student populations. Then, the Higher Education Act of 1965 expanded college support to the poor and historically underserved populations by creating what eventually became known as the Pell Grant, a federally funded grant for students from low-income families. Additionally, the Higher Education Act of 1965 also led to the founding of the Talent Search program, and then Student Support Services, which together with Upward Bound, created the federal TRIO programs. Altogether, the federal college access policies of the 1960s marked the most robust effort to provide college access to people of color in the history of the United States. Upward Bound, for instance, served more than 2,000 students in its first year.[8] Eventually, the program would grow to serve more 60,000 students annually.

However, although federal initiatives, like Upward Bound, the Pell Grant, Federal Work-Study, and Student Support Services were designed to help prepare and support students, the programs were not designed to challenge exclusionary and discriminatory existing admissions policies at colleges and universities throughout the United States. Most of the students who were to attend college were hoping to attend public institutions of higher education. State institutions of higher education, as public institutions, had a mission of providing a college education to residents of their states, and they were supported largely by state appropriations. As public institutions, state colleges and universities were more accessible and more affordable than private institutions of higher education.

Although the federal college access initiatives provided more financial aid and college preparatory programs for underserved populations, traditional college admissions processes remained unchanged. Other than the

2-year "junior colleges" or community colleges, which had more accessible admissions policies, most state 4-year colleges had requirements that included standardized test scores (mostly Scholastic Aptitude Test), grade point average, and high school preparatory curriculum requirements that prevented many people of color from attending their institutions, even with the support of the federal initiatives.

Although every aspect of college admissions requirements—what high school the student attended, college preparatory program of study, grade point average, class rank, standardized test scores, and "extracurricular" activities—presented challenges for students from low-resourced, communities of color, the standardized test scores were the most problematic. The Scholastic Aptitude Test (SAT), gained widespread acceptance as a tool to assess college preparedness in the 1940s and 1950s, as college access opportunities began to expand after World War II.[9]

In his book on the origins of the SAT, Nicholas Lemann writes that in the 1930s, Harvard President James Bryant Conant, perhaps the most influential person in promoting the use of the SAT, pushed for an admissions test as a way to create a "natural aristocracy," as opposed to a hereditary aristocracy, composed of the most intelligent and capable citizens to lead the nation.[10] Conant viewed an admissions test as essential to break the dominance of the northeast elite on access to the elite institutions of higher education, like Harvard. Conant argued that by instituting an admissions exam, students from diverse geographic regions, would be able to demonstrate their "talent" and worthiness of acceptance to elite institutions. By the late 1940s, the Educational Testing Service (ETS), the organization that would administer the SATs, was created, and within the decade, colleges and universities across the country incorporated the SAT as part of their admissions criteria.

Although Conant viewed the SAT as a mechanism to democratize the college admissions process and open doors to students who otherwise would not have the opportunity to attend Harvard, he and the cadre of individuals responsible for instituting the SATs did not consider women and people of color as part of the "democratization" of college access expansion. In the 1930s and 1940s, when the test was being designed and initially implemented, women and students of color, were not considered college "material" and, therefore, not part of the "natural aristocracy" they were trying to create.

Despite the claims that the SATs were ushering a new era of "meritocracy," critics, as early as the 1930s, were arguing that the SATs were not a valid measurement of intelligence, as promoters of the test had claimed.[11] Rather, the critics argued, the SATs were more apt for measuring students' exposure to training and schooling, and not intelligence or potential, as the test purportedly measured. Thus, as the Civil Rights movement and the Women's Rights movement gained momentum in the early to mid-1960s, the meritocracy that Conant and others were attempting to create through the SAT collided with a movement to expand rights, and democracy, to portions of the population that the purveyors of the SAT had not deemed worthy.

As colleges began adopting the SAT requirement, the test, which was ostensibly race-neutral and not aimed at privileging one group above any other, was anything but race-neutral. Results showed that students living in poverty, Black students, and students whose first language was not English, did not perform as well on the SATs as White and wealthier students. The exclusionary effect that the mass adoption of SAT requirements had on poor students and students of color presented a dilemma for a federal government that had expressed an interest in expanding college opportunity for all students as early as 1947, with President Truman's Commission on Higher Education, and to a larger extent with President Johnson's higher education initiatives.

AFFIRMATIVE ACTION

The tension between SAT adoption and expanding college opportunities for all exposed the limits of the meritocracy elite institutions were trying to create. To address the conflict between the exclusionary effects of the SAT and the promise of college opportunities for all, affirmative action emerged as a tentative solution. The policy of affirmative action has its roots in the

1930s and 1940s when Black leaders were demanding policy solutions for the lack of employment opportunities for Black people. However, the term has its origins in an executive order signed by President Kennedy in 1961. Then, in 1965, President Johnson signed Executive Order 11246, the Equal Employment Opportunity order, which prohibited federal contractors from "discriminating in employment decisions on the basis of race, color, religion, or national origin."[12] Moreover, the order required "Government contractors to take affirmative action to ensure that equal opportunity is provided in all aspects of their employment."[13]

The emergence of affirmative action not only affected employment but college access as well. Indeed, Amaka Okechukwu writes that university administrators began implementing "campus-level" affirmative action policies in the early 1960s, "before the federal government began instituting nondiscrimination policies in the employment sector."[14] For proponents of the SAT, including university presidents, affirmative action presented the solution to the dilemma of selectivity through college admissions testing and the rhetoric of expanding college access for all.[15] As Nicholas Lemann writes, "affirmative action evolved as a low-cost patch solution to the enormous problem of improving the lot of American Negroes, who had ongoing, long-standing tradition of deeply inferior education; at the same time American society was changing so as to make educational performance the basis for individual advancement."[16]

Although affirmative action provided a "low-cost patch solution" for colleges and universities, particularly the elite institutions, a more intense battle was brewing between communities of color and their own state institutions of higher education over college access. For years, activists in cities throughout the country had been demanding greater college access opportunities for their students. For some, tinkering with admission requirements to provide a select number of students an opportunity to attend college, particularly elite institutions away from their communities, was not what they envisioned as college for all. As the examples later in this chapter and in the following chapters will demonstrate, community activists concerned with college access viewed college admissions criteria, particularly SAT requirements, as part of the systemic barriers that subjugated Black communities. While the elites were content with offering affirmative action to high-performing students of color, who may not have achieved a benchmark score on the SAT, the community activists rejected the college admissions process altogether.

Their demands for expanding college access to students of color initially reached small audiences consisting of sympathetic college professors and administrators. However, as the urban protests of the early 1960s turned to urban uprisings by 1967 and 1968, the demands for college access among community activists gained a heightened level of attention.[17] Their mobilization forced public colleges and universities and state governments to respond to their demands, which included an alternative, more radical version of affirmative action. Their success in expanding college access opportunities in response to these demands challenge conventional wisdom on the effects of violent protest on public policy.

COMMUNITY-CENTERED AFFIRMATIVE ACTION

Scholars of affirmative action policies in the United States point to the "To Fullfill These Rights" speech President Lyndon B. Johnson delivered at Howard University in 1965 as a seminal moment in the push to advance affirmative action in the United States.[18] Johnson, in acknowledging persistent struggles for Black Americans in various areas, including jobs, housing, and healthcare, vowed that his administration was committed

> to help the American Negro fulfill the rights which, after the long time of injustice, he is finally about to secure. To move beyond opportunity to achievement. To shatter forever not only the barriers of law and public practice, but the walls which bound the condition of many by the color of his skin . . . And I pledge you tonight that this will be a chief goal of my administration, and of my program next year, and in the years to come. And I hope, and I pray, and I believe, it will be a part of the program of all America.[19]

As the political scientist Ira Katznelson notes, Johnson's speech explicitly focused on a class and race analysis by emphasizing that his administration's efforts to address persistent racial inequality would be targeted "not at the black middle-class" but at the Black "poor, the unemployed, the uprooted, and the dispossessed," making this speech and the vision it promoted, one of the most radical statements on addressing inequality by a US president.[20]

Although Johnson embraced a radical program of attempting to close existing gaps between White and Black Americans in housing, employment, healthcare, and education, Katznelson also notes that this vision was undermined by a series of events in the mid-1960s, including the escalating Vietnam War, tensions within the Democratic Party, the resurgence of the Republican Party, and racial violence in American cities. Katznelson writes that "Johnson's revolutionary brand of affirmative action" was no longer possible "after the bloodshed in Watts in 1965" and "the intensification of racial violence in the summers that followed" since public opinion among Whites showed, and many members of Congress expressed an unwillingness "to authorize a comprehensive racially oriented attack upon poverty and disadvantage."[21]

Katznelson's conclusion is consistent with research on violent protests that have suggested that the uprisings of the 1960s had a negative effect on support for policies intended on addressing concerns among race subjugated groups, particularly African Americans. In a study of urban uprisings in the late 1960s, Omar Wasow (2020) found that violent protests led White Americans to shift their support for the Republican Party, which led to the election of the Republican candidate for the presidency, Richard Nixon, in 1968.[22] The implications of Wasow's study is that violent protest leads to greater social control of the protest groups, which is counterproductive to their political objectives. Similarly, Sears and McConahay (1973) and Gilens (2012) find that uprisings contributed to decreasing support for race-based policies among Whites.[23]

However, by focusing attention on politics at the local and state level, we are able to observe more complicated responses to the urban uprisings. The historian Elizabeth Hinton writes that in "the immediate post-civil

rights period, many Black leaders used both the threat and reality of collective violence to make demands for structural change, and to advocate
for community control of resources in Black communities."[24] Indeed, an
examination of the factors that led to the creation of the college access
programs of the 1960s shows a different effect of the rebellions on policy
formation and demonstrates that the uprisings helped advance, and in
some cases, set in motion, a series of political dynamics that were not
visible from an analysis of national politics. The creation of the Education
Opportunity Fund in New Jersey in response to the Newark rebellion of
1967 demonstrates the complicated political consequences of the urban
uprisings in the 1960s.

THE EDUCATION OPPORTUNITY FUND IN NEW JERSEY

In 1967, the city of Newark, New Jersey had one of the deadliest urban
uprisings in the history of the United States. In the end, 23 people were
dead, 21 of them African American. Although the incident was ignited by
the beating of an unarmed Black cab driver by White police officers, the
conditions that led to the rebellion were created by social, economic, and
political factors that had discriminated against the Black community in
Newark. By 1967, Black Newarkers represented the majority of the population in Newark. However, the Black community did not have political
power and experienced discrimination in employment, housing, and education. The lack of educational opportunities frustrated the Black community in Newark, which had demanded improvement of the public schools
and Black representation on the all-White school board but were resisted
by the city's White power structure.

The dismal conditions that Black and, increasingly, Puerto Rican children encountered in the Newark public schools also translated into a lack
of higher education opportunities. For instance, in 1967, only 2.8 percent
of Black men in Newark, who were 25 years or older, had a college degree.[25] At the Newark campus of Rutgers University, the absence of Black
students was striking. In 1967, the College of Arts and Sciences at Rutgers

University in Newark, the main unit at the University, had an undergraduate population of 2,500 students. Only 62 students were Black and a
very small number were actually from Newark.[26] In the wake of the rebellion, Black community organizations in Newark and Black students at
the Rutgers Newark campus began to demand that Rutgers create more
opportunity for Black students, particularly from Newark. At the Newark
campus, Black students created the Black Organization of Students
(BOS) which advocated for Black student concerns on campus, including
increasing the number of Black students, faculty, and staff. Many of the
BOS members were also involved in The Congress of Racial Equality
(CORE), the National Association for the Advancement of Colored People
(NAACP), and other organizations that were dedicated to civil rights issues in Newark.

In response to demands from students and community activists in
Newark, Rutgers-Newark created the Special Entrance Program in 1968
to provide admissions opportunities to "disadvantaged" students. The
University's Admission Committee agreed to accept Newark students
who graduated in the top 10 percent of their high school class. In the
fall of 1968, 90 students were admitted to the program but only half of
the admitted students were Black. In response, Black student activists
demanded greater access for Black students from Newark.

In February 1969, tensions escalated on campus. Frustrated with the
lack of progress with University officials, students from BOS took over
Conklin Hall, located at the center of campus, and renamed it Liberation
Hall. BOS coordinated the takeover of Conklin Hall with Newark community organizations. Junius Williams, the Director of the Newark Area
Planning Association (NAPA) at the time, recalled BOS leader Joe Brown
asking for community support. According to Williams,

> in addition to the BOS members outside Conklin, SDS (Rutgers
> Students for a Democratic Society) and other progressive white
> students on campus, NAPA, the United Brothers, and other com-
> munity organizations supported the students on the outside. . . . We
> conducted press conferences to "explain and warn." During our

watch, some of the guys on our team had to take a battering ram away from local white vigilante Anthony Imperiale's boys,[27] who were planning to break down the door at Conklin to get the black students out. I was off campus, so to speak, on food procurement detail. When I returned, I found our young men flexing their muscles, proclaiming that "ain't nothin' comin' through here!" Such was the nature of the bond between Town and Gown: they supported us, we supported them.[28]

The students demanded better conditions for Black students on campus, including an increase in the number of Black faculty, counselors, and staff. In addition, the students demanded a radical change to the University's admission policies. They made the following admissions demands[29]:

a. The admission deadline must remain open until September 12, 1969.
b. No black applicant holding a diploma from a Newark high school accredited by the New Jersey State Department of Education can be rejected during the period between now and September 1, 1969.
c. No Black student can be dismissed for academic reasons before completing AT LEAST three full semesters of work.
d. The first year's academic record for any Black student cannot be a determinant in the dismissal of Black students for academic reasons.
e. Black students reserve the right to erase the first year's academic record and start anew the following semester with a clean slate.

The takeover of Conklin Hall lasted three days, but BOS members threatened further action, including bringing busloads of Newark students on campus. For a month following the Conklin takeover, BOS members and Rutgers-Newark administrators negotiated without arriving at any agreement. Finally, in March 1969, the Rutgers University Board of Governors, the governing body of the entire Rutgers system, met to discuss the student and community demands in Newark as well as the other University campuses in New Brunswick and Camden.[30] At that March 1969 meeting, the Board of Governors agreed to create "a new and pioneering program by September 1969, which initially will open college doors to educationally and economically disadvantaged graduates of secondary schools in the communities where Rutgers has its primary locations and its most significant community obligations—Newark, New Brunswick, and Camden."[31]

The original program was called the Urban University Program (UUP) and its mission was to admit students from Newark, New Brunswick, and Camden who did not meet traditional admission requirements but were able to demonstrate that they "were motivated to seek a college degree."[32]

At the same time that Black students and community organizations were mobilizing to increase Black students, faculty, and staff at Rutgers University, the New Jersey Department of Education was engaged in a separate effort to address the absence of students of color at New Jersey colleges and universities. Following the 1967 Newark rebellion, state officials at the Governor's office, the Department of Education and the state legislature began to discuss plans to create college access opportunities for Black students in New Jersey. In 1968, the state released the Governor's Select Commission on Civil Disorder, a study of the factors that led to the 1967 uprising. The report concluded that a major reason for the conditions that led to the "riot" was a lack of educational opportunities for Black Newarkers.

In 1968, the governor announced the creation of the Education Opportunity Fund (EOF). EOF had many of the same objectives as UUP, including targeting students who were economically and educationally "disadvantaged." However, EOF was not limited to students from Newark, New Brunswick, or Camden and eligible students could attend a number of colleges and universities, including community colleges, in New Jersey. In its first year, 1968, the state legislature appropriated $2 million for the program and more than 1,600 students participated. Although EOF and UUP were operating as separate programs, Rutgers officials eventually decided to end UUP and participate in the EOF initiative. By 1971, EOF was the only program of its kind in the state of New Jersey.

The EOF program that began in Newark and spread throughout the entire state demonstrated how communities and student groups mobilized to bring down barriers that prevented students of color, particularly Black students, from attending their state colleges and universities. In other words, it was not enough to get the support from the federal initiatives like the Pell Grant, Work Study, and TRIO programs like Upward Bound. The state system of higher education, which remained inaccessible to students of color, had to be challenged.

Between 1966 and 1968, 14 states created similar special college access programs at their state institutions of higher education.[33] In New York, community mobilization led to the creation the Search for Education, Elevation, and Knowledge (SEEK) Program at the City University of New York (CUNY).[34] Black professors and university officials at CUNY, community members and organizations, and Black and Latino politicians primarily from Harlem, Brooklyn, and the Bronx, began to demand greater access for Black and Puerto Rican students, which led to the creation of the program in 1966.[35] The program, which began with 113 students in the first year, expanded to more than 3,000 students by 1968 and provided admissions and academic and financial support to mostly Black and Latino students from New York City.

In 1968, the Southern Education Foundation published a report, "Higher Education for 'High Risk' Students." The report's author, John Egerton, studied what "predominantly White, four year colleges and universities are doing to make higher education available to low-income and minority group students who lack the credentials—but not the qualities—to succeed in college."[36] Egerton found that states across the country were creating special admissions programs for students of color. Among the public universities to create programs were Southern Illinois University, University of Wisconsin, Temple University, Michigan State University, and the California State System. The results of the study showed that in beginning years of the programs, despite the many political and academic challenges of admitting students of color who "lack the credentials to succeed in college," students were meeting and even "surpassing expectations" in several programs across the country.

DEVELOPING SCHOLARS

The creation of these programs were based on a radical idea of higher education. The student and community activists understood that a college education created a path out of poverty. They also understood that decades of racist policies and practices, including deliberate lack of investment in the education systems that served Black and Latino communities, created conditions where the vast majority of students from underserved communities would not meet college admissions requirements. While some concerned groups advocated for college preparation support services, to ensure that students increased their chances of getting accepted to colleges and universities, and others advocated for conventional affirmative action policies, which required colleges to meet an acceptance quota of students of color, the advocates of the special programs had a different vision of higher education.

The special programs advocates demanded access for all students who graduated from high school, regardless of their academic record in high school. Their demands were driven by a philosophy that with adequate support—academic, financial, personal, and social—the students could eventually earn a college degree and transition out of poverty. Although they were visionaries, their demands also took into account the practicalities of progressing through a college experience. For instance, in the case of the Black student demands in Newark, student activists demanded that students have at least three semesters before they could be dismissed from the University for academic reasons. Furthermore, they demanded that students have "the right to erase the first year's academic record and start anew the following semester with a clean slate" if they did not perform well academically in their first year. In other words, the activists were anticipating that the transition for students who were inadequately prepared coming out of high school could be difficult. Therefore, to ensure that students had an opportunity to work through the early challenges and *develop* as scholars, they also demanded for mechanisms to prevent students from being dismissed during their first three semesters at the university.

Despite the challenges and resistance from professors who deemed the students unqualified to be in their classrooms, these programs were successful. The EOF Program in New Jersey serves roughly 13,000 students annually.[37] Although the SEEK program has experienced threats to the program, as of 2015, the SEEK program served roughly 11,000 students across 17 colleges in the CUNY system.[38] Moreover, research by Raj Chetty, David Deming, and John Friedman (2018), found that SEEK "helped boost participants' post-college average earnings to almost double their parents."[39]

The community-centered approach to college access, including the programs activists helped to create, provides an alternative, more radical vision of affirmative action that has received less attention from scholars and higher education practitioners. Additionally, the examples of the special college access programs in New Jersey, New York, and throughout the United States also provide a different perspective on the consequences of the urban uprisings of the 1960s. Katznelson observed that the urban rebellions of the 1960s derailed radical affirmative action policy because his analysis was limited to national politics. Similarly, Wasow concludes that the rebellions were counterproductive to the policy aims of African Americans because they led to the election of Richard Nixon as president. Although these observations are correct, they are incomplete because they ignore how these rebellions were also shaping politics at the community level.

As I demonstrate in the following chapters in greater detail, the violent protests, and threats of future violent protests, allowed community activists who had been advocating for expanding college access opportunities, with minimal success, to strategically use the threat of escalating violence to further their goal of expanding college access. In other words, activists mobilized the fear of escalating violence to convince policymakers to support college expansion programs for students from marginalized communities. These examples demonstrate that the urban uprisings of the late 1960s did not have a uniformly negative effect on Black political interests, as the research suggests. Rather, well-positioned community activists, relied on the violent protests in that moment, as well as the threat of future protests, to advance their policy goals. Research by Enos, Kaufman, and Sands (2019) found that following the 1992 Los Angeles uprising, voters increased support for policy initiatives championed by African Americans. I argue that their research has significant implications for how we view the role of urban uprisings among subjugated racial groups in the United States.[40]

POLICY RETRENCHMENT AND PROTEST AS A MECHANISM FOR RESISTING RETRENCHMENT

Despite the success of the college access programs, by the mid-1970s, many of the programs suffered cuts and some were eventually dismantled. Existing research on the political responses to social movements help explain why. Research by historians and sociologists has shown how the Black student movements in the 1960s led to changes in admissions policies and creation of Black Studies programs, among other things, but over time, universities began to roll back the changes.[41] Ibram Kendi, who researched Black student mobilization on college campuses, argues that many of the concessions on the part of the universities served the purpose of "depoliticizing" the movement. Kendi shows how not long after many institutional changes, historically White colleges and universities (HWCUs) began to stymie their momentum in the veiled language of racial egalitarianism, followed by calls of "reverse discrimination."[42]

Outside higher education, scholars have also shown how US policy changed following the social movements of the 1960s.[43] In policing and incarceration, for instance, political scientist Vesla Weaver (2007) and historian Elizabeth Hinton (2015) document the shift from "the war on poverty to the war on crime" as wholly intertwined with the 1960s rebellions and as an effort for conservative politicians to curry the favor of local officials and White liberals.[44]

The research by Kendi, Weaver, Hinton and others, showing retrenchment following policy gains in the 1960s is consistent with Piven and Cloward's influential work in the 1970s. In their book, *Regulating the Poor: The Functions of Public Welfare*, Piven and Cloward argue that the "key to an understanding of relief-giving is in the functions it serves for the larger economic and political order." They add, "historical evidence suggests that relief arrangements are initiated or expanded during the occasional outbreaks of civil disorder . . . and are then abolished or contracted when political stability is restored."[45]

Therefore, according to the Piven and Cloward argument, as the threats of rebellion subsided, states predictably would cut support for special college access programs. Indeed, as the following chapters demonstrate, states and universities did cut support. In the 1970s, 1980s, and 1990s, state support for higher education in general decreased, and support for programs designed to provide college access to students of color, were particularly targeted as costly and ineffective. As Kim Phillips-Fein describes in her book on austerity politics in New York City, business leaders targeted public institutions like CUNY in the 1970s, which eventually led to the end of free tuition at the University.[46]

Yet, despite the political attacks and disinvestment in college access initiatives like affirmative action and public funding for higher education, which are consistent with the social movement literature, what explains the survival, and even expansion, of some programs? As the following chapters show, part of the answer is that the programs never stopped being a political movement. Equally as important, protest, or the threat of protest, has remained an integral component of that movement.

The continuity of these programs through political mobilization, including protest, by actors "outside" the formal institutions, like students and community activists, helps expand our understanding of how policies can become entrenched. The dominant scholarship on policy entrenchment has focused on national institutions (e.g., Congress and the presidency) and national policies like Social Security, Medicare, and the Affordable Care Act to show how politics, primarily from the perspective of formal officials, shape policy entrenchment.[47] For instance, Patashnik and Zelizer (2013) examine two national policies, the Affordable Care Act and the Dodd-Frank Act, to show how "policy breakthroughs can re-fashion the political context in ways that actually entrench and deepen the reforms themselves" (1072).

In the following chapters of Part I, we see through an analysis of the Talent Development Program, how activists relied on the rebellions to advance a policy agenda at the local and state level that created the opportunity for the type of radical affirmative action that was not visible from the national level. We also see how these activists and the policies they helped enact, inculcated the element of protest in the program they helped create, which has been employed by future generations of students and activists to ensure the continuation of the program. These findings, which are arrived at by observing politics from the view of community mobilization, expand our understanding of how protest, including violent protest, can be a vehicle for policy maintenance.

Finally, while an examination of social movements, race politics, state politics, and federalism help us understand the political, historical, and philosophical underpinnings that led to the creation of these programs and their survival, an important aspect of why these programs have survived is because they continue to adapt to meet the needs of the students they serve. Through the case study of the Talent Development Program, the book demonstrates how the work of developing scholars requires building an infrastructure of support beyond college admissions, academic advising, and financial aid. Chapter 4 shows how, in addition to helping students progress through a course of study and meeting financial aid needs, the program established formal and informal mechanisms to support students dealing with family and criminal court issues, immigration concerns, and housing and food insecurity, among many issues. As recent research by Sara Goldrick-Rab and colleagues have shown, poverty, particularly hunger and homelessness, is a major concern that affects many college students throughout the United States.[48] The college access programs have been at the forefront of dealing with these student concerns since their founding.

Part II of this book (chapters 5–7) examines another puzzle that emerges as a result of learning why the special college access programs were created and how they have been able to survive despite consistent political threats. The case study analysis reveals how, over time, students in the Talent Development Program have found it more difficult to enter certain majors and graduate with degrees like education, nursing, and business. By examining the causes of the increasing challenges to graduate with certain majors for Talent Development students, we learn that these challenges are not unique to Talent Development students.

Indeed, the analysis reveals that additional layers of restriction to the majors and professions have emerged in the decades following the expansion of college access opportunities to previously excluded groups. Part II of this book shows that these forms of restriction, like the emergence of *secondary admissions processes* for students to enter certain majors, and the rise of more stringent certification requirements to enter certain professions promoted by *credential cartels*, have presented students of color with barriers that have gone largely unnoticed but have significant consequences for higher education and its promise of alleviating inequality.

The emergence of hidden forms of restriction in response to the success of college expansion efforts is consistent with the policy change scholarship by Jacob Hacker (2004) and Wolfgang Streeck and Kathleen Thelan (2005). These scholars argue that policy change is dynamic and does not occur in ways that we often expect and propose alternative modes of policy change (displacement, layering, drift, conversion, and exhaustion) to describe the different ways that policy change may take shape.[49]

As the following chapters show, the success of the mobilization efforts to expand college access for historically excluded groups made it difficult for university officials to cut or eliminate programs, although that was their original intent. Instead, university officials, faculty members, and credentialing organizations relied on a "layering" approach to circumvent the success of the political movement. The process of "layering," first described by Eric Schickler (2001) and expanded upon by Hacker (2004), is the process by which "proponents of change work around institutions that have fostered vested interests and long-term expectations by 'adding new institutions rather than dismantling the old.'"[50]

This book argues that *secondary admissions processes* and *credential cartels* are a form of "layering" that emerged as an accepted means of restricting opportunity to students of color in response to the expansion of college access opportunities for historically marginalized populations. In Part II of this book, I explain how these hidden forms of restriction emerged and equally as important, why they emerged. Understanding why barriers to access continue to be erected for students of color requires a critical examination of not only politics but economics as well, and the role of higher education as an instrument of the existing political and economic structure.

DATA AND METHODS

In the pages that follow, I employ various research methods to answer the research questions presented at beginning of this chapter. In Part I of this book, I rely on an in-depth case study of the Talent Development Program at the University of Rhode Island. In Part II of the book, the empirical analysis relies on an original dataset of state colleges and universities, special college access programs, and grade point average requirements for selected majors. I provide a more detailed discussion of the data collection and methodology of Part II in chapter 5 and Appendix B.

For the case study analysis, I conducted more than 50 structured and semistructured interviews with individuals who were identified because of their public role with the University of Rhode Island, the Talent Development Program, campus activism, community activism, and local or state government. The interviews were conducted in person, over the phone, and over Zoom.

The interview participants included former and current program directors, program staff (associate director, assistant directors, and academic advisors), and former students. The interviews of former students were conducted in individual and group settings. Group and individual interviews were conducted with members of the first Talent Development class of 1968. Similarly, group and individual interviews were conducted with students involved in campus protests in the 1970s, 1990s, and early 2000s. I also interviewed students who were part of the program but who were not involved in protests.

In addition to former students and program staff, I interviewed former and current officials from the Rhode Island Office of Higher Education and University of Rhode Island officials, including the offices of admissions, registrar/enrollment management, academic advisement, financial aid, and multicultural services. I also interviewed community leaders who were involved in the creation of the program.

For archival data, I relied on several sources. I was granted permission to examine all the available documents at the Talent Development program, from its founding to the present. I also relied on historical data from the University of Rhode Island Library and the Rhode Island Secretary of State archives for meeting minutes and Annual Reports from the Rhode Island Board of Trustees of State Colleges. I use several newspaper sources, primarily the *Providence Journal*, for historical and contemporary data, including coverage of the founding of the Talent Development Program, civil rights activism and the rebellions in Providence in the mid-1960s, as well as political and education coverage of state board of education, state legislature, Providence city politics, and the Providence public schools.

Finally, I relied on my personal experience as a former student and staff member in the Talent Development Program as an important data source. These experiences, which consist of countless interactions with fellow students, students I recruited and advised, university faculty, public school guidance counselors, teachers, principals, community leaders, and state legislators, among many others, provide a richness of data that extends beyond the formal interviews and formal archival data gathering.

Creating TD Nation

Community Action, Protest, and a

Program for "Disadvantaged" Youth

When I say TD, you say Nation!
TD! Nation!
TD! Nation!

This was the chant led by Gerald Williams, the director of the Talent Development Program at the University of Rhode Island (URI), at a welcome meeting in 2017 for accepted students and their families. During that Saturday afternoon meeting in late March, Edwards Auditorium, a 920-seat hall on the campus of URI, was filled to capacity. An overflow of students and parents filled Swan Auditorium in an adjacent building and viewed the welcoming remarks via live stream. As Williams shouted "TD!" the students and their families shouted "Nation!" in response. The chant of TD Nation also served as a signal to the students and their families that while they were being welcomed to the university, they were entering a program with a history and identity separate from the University.

The accepted students came from all corners of the state of Rhode Island. However, the majority of students came from Providence, the state's capital city. For many students and their family members, it was their first

Developing Scholars. Domingo Morel, Oxford University Press. © Oxford University Press 2023.
DOI: 10.1093/oso/9780197636992.003.0003

time taking the 30-mile trek south of Providence to Kingston, the main campus of URI. Most students in attendance were the first members of their families to attend college. Most came from low-income households. Although there were White students who were part of the program, the majority were students of color. And none of them would have been able to attend URI without the support of the Talent Development Program because they lacked the academic credentials—mostly Scholastic Aptitude Test (SAT) scores—to enter URI through the regular admissions process. The welcoming event, which included more than 1,000 people, and more than 500 accepted students, had come a long way for a program that began with 13 students in 1968 in response to community demands for college access for their students.

THE COMMISSIONS

Throughout the 1940s and 1950s, Black organizations had been documenting and challenging discriminatory state policies in Rhode Island. Although state officials largely ignored complaints from the state's Black communities, by the early 1960s, pressure from Black organizations, including the Providence chapter of the National Association for the Advancement of Colored People (NAACP) and the Urban League of Rhode Island, led to the creation of several commissions to examine concerns with education, housing, and economic opportunities.

In 1963, the city of Providence created the Providence Human Relations Commission to "protect residents' rights to fair housing, education, employment, credit, and public accommodations, free from discrimination."[1] That same year, Governor John Chafee formed a Task Force on Civil Rights to "study the grievances of minority groups."[2] The mission of the Task Force was "to ascertain the extent of unemployment and underemployment among the Negro community in our State; investigate the extent educational opportunities are being used by our Negro citizens; and to study the opportunities that are available to Negroes to obtain decent adequate housing."[3]

Among the key concerns for the Black community was the lack of educational opportunities for Black students, including access to higher education. A specific concern, according to these organizations, was the college admission requirements that prevented Black students from entering the state's colleges and universities. At one of the Task Force's public hearings in November 1963, community leaders urged the state to create special college access opportunities for Black students who "may have high ability and motivation but may score poorly on standardized tests."[4]

Although the Task Force's final report documented these concerns, including concerns with scholarship opportunities for Black students, the Task Force's recommendation was limited to establishing a "scholarship aid committee which would investigate the special problems of Negro students and aid those in need of scholarship assistance to a greater extent than is currently available under present formulas."[5] Then, in 1965, the Rhode Island General Assembly created the Special Commission to Study the Entire Field of Education, or the Thibeault Commission, named after its chairman, Representative Joseph Thibeault.[6] The Commission's report, which was completed and published in 1968, did not specifically address the lack of college access opportunities for Black students.[7]

After two state reports and growing concerns from the state's Black community, at the end of 1967 very little had been achieved to provide college access opportunities for Black students. At the beginning of 1968, the three state institutions of higher education in Rhode Island (URI, Rhode Island College, and Rhode Island Junior College) had a combined enrollment of 11,600 students. There were only 65 Black students enrolled in all of the state institutions combined.[8]

COMMUNITY ACTION

Despite the lack of response from state officials, the Black community continued to agitate for greater college access opportunities for Black students in Rhode Island. In addition to the Providence NAACP and the Urban League, which had a decades-long presence in the state, another organization, Progress for Providence, emerged as a forceful advocate for social justice issues, including education. Progress for Providence was an antipoverty agency, created by the federal antipoverty initiatives of the mid-1960s.

In Providence, federal funds helped create and support several organizations, but by 1968, Progress for Providence was the largest recipient of federal antipoverty funds in Rhode Island. Between 1968 and 1969, the agency was awarded more than $2.5 million from the federal government for antipoverty programming, including medical care, head start, summer programs, and legal services.[9]

The federal programs of the 1960s, including the community action programs, had an explicit objective of promoting participation among the most marginalized members of the society. The community action programs required "maximum feasible participation" among the poor, a phrase that became highly controversial but was intended to ensure that the targeted recipients of the federal funds were involved in how the funds were utilized.[10] These federal initiatives, the programs and organizations they helped launch and support, and the explicit expectation of participation among the poor created pathways for political mobilization for Black communities in cities across the United States.[11]

In Providence, like in Chicago, Detroit, Oakland, Newark, and other cities, these community organizations began challenging existing political, social, and economic injustices in their respective cities. Education was among the key focus areas for these community organizations. Although K–12 public education was a main focus and received the most attention, including issues concerning adequate school funding, segregation, and school board representation, access to higher education also became an important part of the struggle for political, social, and economic justice.

In Rhode Island, Progress of Providence became a leading voice in demanding greater opportunities for poor people and people of color in the state, and access to education, including higher education, became a major focus area for the organization. At a panel discussion at URI in 1968, Deputy Director of Progress for Providence Reverend Benjamin Mitchell said: "Negroes are excluded from good jobs, housing, higher education and meaningful political power. . . . Our society and our institutions have built this. White society should face this reality and once having faced it, do something about it."[12]

One of the organization's most forceful advocates was Charlie Fortes. Fortes was born in 1922 in New Bedford, Massachusetts, and was involved in worker and community organizing from an early age. As a merchant seaman in New Bedford, Fortes helped organize Black and Puerto Rican longshoreman. After suffering a heart attack in 1966 and no longer being able to work as a seaman, Fortes began working for Progress for Providence. During this time, he emerged as a respected leader in the Cape Verdean community in the Fox Point neighborhood in Providence.

Fox Point is located on the east end of Providence and is home of the city's first port, India Point, created in 1680.[13] The neighborhood has a large Cape Verdean community, which traces its roots in Fox Point to the mid- to late 1800s.[14] Although highway construction and gentrification have displaced many of the long-standing families in the neighborhood,[15] Fox Point continues to be the center for many in Providence's Cape Verdean community. Over the decades, generations of Black community activists in Rhode Island, including URI, would trace their community roots to Fox Point. Charlie Fortes emerged from this community and in addition to advocating for workers' issues and racial justice, he also became an influential actor in the movement to expand college access opportunities for people of color in Providence.

URBAN REBELLION

Although community groups continued to advocate for greater access to higher education, by early 1968, the state of Rhode Island had not created any special college access initiative for students of color.[16] However, in April 1968, that changed. On April 4, Dr. Martin Luther King Jr. was assassinated in Memphis, Tennessee. The killing of the civil rights leader shocked the nation and sparked more than 200 uprisings in cities throughout the

United States.[17] The uprisings during Holy Week surpassed the more than 160 urban revolts in the "long hot summer" of 1967.[18]

While the Newark and Detroit rebellions of July 1967 received most of the national attention, many mid to small size cities experienced urban unrest as well, including the city of Providence. Late in the evening of July 31, 1967, roughly 200 people were involved in civil unrest on the Southside of Providence. A large police force was called in to quell the unrest near the Willard Avenue shopping center in Providence.[19] The following day, a large police force, including state police, was called in to respond to continued unrest, which included shootouts between civilians and police officers. Over the two-day period, dozens were arrested and injured, including six police officers.[20] The violent unrest in South Providence in 1967 occurred almost exactly one year after police were called in to put down a racial disturbance in August of 1966. The unrest in 1966, which occurred nearly in the same location as the disturbances of 1967, led to the arrest of 40 people.

The racial tensions in the summers of 1966 and 1967 in Providence had many worried about the possibility of future escalations in the summer of 1968. On the day before Dr. King's assassination, the *Providence Journal* published an article about a county sheriff in nearby Massachusetts who was "recruiting young men in every neighborhood in the county for a 'watch society' aimed at heading off summer riots."[21] The assassination of Dr. King on April 4 and the civil unrest that followed concerned state and local leaders in Rhode Island who feared similar unrest in Providence.

One of the swiftest responses in the aftermath of King's assassination came from the Board of Trustees of State Colleges in Rhode Island. On April 9, the board approved plans "to correct its own admitted failure to give significant help to Negro students."[22] The board approved the creation of a "free university" in "the black ghetto of Providence" to expand educational opportunities in the Black community. In addition to the free university, the board approved a measure to increase the number of Black students at the three state institutions of higher education. During the board meeting, Board Chair Lila Sapinsley stated that following King's assassination, she realized that "despite a lot of talk," the board "had done nothing significant for Negro students in Rhode Island."[23] To increase the number of Black students, the board agreed to create 120 to 180 full scholarships for Black students at the state institutions of higher education.[24]

Although the proposals seemed spontaneous, a plan to create scholarship opportunities for students of color had been in the works months before King's assassination. Rhode Island College Professor Raymond Houghton and Robert Spencer, dean of the graduate school at URI, were part of a group, along with Black community leaders in Providence, that worked to develop plans for a "free university" and a scholarship program for Black students. In fact, earlier that year, members of the working group warned the board of trustees that without adequate action to address the needs of the Black community, the state was likely to experience future racial unrest.

To convince the board to take action, Robert Spencer provided copies of the recently published report by the National Advisory Commission on Civil Disorders, or the Kerner Commission Report, which examined the causes of the 1967 uprisings.[25] The report provided recommendations on a number of policy issues including employment, policing, housing, and education. On education, the report specifically mentioned the need to expand opportunities for higher education, including expanding the Upward Bound Program, removing "financial barriers to higher education," and providing federal funds for "special 1-year educational programs with the function of providing college preparatory training for disadvantaged youth."[26]

Although the board of trustees had not agreed to support the recommendations of the working group prior to Dr. King's assassination, Board Chair Sapinsley, confident that the assassination and the unrest that followed had changed the climate around supporting college access programs for Black students, invited Houghton and Spencer to the April 9 board meeting to present the proposals. Additionally, Lawrence Dennis, who became chancellor of the state system of higher education in 1967, helped initiate discussions on an urban campus and scholarship programs for Black students and strongly supported the plans when they were presented to the board of trustees. Both of the proposals received strong support from the board of trustees which launched the process of creating a program for "disadvantaged youth."

The creation of a college access program for Black students in Rhode Island finally came to fruition after years of demands from Black leaders and community groups in Providence. It was also created because of the advocacy of faculty and university officials who worked alongside community leaders to champion the cause within the institutions of higher education. However, the urban uprisings across the country and especially in Providence between 1966 and 1968 also influenced the creation of the program.

Community leaders and university officials warned state officials that without creating opportunities for young Black people, the threat of violence, which had been experienced in Providence and on television screens, would escalate. After two years of disturbances in Providence, and then the nationwide explosion of violent protest following the assassination of Dr. King, state board officials, who had failed to create a program for Black students after years of demands from community leaders, finally relented. In future years, state leaders and others would say that the program for "disadvantaged youth" was created in response to the killing of Dr. King. However, the more accurate characterization is that the program was created in response to the urban protests in the years leading up to and following the assassination of Dr. King.

A PROGRAM FOR "DISADVANTAGED YOUTH"

On May 1, 1968, the Rhode Island Board of Trustees of State Colleges received a plan for "modifying the state college system to fit the needs of Negro and other disadvantaged students."[27] The proposal was written by a committee of ten faculty members from URI, Rhode Island College, and Rhode Island Junior College in consultation with Black community leaders, including members of Progress for Providence.[28]

The committee's proposal consisted of a 5-point plan[29]:

1. A state-sponsored program to provide summer school work and year-round counseling designed to create a "pool" of high school students in or below the 11th grade who would not otherwise consider going on to college because of repeated failures in public schools.
2. A special, limited program of recruitment, intensive summer preparation, and scholarship help for about 50 students who will finish high school in June.
3. A long-range scholarship program designed to pay full or partial costs of 150 disadvantaged students attending the three state institutions of higher learning.
4. A variety of "institutional involvement programs" designed to change the environments of the campuses, their administrative structures, student organizations, and academic programs for the purposes of carrying out all of the objectives of the report.
5. The establishment of an "urban educational center" under the board of trustees in Providence, to open in September, that would provide a variety of educational and reference services to the members of the Negro community and any other interested persons.

The proposal was approved by the board of trustees. However, the vote was not unanimous. Several board members voiced concerns that creating special programs for the Black community would "support black separatist ideas within the Negro community."[30] Others opposed the board's involvement at the high school level by creating "compensatory programs" to help high school students prepare for college.

The other point of contention involved the summer program for about 50 high school students who expected to graduate in June of 1968. The program was to provide an "intensive" summer college experience at URI. At the conclusion of the summer program, the students who successfully completed the program would be accepted to one of the three state institutions of higher education. The committee that wrote the proposal and the Black community leaders who advised the committee strongly recommended that the coordinator of the summer program should be Black.

However, some board members objected, arguing that race "should never be a qualification" for employment. Robert Spencer, the chair of the committee, argued that the committee recommended that the person leading the program should be a "Negro" because "it was necessary for the self-image of the Negro students and the education of white students."[31] Board Chair Lila Sapinsley supported the committee's recommendation, arguing that while she agreed that race should not be typically a qualification for employment, "I look at these appointments as exceptions because the whole program is an exception."[32]

Despite objections from several board members, the proposal was adopted and several weeks later Louis G. Davis was named the coordinator of the summer program for "disadvantaged youth." Davis, a member of the committee, was a professor of English and music at the Rhode Island Junior College and one of the few Black faculty members in the state's entire system of higher education.

By mid-May, the committee and Davis were in a rush to recruit 50 students to begin the summer program in June. To help Davis run the program, the board hired Harold Langlois Jr. Harold Langlois graduated from URI in 1966 with a double major in English and Sociology. His father, Harold Langlois Sr., was the warden of Rhode Island's Adult Correctional Institutions (ACI). After graduating from URI, Langlois attended Indiana University to pursue a master's degree in English with the plan of continuing his studies at the PhD level. However, after earning a master's in his first year, Langlois was drafted by the Army for the Vietnam War. Langlois applied for a deferment, based on his status as a graduate student, but the draft board rejected his deferment application.

Langlois was opposed to the war and feared the possibility of having to go to Vietnam and "decided that was not going to happen."[33] After being turned down by the draft board, Langlois returned to Rhode Island and decided that "although I was not going to go to Canada, I had to find a way to not go to Vietnam." His opportunity came at a party in Kingston, Rhode Island, in 1968 when he met Louis Davis, who had been recently named the coordinator of the summer program for disadvantaged youth. In their conversation, Davis mentioned that he was working on starting a program for Black students at URI and asked Langlois if he would be willing to join him and invited him to attend a planning meeting on the campus of URI.

Langlois accepted the invitation and joined Davis at the planning meeting. The meeting was attended by university administrators, faculty, members of the board of trustees, and community activists. Among the community members in the room was Charlie Fortes from Progress for Providence. "I don't remember everyone who was at that meeting," said Langlois, "but I remember Charlie Fortes being there. He was one of the leaders pressuring the University." That June, Langlois was officially hired by Davis and the board of trustees as an assistant director.

SUMMER OF 1968

As the summer of 1968 quickly approached, and in the midst of American turmoil that would see the assassination of Bobby Kennedy and what became the peak of US involvement in the Vietnam War, the Rhode Island state colleges were scrambling to put together the summer program for "disadvantaged youth" at URI. Lacking the institutional connections to the urban communities, University officials relied on community organizations and leaders in the Black community to recruit students for the program. We "recruited people off the streets of Providence. We went to barbers and policeman and not to guidance counselors," stated Robert Spencer, the dean of the graduate school at URI. "This was off-beat and had to court probation officers" and ask "where is the talent going?"[34]

Charlie Fortes from Progress for Providence, who had been instrumental in pushing for the creation of the program, was also involved in recruiting students for the program. "I must have interviewed 125 kids" stated Fortes, who went "house to house to tell students the state had agreed to give 50 poor youngsters a crack at higher education."[35] Black teachers and high school coaches in Providence were also informed about the program and encouraged to recommend students.

Frank "Chico" Santos, who grew up in the Chad Brown Housing Projects in Providence, was a senior at Mount Pleasant High School in 1968. When he started high school, he was not placed in a college preparatory track. "We weren't encouraged to take a college preparatory curriculum. We were encouraged to go into the armed forces," stated Santos. However, "I played football and basketball at Mount Pleasant and my head coaches, Irv Nelson, a Jewish guy and Jimmy Ahern, an Irish guy, walked me into the guidance office during my junior year and told the guidance counselor that I had to be put into a college preparatory program because I could do the work."[36] Following that meeting, Santos was placed in a college preparatory track. However, his late entry into the college preparatory curriculum did not allow him to earn all of the course requirements to enter URI by the time he was a senior.

Like most Black students in Providence, the state university was not an option for Santos after graduation. However, weeks before he was to graduate, he learned about an opportunity for Black students to enter URI through a summer program from one of his football coaches, and the only Black teacher he had at Mount Pleasant, Melvin Clanton. "In the spring of my senior year I applied to the program and I had to go for an interview at the RI Junior College and I remember seeing a bunch of other Black kids I knew from Central High School and Hope High School going for the interview as well." Santos added, "We didn't know it at the time but the Black community in Providence was trying to identify as many of us as possible to go to the university."

Although some students were being recruited directly from high school, some students had been out of school for several years. Some had been working and others had recently returned from Vietnam. Donna-jean Freeman (later Donna-jean Wosencroft) was working at the time for the phone company. She had graduated several years earlier but heard from a close friend, Georgia Machado, who had also been out of high school for several years and also worked for the phone company, about the program. Wosencroft called to learn about the program and decided to apply shortly before the start of the program. "When I went in for the interview they decided to accept me without my official transcript. They had to take

my word for it because they had to make a quick decision."[37] Wosencroft,
was joined by her close friend Georgia Machado, as well as Frank Santos,
and 40 other students who started the first "prematriculation program" at
URI in the summer of 1968.

After years of community efforts to create opportunities for Black
students to enter their own state college and university, the Program for
Disadvantaged Youth began in June of 1968. Students were informed to
check in to Dorr Hall at URI in Kingston. Some students arrived by bus
provided by the program and others arrived on their own. "It was a fun
time" said Katherine Soares (Katherine Franklin at the time). Katherine
and her close friend Eva Smith, both graduates of Hope High School, were
roommates in the summer and recall the first couple of days being con-
fusing but exciting.

The program was structured to provide academic, social, and economic
support to the students. Students were assigned a counselor and had math
and reading courses throughout the day and structured study periods.
The program provided three daily meals and a weekly stipend of $25. The
weekly stipend was provided to allow students to complete the summer
program, since many families counted on their summer earnings to cover
household expenses.[38]

In addition to academics, the program provided social activities for
the students as well. "We went to the Apollo to see Isaac Hayes" said
Wosencroft. "They also brought us to Boston to go see a concert. We went
to plays, and to the beach," remembers Santos. There weren't any buses
that traveled between Kingston and Providence, where most students
were from and most of the students did not have their own vehicles. "So
the program organized all of these activities because we spent most of
the summer on campus. We didn't really go home" added Santos. "I remember we snuck out one time and went to a club down in Kingston" said
Eva Smith. "We couldn't move around much, but we had fun down there."

The students also took one trip that they did not appreciate. Deborah
Nelson (now Deborah Bush), who graduated from Hope High School
said, "the only negative thing that I remember" about these trips, "was
when they took us to South Providence. That was awful." Harold Langlois,

who was running the program, thought that it would be helpful for students to see "the life they could achieve by earning a college degree." The students referred to it as the Blackstone trip. The program brought students by bus to tour Blackstone Street in South Providence and then Blackstone Boulevard on the East Side of Providence. Blackstone Street, was a majority Black and low-income section in Providence and Blackstone Boulevard was, and still is, in the wealthy section of Providence, close to Brown University.

"They brought us to Judge Wiley's house on the East Side" said Wosencroft. Judge Alton Wiley Sr. was the first African American appointed to the Rhode Island Superior Court. "We had lunch at his house and they had a maid that brought out the lunch for us. They were trying to show us what people have and what people don't have. We didn't think that was a positive experience." Donna-jean Wosencroft and her friend Georgia Machado approached Langlois about the trip. "That was the thing about Harold, he really respected us." Wosencroft and Machado, who were older than the majority of the students and were about the same age as Langlois, told Langlois "that we didn't appreciate this trip. He listened to us and understood."

In addition to the negative experience with the tour of the East and South sides of Providence, the students recall another negative experience on campus. Although URI was an overwhelmingly White campus, the campus was mostly empty in the summer and for the most part, the students in the program had the campus to themselves. However, when the Black students entered the academic buildings, the dining hall, the bookstore, and the library, they had to wear a badge that said "Special Program for Disadvantaged Youth." "That made us feel terrible," said Bush. "We didn't like it and a group of students approached Harold about that as well. But for several weeks, we had to walk with that badge around campus."

Despite the feelings of anger, humiliation, and disrespect that students felt for having to walk around campus with a label of "disadvantaged youth" and going on the Blackstone tour of Providence, they also felt a sense of mission. They were the first in their families and their communities to have an opportunity to attend URI or Rhode Island College. Deborah Bush, who eventually became a teacher at Central High School in Providence, said, "We knew we had to do well. If we didn't succeed, there wouldn't be Black students coming after us. We had to pave the way. So we had to put up with some things." That sense of "duty," as Donna-jean Wosencroft, who also became a public school teacher in Providence, described it, was indeed an ethos of the program that would be instilled in future students and would serve as a catalyst for student mobilization when the program would be threatened in future years.

As the summer of 1968 came to a close, 43 students had reached the end of the program. Although students were aware that there were three possibilities—admission to URI, Rhode Island College, or the Junior College—many believed that they would have the opportunity to attend URI if they did their work and completed the summer program. For the students, there was much at stake in the admissions decisions. Some feared disappointing their families and their communities if they did not get accepted to URI or Rhode Island College.

There was also the fear of getting drafted to go to Vietnam. In 1968, the United States would be at the peak of the number of soldiers in Vietnam and soldiers drafted.[39] It was also the deadliest year of the war. By gaining admission to the University, Black students would be eligible to apply for a college deferment, as many White students had been able to do across the country. It was not just the Black students who feared the possibility of being drafted. Harold Langlois, whose title was assistant director but actually directed the program that first summer, was also concerned about his draft status.

Around the fourth week of the program, Langlois approached Dean Spencer and asked him what his plans were for the program in the fall. The University had not assigned anyone as director for the fall and Langlois thought he should be that person. "I have been directing the program throughout the summer and have built a rapport with the students and would like to continue to work with them in the fall," said Langlois. When Spencer agreed to hire him for the fall, Langlois asked him to write a letter to the draft board in Providence. "Tell them," Langlois said, "that with Detroit burning, Harold is putting out fires here. He is much more important here, than he is there [Vietnam]." Spencer agreed to write the letter and by the end of the summer Langlois had been granted a defer-ment for one year. Langlois never did go to Vietnam. His work with the program and later on in different positions at the University and in higher education in Rhode Island allowed him to gain deferments until he aged-out of draft status. "The program which I helped create," said Langlois, "might have saved my life."

All of these things were going through the minds of the students when they were called into a room to be informed of the admissions decisions at the conclusion of the summer program. In this meeting, the students learned that only 13 students of the 43 were to attend URI in the fall. "We were pissed," said Santos, who was not one of the 13. "We were angry. We thought we were going to URI and they said only 13 will start in the fall, although we all passed our classes."

Santos and other students believed that it may have been their high school record that prevented them from gaining admission to the University. "We thought it may have been a missing class or something. Or that our SAT scores were too low," said Santos. In reality, Dean of Admissions at URI James Eastwood "had no intentions of accepting the students. None," said Harold Langlois. According to Langlois, Eastwood had made it clear that he "was not going to accept these kids off the streets of Providence because Charlie Fortes said they should be in college."

Unbeknownst to the students, there was a battle between Eastwood and Charlie Fortes over the number of students the University should accept. By mid-summer, Fortes had been alerted by prematriculation staff that the University was planning to accept only a small number of students at the conclusion of the summer. Indeed, Eastwood had informed uni-versity officials and Langlois that only "4 students were judged O.K." for admission to the University "on the basis of college board scores" but he was willing to accept 8 students.[40] At a meeting of the Board of Trustees of State Colleges on July 17, Fortes raised concerns about the University meeting its obligation to accept students who had completed the summer program.

Frustrated but understanding that the University was not going to accept the number many had envisioned, the summer program staff agreed on recommending 14 students and informed Fortes of their recommendation. On July 30, Fortes called Chancellor Lawrence Dennis, of the state system of higher education, to express further concerns about Dean Eastwood's refusal to accept more students and threatened to alert federal officials and the Governor's office, since the programs was "mounted with the help from Federal funds and endorsed by the Governor's office."[41]

Chancellor Dennis contacted URI President Werner Baum about Fortes's concerns and agreed that the University should accept the 14 students recommended by the prematriculation staff. In a letter to University Vice President Jerome Pollack, Baum asked Pollack to "pursue" the matter with Eastwood. Baum added, "I think we must admit all 14, or certainly any who have qualifications at least equal to the least qualified student already admitted."[42]

The pressure from Fortes led the University to agree to accept 13 students. At the banquet, students learned about the admissions decisions. The staff read the names of the 13 students who were accepted to the University, followed by the names of 5 students accepted to Rhode Island College, and the 23 students accepted by the Junior College. Two students were accepted to Providence College.[43]

It should have been a time of joy for every student. However, even among the 13 students who gained admissions to the University, there was anger. "We were all in this together," said Deborah Bush, who was among the 13. "They were bright and talented students who should have gotten a chance to be at the University."

Frank Santos was among the students who attended the Junior College after being denied the opportunity to attend URI. "We appreciated it but it was not the same as attending URI," said Santos. "It was difficult because you had to go back to your community and deal with everything that was going on in the community. You had to deal with the distractions at the same time that you had to be a student," he added. "It was just difficult."

Indeed, students who attended the Junior College did not receive the academic, financial, and emotional support from the Junior College and after a year, many of the 23 students were no longer attending college. One study, which examined the first four years of the special program for disadvantaged youth at URI, compared the success rates of the students who were admitted to URI and the students who attended Rhode Island College and the Junior College. The study found that by 1971, only 5 of the 23 students had graduated or were still enrolled at the Junior College.[44] Most of the students entered the workforce and at least one of the original 43 students, Robert Blue, was drafted and served in Vietnam.

As they look back at that time, several of the students who did not get accepted to URI still consider the summer program a transformative experience. "Before that program, no one had talked to us about college," said Santos. "Living on that campus that summer of 1968 impacted all of us and encouraged us to finish what we started, inevitably." Santos was one of the students who continued his studies and eventually returned to URI, not as a student, but as an admissions officer. In 1989, Santos was hired by the Office of Undergraduate Admissions at the University as an admissions officer. One of his major responsibilities was to review applications for what had become the Special Program for Talent Development. "How ironic," said Santos, "that the same office that denied me admission, hired me as an admissions officer all these years later. I made sure that I provided an opportunity to as many students of color as possible to attend the University."

The students of that first summer consider themselves part of the same pioneering class, even if most of them did not get an opportunity to attend URI that fall of 1968. "We came from all parts of Providence, the East Side, the South Side, the West Side. We were able to come together, no fighting, no problems, and forged friendships with one another," said Katherine Soares, who eventually attended Bryant College. "I think it's important that those of us who did not go to URI, still be part of the record. They only consider the 13 students but we were all in there together."

At the conclusion of the summer program, the 43 students went their separate ways. URI, which had historically refused to accept Black students from Providence, was forced to accept a class that began with 13 students in 1968 and would grow to more than 600 accepted students in 2019. However, the program's growth would not be easy and it would face challenges—external and internal—that would threaten its existence at several critical junctures. Some of those challenges would start to become visible as the University welcomed its incoming class in the fall of 1968.

Resisting Retrenchment

As the fall semester of 1968 began, the University of Rhode Island (URI) welcomed the students back to campus. Among the 6,572 undergraduate students enrolled at the URI, there were 13 Black students from the Program for Disadvantaged Youth.[1] For the 13 students, the fall experience could not have been more different than their summer experience on campus. They no longer had the campus to themselves and the comfort of being surrounded by other Black students from Providence. They were on their own, and it was a different experience.

"It was terrible, we were just a few and the racism we felt was unbelievable," said Donna-jean Wosencroft. The faculty were particularly challenging. "The faculty were very racist," she said, and remembered one time being asked "why [I wore] a wrap on my head?" Deborah Bush remembers the students in the program being asked to "see a school psychologist or social worker" to "talk about what our experience was like being one of the few Black students on campus and how we were adjusting."

The faculty had expressed support for the program in a bill the Faculty Senate adopted in the spring of 1968. The bill, which focused on Admissions Policy, "instructed" the admissions staff to consider the applications of "culturally disadvantaged students" who "for social or economic causes have not enjoyed the normal opportunities in preparatory work" to gain admission to the University.[2] Theoretically, the faculty supported the creation of the program, but in practice, as a body, they resisted the program. Indeed, the program would continue to experience challenges from the faculty in the years that followed for accepting and enrolling students who, in their view, were not academically qualified to be at the University.

Harold Langlois, who was directing the program in the fall, tried to work with several faculty members to deal with the racism the students were experiencing. Langlois worked with the dean of Arts and Sciences, Frank Woods, to provide "sensitivity training" to some of the faculty members in Arts and Sciences. While some of the faculty members participated in the trainings and were interested in creating a better campus climate for the Black students, most faculty members were not involved, and the students had difficult experiences in their classrooms.

In addition to working with faculty to be more supportive of the students, Langlois was also beginning to plan for the program's upcoming summer component in 1969. The previous summer, 43 students completed the summer program and only 13 were accepted to URI. Members of the Black community had made it clear to Langlois and other university officials that they expected URI to accept more students the following summer. Langlois developed a plan for the University to accept 50 students the up-coming summer and asked to meet with URI President Werner Baum to present his plan.

"I walked into his office, he had a bowl of flowers on his desk," remembers Langlois. "I asked him for a budget for 50 students" to enter the University the following year "and he said, no. We don't have the money." Baum was not interested in growing the program, according to Langlois. "All he cared about was the academic reputation of the University, and building this program was not part of that plan." That evening, Langlois called several leaders in the Black community, including Charlie Fortes, to alert them to the problem with Baum. The following morning, Langlois received a call from Baum summoning him to his office.

"I said OK, I must be in trouble," recalls Langlois. When he arrived at the president's office, he was greeted by Vice President Pollack, who said, "Your career is done! You ruined your career. You had people call the President and threaten to blow the house down?" Fortes and others had called the president and demanded more slots for students and threatened to bring the community to the campus and indeed "burn the house down."

In the fall of 1968, the smoke of the uprisings following the assassination of Dr. King was barely gone and officials feared the possibility of future uprisings. The Black leaders and Langlois understood the power of that threat and used it to push the University to grow the program.

When Langlois finally met with Baum, the president agreed to support the budget for 50 students but he told Langlois, "You have your budget but you don't have a renewed contract. You're done here." Langlois, who was relying on the University job for a draft deferment, had lost that protection and would have to look for another job in a year. In the meantime, he had the budget he needed to grow the program and he received even better news from a family friend, Romeo "Buck" DeBucci, the director of Financial Aid at the University. Following the meeting with Baum, Langlois met with Buck to discuss the budget and financial aid package for students. Buck told Langlois, that with that budget, "You can actually accept 100 students." He mentioned that with the Federal Supplemental Opportunity Grant (FSEOG), a federal grant created in 1965 to help support the financial needs of low-income students, Langlois could cover the costs of 100 students.

Based on the budget the president provided Langlois, and the news that the FSEOG could help cover the costs of 100 students, the plan was to recruit enough students to enroll 100 students in the fall of 1969. But Langlois would not be part of that program. It was time to find his replacement and the Black community had their wishes. They wanted a Black person to lead the program and the person they had in mind was the Reverend Arthur L. Hardge.

REVEREND HARDGE

Rev. Arthur Hardge was a well-respected community leader in the state. He arrived in Rhode Island in 1963 to become pastor of the Winstor Street A.M.E Zion church in Providence, which later became the Hood Memorial A.M.E. Zion Church. Born in Indianapolis, Indiana in 1927, Hardge's family moved to Jersey City, New Jersey, and after graduating from high school, he attended New York University and then Morgan State College in Baltimore, Maryland, where he earned a bachelor's degree.[3] Rev. Hardge then attended Temple University School of Theology and became pastor of the Union A.M.E. Zion church in New Britain, Connecticut.

In the summer of 1961, while serving as pastor of the Union A.M.E. Zion church in New Britain, Rev. Hardge joined the Freedom Ride movement which began in Washington, DC, and, for him, ended with his arrest in Tallahassee, Florida. He and nine other clergymen from northern states were convicted for protesting segregation in the Tallahassee airport. Hardge and the other clergymen served three days in jail before posting bond. The clergymen appealed their charge and their case made it all the way up to the Supreme Court in 1963. However, the Court decided to send the case back to the local Florida court and in August of 1964, Hardge was ordered to turn himself in to serve a 60-day jail sentence for his role in the Tallahassee protest. Rev. Hardge and the other clergy members were released after 4 days when the municipal judge, who gave the 60-day jail sentence, reversed his own decision.[4]

In May of 1963, while going through the court appeals process, Rev. Hardge moved to Rhode Island. Immediately after arriving in Providence, Rev. Hardge became active in the state's civil rights efforts. That year, Hardge founded and became the first director of the Rhode Island chapter of the Congress on Racial Equality. All throughout the mid-1960s, Hardge was involved in organizing sit-ins, protests, legal actions, and legislative efforts to demand action on fair housing, poverty, and racial discrimination in Rhode Island.

Rev. Hardge was also active with education issues in the state. In 1966, he was part of a group working to desegregate the Providence public schools.[5] In 1967, he was involved in efforts to demand action from the state board of education to end racial discrimination in public school systems throughout the state.[6] Then, in 1968, he was part of the advisory board of Black community leaders who advised the higher education committee on the plan that led to the creation of the "Program for Disadvantaged Youth."

By 1968, Rev. Hardge had gained prominence in the Black community and with the White political establishment in Rhode Island. On July 25, 1968, John Chafee, the Republican Governor of Rhode Island, named Rev. Hardge the first director of the State Department of Community Affairs.[7] Hardge became the first Black person in the history of Rhode Island to head a state department.

In the 1968 gubernatorial election, Chafee was narrowly defeated by Democrat Frank Licht, an Associate Justice in the Rhode Island Supreme Court. Licht's upset victory ended Chafee's three-term governorship and Rev. Hardge's directorship as well. When Frank Licht assumed office in January of 1969, he did not reappoint Hardge as head of the Department of Community affairs.

After learning of Hardge's removal from state government, Black leaders, including Clifford Monteiro and Michael Van Leesten, who had been involved with the development of the Program for Disadvantaged Youth, began to push Langlois, university, and state board officials to hire Hardge. Langlois, who only had several months left as director of the program, did not know Hardge personally and had someone else in mind to replace him. Langlois was trying to bring Leo DiMaio, who worked for Langlois's father, as the head of recreation and acting supervisor of education at the Adult Correctional Institutions in Rhode Island to work for the program. However, after consistent pressure from community leaders, on June 5, 1969, one month before the start of the second summer program, the Board of Trustees for State Colleges officially announced the hiring of Rev. Arthur Hardge as assistant director of the Program for Disadvantaged Youth.[8]

Rev. Hardge's addition helped the program in two immediate ways. His stature in the community helped increase the visibility of the program, which would help in the areas of recruitment and resource allocation from the state and the University. Upon his hiring, Hardge stated that his plan was "to explore new possibilities for recruitment" and added that it was "necessary to have a program of this type because in the society which we live, there are still many disadvantaged students who don't believe that the opportunities are present and available."[9]

Indeed, in 1969, very few people in Rhode Island were familiar with the Program for Disadvantaged Youth. The program conducted a survey of Providence residents in 1969 and asked the question, "Have you heard about the program at URI this summer to help disadvantaged high school graduates going to college this fall?" Nearly 80 percent (78.2 percent) of the Providence residents surveyed answered that they did not know about the program.[10]

Rev. Hardge's presence also helped the Black students on the campus, who for the first time had a Black administrator who could advocate on their behalf. In addition to recruiting students, Hardge viewed his role as a conduit for addressing the racial discrimination that Black students on campus were experiencing. In this position, he stated that his role was to also "talk to professors and other personnel who deal with students to acclimate them to the peculiar problems of the disadvantaged."[11]

The dual role—informing students of possibilities and challenging systemic barriers—that Hardge engaged in as he began his work with the program would become a central tenet of the program then and in the decades that followed. On the individual side, the program would work with students, inform them of opportunities, and advise them on how to navigate the racist terrain of life in a majority White campus and society. In this sense, Hardge and others would engage in a "politics of respectability" where he would advise students to "be at their best, not just for them, but for the race."[12]

At the same time, Hardge and program officials would also engage in systematic battles with professors, admissions officers, financial aid officers, university presidents, high school teachers, guidance counselors, state legislators, and governors to remove barriers to access for Black students and other students of color to the University. This dual approach, of supporting the needs of the student at the individual level while simultaneously engaging in systemic struggles against the machinery of marginalization constituted a major philosophical approach for the program.

As the summer program of 1969 began, 53 students started the program; roughly half the number Langlois was hoping to have on campus. Once again, the community was fighting against the administration to increase the number accepted to the University. By the end of the summer program in 1969, 19 students were accepted to the University, 17 students were accepted to Rhode Island College, and 9 accepted to the Junior College. The 19 students were far from the increase Langlois and others were pushing for to start the fall at URI. However, beyond the small increase in students, there were signs that the state and University were beginning to make long-term investments in the program.

In addition to hiring Rev. Hardge as assistant director before the start of the summer program, the University also hired Leo DiMaio in the summer of 1969. Langlois recruited DiMaio from the ACI, when his father, Langlois Sr., was getting ready to retire as warden of the ACI. DiMaio wanted to become the next warden but that position "would have killed him," said Langlois. "His heart was too big for that place." Eileen DiMaio, Leo's wife, agreed with Langlois. "Eileen thanked me. We all knew that he would be great with the students in the program."

Indeed, Mr. D, as he would become known by the students, was loved by the students. "We saw him as a father figure. He protected us from so many things on campus," said Wosencroft. Future generations of students would share similar sentiments about DiMaio. To the students, he was viewed as a source of support and to university administrators, a source of angst due to his advocacy for the program. Robert Carothers, who became president of the University in the 1990s and would have his battles with DiMaio, said he was "a man who carries a big stick but carries it with love."[13]

At the conclusion of the summer program, and as the fall began, the program had a new leadership team. On September 4, 1969, the Board of Trustees of State Colleges announced several changes to the Program for Disadvantaged Youth. Harold Langlois left the University to become a special assistant to Higher Education Commissioner Lawrence Dennis. The program's assistant director, Rev. Hardge, was named the new director of the program and Leo DiMaio was named the assistant director of the program.[14]

In addition to the new leadership, the program also had a new name. Since the summer of 1968, students in the program had questioned the name "Program for Disadvantaged Youth." Several students, including Donna-jean Wosencroft and Georgia Machado, complained to Harold Langlois about the name. By the end of the summer, as Langlois was leaving, the program changed its name to Special Program for Talent Development (TD). According to Hardge, the new name of the program was chosen "to emphasize the aspirations of higher education and development of potential, rather than to focus on the students' background as the previous title did."[15]

In the fall of 1969, the program also hired John Wills as a full-time recruiter. Wills, who had previously worked as a counselor for the state's Vocational Rehabilitation Program, was responsible for expanding the program's recruitment efforts in the city of Providence as well as other cities in the state, including Central Falls, Newport, Pawtucket, Warwick, and Woonsocket.

Wills was also responsible for coordinating a new partnership between the program and the Providence public schools to provide tutoring and advising to students in the 11th and 12th grades. "It was necessary to devise a mechanism to salvage these students before they become totally discouraged and disillusioned by the failure of our social and academic systems," said Hardge. The program did not trust the teachers, guidance counselors, and school administrators in Providence with creating a pathway for Black students to attend college. "Everything militates against the black as a professional person," stated Hardge. "In the schools, these students are discouraged from attempting to pursue courses that lead to higher education. Instead they are directed toward vocational type courses."[16] The program had decided that if there was to be a pipeline from the high schools to the University for Black students, the program had to create it on its own.

The partnership with the Providence schools and statewide recruitment efforts began to bear fruit in 1970. The summer program accepted 94 students in 1970. Eventually, 40 of the 94 were accepted to the URI. Twenty-seven students were accepted to Rhode Island College and 20 to the Junior College. In addition to having its largest summer class, the program had its largest geographic diversity. Although most students were still from Providence, the program saw an increase in the number of students from other urban areas, including high schools in Cranston, East Providence, Newport, and Pawtucket.

Race was another area of increased diversity. In the summer of 1970, 18 of the 94 students were White. The program had made it clear that its mission was to accept "disadvantaged" students, and that included low-income, White students who were the first members of their families to attend college. The decision from the onset of the program to include White students turned out to be an important strategic decision in the years that followed. As anti-affirmative action lawsuits and conservative attacks on government spending began to emerge in the 1970s, special college access programs for students of color began to lose support from state governments and universities.[17]

As Alan Sadovnik, who examined compensatory programs in higher education in the 1960s, noted, "In the 1970s, liberal education reforms were placed under both critical and skeptical examination. As part of the conservative attack on government spending, funding for various programs was cut back." Moreover, Sadovnik argued, "conservative critics argued that the goals of equality of opportunity had been superseded by the attention to equality of outcomes, threatening the meritocratic selection process by destroying traditional academic standards."[18]

The challenges to college access programs for students of color began to gain traction in the 1970s. In New York City, the City University of New York, which had been at the forefront of providing college access opportunities for historically marginalized people by providing a tuition-free college education, began to charge tuition for the first time in the 1970s, as the Black and Latino student population began to increase.[19] Additionally, the *Bakke* decision in 1978, which upheld the right of universities to use race as one factor in determining admissions decisions, also made "affirmative action vulnerable to legal challenge," according to Okechukwu (2019, 6), because the split decision by the Supreme Court "raised questions" about the legal precedent of affirmative action.[20]

Therefore, at the same time the special college access programs created in the 1960s began to experience legal and political attacks in states and universities across the country, the TD Program in Rhode Island seemed to be gaining support from state and university officials. At the end of the 1969 summer program, Rhode Island's Lieutenant Governor J. Joseph Garrahy, who visited the program to observe it in action, stated that he was "impressed" with the program and was going to "recommend to Gov. Licht that it be expanded next year."[21]

As of 1970, the future of the program looked promising. The state's lieutenant governor was in support of the program. The state board of higher education had hired a new director, a new assistant director, and a full-time recruiter to expand the reach and support of the program. Faculty members at the URI, who had been reluctantly in support of the program, had also begun to express more support for the students by agreeing to participate in conferences organized by the program to learn about how to support Black students at the University.[22] Additionally, in 1970, the summer program had seen the largest number of students since its founding in 1968 and the URI had accepted its largest class of TD students since its founding. Moreover, the program had increased its geographic and racial diversity.

However, as 1970 came to a close, there were problems for the program and the University. The Black students on campus had begun to challenge the administration for its failure to increase the number of Black students, staff, and faculty, as well as courses in Black Studies. The University was also preparing to grapple with the financial implications of the program. In a letter from University President Werner Baum to Vice President Jerome Pollack, dated April 9, 1969, Baum discussed the pending financial predicament of the program[23]:

There appears to be a distinct possibility that we shall raise more than $50,000 of grants and gifts in support of the pre-matriculation program and directly associated activities.

I want you to be absolutely certain that we do not exceed the authorized expenditure level, even if funds should be available. I envision serious difficulties for the fiscal year 1970-71, when we will presumably have a third group of students participating in this program, and I wish to carry forward into that fiscal year as much of the gift and grant money as possible. If we do not take every precaution, we may have a serious problem on our hands during that year.

Indeed, the University had a serious problem in 1971, and it was a result of the student mobilization on campus.

STUDENT MOBILIZATION

In the late 1960s, the Black Power movement had gained momentum in cities throughout the United States. The movement also had a profound impact on college campuses. In the late 1960s and early 1970s, Black student protests took place at public universities, historically Black colleges and universities, and private universities.[24] The students were demanding an end to the political, social, and economic structures that led to the oppression of Black people. On the college campuses, the goal of the Black Power movement translated into the demands for greater access for Black students, Black professors and staff, and Black Studies programs.

In Rhode Island, Black students on the campus of the URI were experiencing similar conditions to Black students on other campuses and also organized to demand action from university officials. In the late 1960s, the URI-Afro American Society (AAS) mobilized to make demands on behalf of Black students at the University. Although the URI-AAS focused its action on the URI campus, they were supported by the Black community in Providence, where most of the students came from. In fact, Providence's Black community was not only supporting the URI-AAS, it was also instrumental in the support of the AAS at Brown University.

In his book on Black student protests on Ivy League campuses, Stefan Bradley writes about how leaders of the Brown University AAS "benefited from external support" from the Black community in Providence. In a press conference held by the AAS on December 9, 1968, the group wanted to "express gratitude" to the local Black community "not only because of their support in giving us money and food but most important of all they gave us moral support."[25]

In the spring of 1969, as the semester was coming to an end, students from the URI-AAS sent a letter to the university administration. In addition to sending the letter, the students also planned to organize a boycott of classes if the University was not responsive to their demands. The letter, dated May 5, 1969, stated:

"[The] Afro-American Society at URI has evaluated the progress made by the Administration in solving the inequalities that exist in the areas of enrollment of black students, recruitment of black professors, administrators, and development of black courses. We have concluded that the following demands must be met before the University of Rhode Island can serve the Black, as well as the white, community in a meaningful way."[26]

The students made five demands:

1. Increase the number of Black students to 2.5 percent of the total enrollment at URI by the fall of 1969, with a further increase to 5.0 percent by the fall of 1970.
2. Appoint a Black director who would recruit black students for admissions to this University, starting now.
3. Recruit additional Black faculty members and administrators.
4. Appoint a Black administrator to the Admissions Board, starting now.
5. Add additional Black courses to the curriculum at URI

In response to the student demands and the threat to boycott classes, URI President Werner Baum issued a statement to the campus community. He opened the statement by stating, "I shall be sorry if our black students cheat themselves by boycotting classes for a day. They shall be the losers of a day's teaching. So long as they do not interfere with the rights of others or the normal operation of the University, they are free to deprive themselves if they wish."[27]

Then, the statement listed the University's accomplishments in "improving opportunities for the black citizens of Rhode Island," which included becoming the "first major state university with a black vice president" and "the appointment of another well-known black citizen of Rhode Island to an administration post dealing specifically with the problems of the underpriviledged." The appointment he mentioned was in reference to the hiring of Rev. Hardge who would be officially hired by the University the following month, in June of 1969. Baum also stated that they "expect to have three black teaching faculty this fall."

On the issue of Black student enrollment, Baum touted how the "University initiated a state-wide program to recruit black students from Rhode Island high schools" and the University's plan to expand the summer program. However, he also added that many of the students were not prepared to enroll at the URI and "[I] believe it is an injustice to any student to admit him if he is unprepared or enroll him in a watered-down curriculum." He concluded by stating, "I am willing to discuss other recommendations with any individual or group. However, such talks must proceed in a rational manner around the conference table."

The day following Baum's statement, the students carried out the boycott "to express our dissatisfaction with the existing conditions relating to the Black students at URI." They added, "We hope the faculty will show their support by attending our protest rally in body as well as spirit."

The students did not view Baum's statement as meeting their demands. Although the University would eventually hire Rev. Hardge as an administrator and then John Wills as a recruiter, in May of 1969, these Black administrators had not yet been hired by the University. Furthermore, although the summer program of 1968 had enrolled 43 students, only 13 of the 43 students were accepted by the University.

To the students, the University's claim that the students were not prepared to be at the University was also hollow. They understood that most of the Black students coming out of the Rhode Island high schools did not meet the traditional requirements for university admission. However, they viewed the purpose of the program to provide the academic tutoring and support to ensure that students would be successful at the University, despite the high school shortcomings, which they considered a reflection of a racist system of education and not of their ability to be college students. According to the students, it was the University's responsibility to provide the tutoring and support for students to be successful and that had to be done at the URI, not at the Junior College, as the president had suggested in his statement.

Furthermore, the students, who had been working with and were supported by the Black community in Providence, were fully aware that all of the "accomplishments" that Baum and the university administration were touting on "improving opportunities for the black citizens of Rhode Island" had been achieved by community pressure and not out of the University's own initiative. They knew that if conditions were to improve, they would have to demand it.

Additionally, many viewed Baum's statement and approach to the student and community demands as condescending, which contributed to tensions that would escalate in the years that followed and reach a boiling point in 1971. Although the program did experience growth in 1969 and 1970, in 1971, summer enrollment dropped to its lowest number since 1968. At the end of the 1971 summer program, only 23 students were accepted to the University, 17 less than had been accepted in 1970. A number of political and economic factors at the national, state, and university level had placed the program under serious threat, only three years after its founding. In the face of this threat, the students responded.

STUDENT TAKEOVER

At the start of 1971, as Governor Licht was inaugurated for a second term, the state of Rhode Island was facing a fiscal crisis. After Licht's 1970 reelection, his administration revealed that the state had a $25 million deficit.[28] Licht attributed the financial crisis to Richard Nixon's administration policies, which led to "rising welfare and medical assistance costs and declining revenues."[29] The deficit forced Licht, who had promised not to raise taxes in his campaign, to implement a state personal income tax for the first time in the state's history.

The financial crisis was projected to have an effect on the state budget, and government agencies were required to adjust their annual budget to deal with the state's shortfall. The state's institutions of higher education were included and in the winter and early spring, the URI, Rhode Island College, and Rhode Island Junior College began making adjustments to deal with the new budget realities. In April and May, higher education officials made several trips to the state house in Providence for negotiations and hearings with state legislators and the governor's office.

As news of the budget situation began to spread, officials in the TD Program became concerned about the future funding of the program. Rev. Hardge and Leo DiMaio were discussing the state of the budget with their connections in the University and in state government but received no assurances that the program would avoid any cuts. Their concerns were confirmed when they learned in April that the program was not going to accept the number of students that had been initially expected and the program planned for.

In 1970, the summer program enrolled 93 students, the largest class since the founding of the program. As the program prepared for the summer of 1971, Hardge, DiMaio, and John Wills, who had been recruiting throughout Rhode Island, expected to enroll its largest class. The program had received 232 applications, the largest number to date. After reviewing applications the program had decided that 123 students were eligible for the summer program but were informed by the University that only 110 students could enroll. Although TD officials were not happy with the decision, they did not confront the University, since the 110 students represented an increase from the previous summer's class. However, after the University had to change its budget, administration officials informed the program that only 70 students would be able to participate in the summer program. Furthermore, only 32 students of the 70 would be accepted to the University in the fall. To Hardge and DiMaio, the decrease in summer program students and URI acceptances in the fall was unacceptable.

As the University prepared to make the cuts to the program, the Black students on campus began to mobilize. The URI AAS, whose membership consisted mostly of TD students, learned about the pending cuts from Hardge and DiMaio and added this new concern to their list of demands. The demands, which originally included increasing the number of Black students accepted to the University, as well as increasing the number of Black professors, administrators, and staff, now included the demand for the survival and expansion of the TD Program. The students, whose boycott of classes and protest in 1969 did not lead to the fulfillment of their demands, decided to take more direct action against the administration.

On Wednesday, May 5, 1971, two years to the date of the AAS demand letter to President Baum, 35 members of the AAS walked into the university administration building at 7:20 am.[30] "We went into the [Carlotti] administration building and told everybody to leave, we're going to lock the doors. They realized we were serious; they all left, and we chained the doors," said Valerie Southern, one of the students involved in the takeover.[31] The students chained the 5 building doors and demanded to see President Baum. Baum, who had not been feeling well and was not in his office, was called by administrators in the building and asked to come meet with the students. Baum arrived at 8:00 am in pajamas and overcoat and was let in the building by campus security who had cut the chains to enter the building. When Baum walked in to see the students, leaders of the AAS told the president that they had 13 demands and they had placed a document with their demands on his desk and wanted a meeting with the president immediately to discuss their demands. Baum met with three AAS leaders in his office (AAS President Thomas P. Ellison, Vice President Louis S. Francis Jr., and Rebecca Rocha). The president told the leaders that he was scheduled to be in Providence for a hearing at the State House at 1 pm but that he would meet with the students at 4:00 pm.

The students agreed to return later that afternoon for the 4:00 pm meeting. However, after they left the president's office, the 35 members met as a group and decided that they were not going to wait until 4:00 pm (see Figure 3.1). They decided to return to the administration building. At 11:00 am the students returned and Ellison said, "We don't plan to leave until the demands are met. We are not going to sit in any conference room and have him [Baum] cut us up. We're not going to class."[32]

The students staged a sit-in in the first-floor lobby. Students were eating chips, playing cards, and singing (see Figure 3.2). One student, Georgia Machado, who was part of the first TD class in 1968, was reading a book. "Georgia was really smart and always doing schoolwork," remembers her close friend Donna-jean Wosencroft. "She was in there reading but we were all worried for her because she had Lupus and we were concerned with what [might happen] to her." Langlois, the former director, remembers Machado being "one of the smartest students I have been around." Machado, who was a couple of years older than the rest of the students, was seen as a leader by her fellow students and would be one of the leaders during and after the student takeover in 1971.

As the students waited, Vice President for Financial Affairs Joseph O'Connell pleaded with the students to leave before the state police came in an arrested them. However, the students responded by saying that they "were going to stay until their demands were met." By the early afternoon, university administration, recognizing that the students were not going to leave, asked Rev. Hardge and Leo DiMaio to convince the students to leave, but they had no success. Additionally, the 4:00 pm meeting that Baum had scheduled with the students did not happen.

As the afternoon turned into early evening, students on the campus were being told about the student takeover of the administration building. By 10:30 pm, more than 1,000 students, mostly White, had come to the administration building to support the 35 students who had barricaded themselves in the Bursar and Registrar's office. The campus police, seeing the growing body of students, called the South Kingstown police for backup. Then the state police were called in.

Shortly after 10:30 pm, more than 20 state police officers arrived in riot gear. Once they arrived, they were confronted by the students outside the building who attempted to keep them out. Although the chains to the doors were cut, the students inside the building used desks to block the doors and the state police used a metal stanchion to batter down the door. As the state police tried to make their way into the barricaded room, a

South Kingston police officer opened a side window and began to spray mace into the room where the students were staying. As the police officer sprayed mace, a group of students outside the building grabbed the police officer's hand and shut the window to stop him from continuing to mace the room. A state trooper, who saw the students struggling with the police officer, ran in to help the officer and used a club to break the window and the police officer continued to mace the room.

As the South Kingstown and state police forced their way into the building, the students gathered outside the building began throwing rocks at the police and at their vehicles. In the melee, at least 7 students were hurt and required medical attention at the URI health center and South County hospital. One student was knocked unconscious by the encounter with the state police. As the state police entered the building, Leo DiMaio, the TD assistant director, tried to shield the students with his body but he couldn't stop the state police from entering the room. "We were all lying on the floor with our arms interlocked," remembers Daniel Price, Jr, one of the student leaders. "And just when the police hit the door with a battering ram (or whatever they used), a photographer's flash bulb went through the door—very scary. The first person to enter the room was Mr. D, scurrying over the file cabinets and desks we had used for the barricade, shouting to the state police captain by name—'Don't lay a hand on any one of my students in this room!!' "[33] As the police entered the room, the 35 students waited calmly on the floor with their Black Power fists clenched in the air.

By 11:15 pm, the incident was over and the students walked out peacefully. As they walked out of the building, the AAS students were greeted by cheers from the students who had gathered outside the building to support them. The gathering turned into a rally and AAS leaders spoke about their demands to roars of approval. "We don't want to meet with Baum tomorrow," shouted AAS President Thomas Ellison. "We want to meet him tonight!"[34] The president, who had previously said that he would only discuss student demands "in a rational manner around the conference table" and who issued a statement earlier that week declaring zero tolerance for campus disturbances, agreed to meet the student leaders in his residence that evening. Shortly after 12:00 am, the AAS students walked to president's home to discuss their demands.

As the state learned about the student protest at the URI, many began to express their displeasure with the Black students and their demands. Some state legislators called the students "ungrateful" and objected to the timing of their actions and demands. According to some, the student demonstrations were "ill-advised, particularly because the state is in such a fiscal bind that legislators are seeking state budget items to eliminate, not increase."[35]

Although some viewed the timing of the student demands as irresponsible, given the state's fiscal woes, the students disagreed. "We're not asking for privileges," said Georgia Machado. "If legislators, the Board of Regents, and the presidents were doing their jobs, there would be no list of demands."[36] Another AAS student added, "We saw what they were trying to do. We looked around and found that the whole feeder program for black students might be wiped out." For the students, the timing was right. If they did not take action at that moment, the TD Program may have been "wiped out" and their concerns about Black student enrollment and other issues would not have been addressed. "We're fed up, we ain't taking it no more," said Rebecca Rocha, one of the student leaders.[37]

Although many in the state opposed the students, their demands were supported by many within and outside the University. Charlie Fortes and the community organizations he was part of in Providence supported the students. The new Commissioner of Education, Fred Burke, also supported the student demands and stated that "to cut back" the TD Program, "is to serve notice to the disenfranchised that they once again are being left behind." Within the University, Rev. Hardge and Leo DiMaio became forceful advocates of the program and the student demands. Additionally, the presence of White students during the takeover of the administration building and other protest rallies also showed that there was a level of support within the student body beyond that of the Black students and the AAS.

The student actions may have indeed saved the program. In the 1970s, several political and economic factors converged that posed a significant

Figure 3.1 Student rally after takeover of administration building (1971).
(Credit: University of Rhode Island Archives)

threat to programs like TD. Richard Nixon's election in 1968 began the
process of withdrawing the federal government's support for Lyndon
Johnson's "Great Society" programs.

Additionally, Nixon's "New Federalism" began to shift power in various policy areas from the national government to the states. As the states
began to gain more power, a shift that would start with Nixon and expand with Reagan's presidency in the 1980s, state governments also became increasingly conservative. Conservative policy organizations like
the American Legislative Exchange Council, Cato Institute, and Heritage
Foundation all emerged in the 1970s and their influence helped shaped
tax and education policies, among many other issues, particularly at the
state level.[38]

The ascendency of these organizations and the emergence of conservative state legislators and governors in the 1970s had a profound effect on tax
policies and race-based initiatives, including affirmative action policies in
colleges and universities. As was discussed earlier in this chapter, the City
University of New York, which provided tuition-free education, began

Figure 3.2 Student takeover of administration building (1971). (Credit: University of Rhode Island Archives)

charging tuition in the 1970s. Additionally, legal challenges to affirmative action began to emerge in the 1970s as well.

The Black students at URI could not have known the factors that were coming together in 1971 that would shape American politics and higher education policy for the years and decades that followed. However, they knew at that moment in 1971 that their struggle for greater opportunities for Black people at URI was in serious jeopardy. History has proven the students right.

In 1971, the program did experience a decline. The number of students who participated in the summer program and were eventually accepted to URI decreased from 1970 to 1971. However, after 1972, the program began to see increases in the number of students accepted. President Baum, while stating that he could not meet all of the demands of the students, did deliver on many of the demands, including hiring a Black admissions officer, waiving the admissions application fee for low-income students, providing free public transportation for students to go to their communities, and a Black Studies concentration. Additionally, Baum stated that while he could not control state appropriations to the University, if the University had to make cuts, "the talent development program would be near the bottom of the list of things to be cut."[39]

As the decade entered its midpoint, the program survived its first serious threat. Similar programs would experience a decline and some were eliminated altogether, but the TD Program grew in the mid-1970s. The student protests were critical to the survival of the program at this moment of widespread retrenchment, showing the power and importance of protest as a tool for policy maintenance that would be relied upon by future generations of TD students.

At the same time, with growth came another set of concerns, primarily how to serve the needs of the growing student body in the program. Although Rev. Hardge and Leo DiMaio were prominent figures at the University and in statewide circles, whose influence provided the political support the program needed then and in the years that followed, their responsibilities increasingly took them away from the day-to-day needs of the students in the program.

The program lacked an institutionalized form of understanding and addressing the needs of the students. A report, commissioned by the program in 1972, stated that although the program had achieved significant "accomplishments," it was "in need of additional staff, particularly counseling personnel, to meet the needs of their student population."[40] The report confirmed what the program administrators understood, that the program had to create an advising and support structure capable of serving the needs of their students.

The Work of Developing Scholars

By the mid-1970s, the Talent Development (TD) Program was once again growing and seemingly free from external threats. Politically, the program had been able to survive because it had an "inside" and "outside" strategy. From the inside, the leaders of the program relied on their relationships with university officials and statewide leaders to gain support for the program. From the outside, community leaders in Providence made sure to keep pressure on the University and statewide leaders to support the program as well. Additionally, an important aspect of the outside strategy, student mobilization, which included protest and a takeover of the administration building, created the political pressure to continue support for the program.

In addition to implementing the political strategies necessary for the continuation of the program, the program also had to provide support for their students to ensure their academic success. The work of "developing" scholars who were not considered college ready required the type of academic, financial, and personal support that the University was neither equipped to provide nor concerned about providing. Therefore, achieving the goals of community-centered affirmative action also required political attention. How does a program that admits students who do not meet the traditional admissions requirements and who are not considered to be academically prepared to be at the University help students earn a college degree? This chapter turns its attention to the political and individual

Developing Scholars. Domingo Morel, Oxford University Press. © Oxford University Press 2023.
DOI: 10.1093/oso/9780197636992.003.0005

work the program had to undertake, and continues to undertake, to develop scholars.

CREATING AN INFRASTRUCTURE OF SUPPORT

In the 1970s, as the program grew, so did the needs of the students, and the program was ill-prepared to deal with these growing needs. Rev. Hardge, or Rev, was a formidable political force as the director of the program and could call on the likes of John Chafee for political support. Chafee, who became Secretary of the Navy after his gubernatorial defeat in 1968, had been elected US Senator from Rhode Island in 1976. Rev also counted on the support of the Black leaders from Providence and Newport, among other cities, with whom he had worked on civil rights, housing, and education issues since his arrival from Connecticut in 1963.

Leo DiMaio, or "Mr. D," as he was affectionately called by the TD students, was also a political force in Rhode Island. DiMaio had cultivated political relationships during his time at the Adult Correctional Institutions in Rhode Island. He also built relationships with the Black community in Providence as the head of numerous recreational leagues in the city. Additionally, DiMaio, who grew up in the poor and working-class Italian community of Federal Hill in Providence, had deep connections with the growing political class in Rhode Island. In the 1970s and 1980s, Italian-Americans in Rhode Island emerged as a political power in the state, with increasing numbers of elected officials to city council seats, the state's General Assembly, and the Providence mayoralty. In 1974, Providence elected its first Italian American mayor, Vincent "Buddy" Cianci. DiMaio relied on these childhood relationships to provide the political support the program needed throughout the 1970s and 1980s.

Despite the political muscle Rev and DiMaio provided for the program, their strength was not in providing the day-to-day needs of the students in the program. In addition to Rev and Mr. D, the only other individuals working for the program were John Wills, who was mainly responsible for recruitment, and Laura DiSano, who was the academic officer for the program. DiSano was responsible for providing most of the academic support to the students in the program, which by 1974–1975, had reached more than 200 students. As the program grew in size, the limited staff members were finding it increasingly difficult to stay in touch with the students.

The growing disconnect between the students and the program began to have consequences for the program's retention rates. While the first three classes of the program between 1968 and 1971 had retention rates that surpassed the retention rates of students accepted through regular admissions at the University, by the mid-1970s, the program's retention rates began to suffer, which posed significant challenges for a program whose main argument was that "with our help and support, students could be successful at the University." By the mid-1970s, the program could no longer make that argument with confidence.

However, in 1974, the program began to stabilize its internal challenges when Sharon Reynolds and Frank Forleo joined the program. Sharon Reynolds was a student teacher and then substitute teacher in South County, Rhode Island in 1973 when she learned about the TD Program. "I didn't know much about the program but learned that it was a program to provide equal opportunity," said Sharon.[1] She learned about a residential counselor position for the summer program and applied. However, she was never interviewed or offered a position. In 1974, she applied for a tutor position in the summer program and sent "a ton" of documents to "prove that I was qualified for the position," she said.

Before the start of the summer program in 1974, Sharon was called in for an interview with Rev. Hardge and DiMaio. She felt that the interview was going well and toward the end of the interview, Sharon discussed her experience teaching a group of 9th-grade students who had been separated from their regular classes for behavioral reasons. "I told Rev," said Sharon, "that with these kids you can teach, but with a little bit of love, you get a whole lot farther." "He leaned across the table and said, 'What did you say?'" At that point I thought, "That's it. I shouldn't have talked about emotions." Sharon grew concerned and thought that by discussing her "emotions," she was not going to be offered the position. However, she was pleasantly surprised when "he smiled at me and said, that's what he wanted to hear."

As Rev and DiMaio were trying to build a program to meet the needs of the students, they were deliberate, as Harold Langlois was before them, about hiring people who understood their needs. They were deliberate about hiring individuals who viewed the TD students as potential scholars rather than students with deficiencies that made them ineligible for admission to the University. Rev. Hardge said that they were looking for students "who do not look, talk, or behave like college material but who express something nobody else is looking for, who demonstrate an illusive spark that suggests ability that has been turned off."[2] Rev Hardge and DiMaio decided to hire Sharon as a tutor for the summer program in 1974.

In 1974, the program also came into the life of Frank Forleo. Frank had started at the University of Rhode Island as a first-year student in 1965. By the spring of 1967 he was not doing well at the University and "experienced academic dismissal." That fall of 1967, Frank was drafted by the US Army and sent to fight in the Vietnam War. Upon his return from Vietnam, Frank decided to return to the University to complete his degree and began as a part-time student in 1969. After earning his bachelor's degree, he entered a graduate program in English and became a teaching assistant. While teaching a course in writing for the department, he received a "mid-semester evaluation form" from the TD Program.[3]

"I didn't know anything about the program," said Frank.[4] "I had students of color in my class but I didn't know they were part of any program," he added. After receiving the mid-semester evaluation forms for some of the students he had in the class, he made it a point to meet the program administrators and walked over to the TD office in Ballentine Hall to introduce himself to Rev. Hardge and DiMaio. Then, that following spring he learned that the program was looking to hire tutors and instructors for their summer program and he decided to apply. The program hired him as a writing instructor for the summer program in 1975.

That prematriculation summer of 1975, Frank and Sharon met for the first time. That started a courting relationship and eventual marriage. It also started a relationship with the program that would last for more than 40 years. Frank and Sharon Forleo would serve as tutors, writing instructors, academic advisors, and eventually assistant, associate, and interim directors for the program in the years that followed. Equally as important, Frank would also become the program's institutional historian, making sure that as new generations of students entered the program, they would know about its history, particularly the history of student struggle on campus. By ensuring that students understood their history, they would also be politicized and mobilize when threats to the program emerged.

Although the program had made student support a central part of its mission, what we consider academic advisement today did not exist then. Academic advisement and support was a new concept and staff members could not consult existing manuals, lists of "best practices," or scholarship on advising which they could rely on to help them build a support infrastructure for the students. The program's model of support and advisement was built on the fly, based mostly on what the students told them they needed. "The students were their best advocates," said Sharon. "They took ownership of their experience at the University and told us what they needed. And they taught me. I was a White girl from East Bay who had to learn what their experience was like."

Using student feedback as the foundation for developing an advising model, the program began to put steps in place that would bring the students back in. "We did what we needed to do to reach them," said Frank. By meeting the needs of the students—academic, personal, emotional, and financial—the program provided a reason for the students to reconnect. "We didn't have phones in dorm rooms back then," said Sharon, "so that meant that at times, we knocked on their dormitory doors to speak to them."

I can attest to the approach Sharon mentions. Two decades later, when there were phones in the dorm rooms, I was a first-year student at the University. During the fall semester, my friends and I, all TD students, were enrolled in an introductory sociology course. The class was a large lecture and met on Tuesdays and Thursdays at 8:00 am. Several weeks into the semester, we figured out that we might be able to get away without attending the lectures. Slowly, our group of friends, all first-year students of color, began to miss the class lectures.

One Tuesday morning shortly after 8:00 am, I received a call in my room. It was Sharon Forleo. Sharon was my academic advisor in the program and said, "What are you doing in your room? You're supposed to be in class." Professor Peters, the sociology professor who had a long relationship with the program, had alerted Sharon about the TD students missing his class. "You should go to his office hours after class today to speak to him before you fail the class," she told me. I went to the professor's office hours, which were held after his 8:00 am class and when I arrived at his office, there was a line of TD students waiting to speak to the professor as well. We had all received that call.

Over time, the structure of support the program created for the students consisted of academic services that included assigning each student an academic advisor with whom they would meet with on a regular basis, providing advice on course selection for a major of study, and developing a tutoring program to support students with a particular course or broadly in the areas of math, science, reading, and writing. In addition to providing academic support, the program also had to develop a system of support that went well beyond the traditional "academic" support services. At times, it meant providing emotional, professional, and legal support for young women who were sexually assaulted or had experienced domestic violence. At other times, it meant providing shelter and food for students who did not have a home to go to during the summer and winter school breaks. Or ensuring that a student received adequate medical attention for a physical ailment or mental illness.

As the students enrolled in the program, they brought their individual, community, political, social, and economic realities through the doors of the program. For the program, this meant always learning how to address the needs of the students as they emerged, well before the scholarship identified the issues and recommended possible solutions to societal concerns. In the 1970s, the program began to experience demographic changes. Although the Black student population served as the foundation of the program, by the 1970s, Rhode Island's demographics began to change, and so did the program's.

One of the changes occurred after the fall of Saigon in 1975 and the end of the Vietnam War. The Indochina Migration and Refugee Act of 1975 and then the Refugee Act of 1980 created an opportunity for refugees from Vietnam as well as Cambodia and Laos to settle in the United States. Between 1975 and 1980, roughly 250,000 refugees from Southeast Asia arrived in the United States.[5] With the help of the International Institute, an immigrant support agency in Rhode Island, and the Catholic Social Service, Providence was one of the destination cities for the newly arrived refugees from Southeast Asia, particularly Cambodians, Laotians, and the Hmong.[6]

In the 1970s and 1980s, the Latino community in Rhode Island began growing as well. Immigrants from Colombia started arriving in the mid- to late 1960s to work in the textile mills and factories in the city of Central Falls.[7] Puerto Ricans, and then Dominicans, started arriving in larger numbers from New York City in the late 1970s and 1980s. In the 1980s, Guatemalans escaping the country's civil war began arriving in Rhode Island as well. The arrival of Colombians, Puerto Ricans, Dominicans, Guatemalans, and immigrants from other Latin American countries led to a 132 percent increase in the state's Latino population between 1980 and 1990.[8]

In the 1970s and 1980s, Rhode Island also experienced an increase in immigrants from Africa. Although Cape Verdeans can trace their presence in New England to the late 19th and early 20th century, as whalers and fishermen in port cities like Boston, Fall River, New Bedford, and Providence, a later wave began arriving in Providence in the 1970s.[9] Additionally, the civil war in Liberia in the late 1980s led to roughly a third of the population fleeing the country. While most of the Liberians went to the neighboring countries in West Africa, many arrived in the United States, and Rhode Island was among the top destination states for Liberians.[10] Immigrants from Nigeria and Ghana also began arriving in Rhode Island during this period.

The arrival of immigrants from Africa, Latin America, and Southeast Asia in Rhode Island in the 1970s and 1980s began to change the state's demographics, particularly in the city of Providence. As the immigrant population grew, and the school populations reflected these changes, the TD Program's student population also began to change.

In addition to the growing racial and ethnic diversity of the program, TD also experienced growing geographic diversity within the state. Although the majority of the students were still coming from the Providence high schools, students from high schools from all corners of the state were increasingly participating in the program as well. By expanding college access opportunities to students throughout the entire state, the program began building a statewide political coalition that was difficult to challenge.

In addition to the equal opportunity arguments that the program would make to university and state officials to continue receiving support, the program could now also count on support from formal and informal partnerships with teachers, superintendents, school board members, city council members, mayors, and state legislators in each of the communities the students came from.

Formally, the program entered into an agreement with the Providence public schools to create a tutoring program that would serve as a pipeline for students from the Providence schools to the TD Program.[11] By the end of the 1970s, program officials had also built informal partnerships with guidance counselors in every high school in the state. Guidance counselors had been and have continued to be a problem for students of color, since they serve as gatekeepers who were more prone to discourage students of color from pursuing a 4-year college education. However, by providing opportunities for students who otherwise would not have an opportunity to attend college, guidance counselors, particularly in the urban high schools, viewed the program as an asset worthy of cultivating a relationship with.

Moreover, to limit the role of the guidance counselors as gatekeepers, who would select who was deserving of the opportunities the program provided, the program's recruiters asked to speak to as many high school seniors as possible during recruitment events. By speaking directly to the students about the program and debunking the myths of college attendance that discouraged students of color from applying for college, the TD recruiters attempted to minimize the discouraging effects that guidance counselors and teachers might have had on their Black students and other students of color. In later years, recruitment events at the largest urban high schools in the state—Central, Hope, Mount Pleasant, Central Falls, Cranston East, East Providence, Shea, Woonsocket—saw the entire senior class fill the auditorium to listen to the TD presentations.

Additionally, by the late 1970s, alums began to play an important role for the program. High schools invited their former students, who had graduated from the University, to speak to the younger students about their college experiences. TD recruiters also brought students back to their former high schools during recruitment events. In addition, TD graduates like Deborah Bush and Donna-jean Wosencroft, who became teachers and taught in the Providence schools, informed their students about the program and encouraged them to apply.

These formal and informal ties with the schools, school districts, and their communities provided a formidable support network for the program. These networks became an important part of the program's political community. When the program faced threats of cuts by the University or the state legislature, TD would rely on this community to mobilize in support of the program.

By serving the newest arrivals to the state of Rhode Island, the program was on the forefront of immigration issues in the state and had to adapt its approach to advising and meeting the needs of the state's new arrivals. However, immigration was not the only issue the program had to quickly adapt to. By the late 1970s, what has become known as the era of mass incarceration in the United States was beginning to affect families in Rhode Island, particularly Black families.

"LIKE AN UNDERGROUND RAILROAD"

Between 1978 and 1988, the rate of incarceration in Rhode Island more than doubled, from roughly 70 incarcerations per 100,000 people in 1978 to 170 incarcerations per 100,000 people in 1988.[12] By 1994, the rate had increased to 300 incarcerations per 100,000 people in the state. Like most of the United States, the rise of incarceration rates was largely a result of the increase in incarceration of Black people. Although Black residents represent only 7 percent of the state's population, they represent roughly 30 percent of the incarcerated population.[13]

The consequences of changing policing and increasing incarceration rates in the state became another one of the major issues the program had to account for as it grew in the 1970s. From the program's founding, the Rhode Island prison system (Adult Corrections Institute, or ACI) had a ubiquitous presence within the program. Harold Langlois, the program's first director had deep connections to the state's prisons since his father was the warden of the ACI for nearly two decades. Then Leo DiMaio, who became assistant director in 1969, had worked in the ACI as well. Both Langlois and DiMaio often referred to stories about "the can" to warn students about what the alternative may look like if they did not "take care of their schoolwork."

The stories that Langlois and DiMaio shared about prison life to motivate students were personal for an increasing number of students. They were coming from communities where policing had begun taking a toll on their families. These interactions with the police and the court systems increasingly became a part of their world. Some of these interactions involved students themselves, who dealt with legal issues like drug arrests, but much of it also involved dealing with family members who were ensnared in the prison system. Court hearings, probation, parole, legally mandated counseling, and prison became an increasing reality for the students and their families, and supporting these students became part of the work of the program. Writing support letters, making calls to prison officials, helping secure legal counsel, accompanying students to court hearings, and serving as character witnesses became a part of the work the TD staff did to support their students.

Thus, part of the work of bolstering students and ensuring their academic success at the University involved adopting an approach that included a support system that dealt with their students' encounters with policing and the criminal justice system. However, while the program was helping students deal with outcomes of encounters with the criminal justice system, the program provided a sanctuary from incarceration as well.

"I remember going down to campus and thinking, these White kids are doing the same things we're doing in the projects but they're not getting locked up like we were," said Matt Buchanan about his experience as a TD student at the University of Rhode Island. "And basically we did the same things our friends were doing back in Providence but we weren't harassed by the police like they were," he added. While campus police always presented a problem for the students of color at the University of Rhode Island, a reality that eventually led to the second movement of student protest in the early 1990s, the Black students on campus did not face the same type of police abuse that they, and their friends back home, experienced with police.

"It was like an underground railroad," said Gene Kelly about the University of Rhode Island. Gene Kelly did not attend the University of Rhode Island. He graduated from Central High School with Matt Buchanan and me in 1994. Gene, who played basketball for Central, attended Paine College in Georgia after graduating from high school. Paine, a historically Black college, recruited Kelly to play basketball. However, after his first semester at the college, he never returned. For various reasons, Paine College did not work out for Gene.

Gene and Matt were childhood friends who grew up together in the Roger Williams Housing Projects in South Providence. When we returned for our second semester in late January, Gene began spending more time with us at URI and eventually started staying in the dorm room suite we shared with our other friend from Central High School, Richard Hinds. "I didn't know what I wanted to do. I just left the school and didn't have a job or a plan, really," said Kelly. "So I started hanging out with you guys at URI. I didn't want to be back in the projects. You guys had it good down there. You had a meal plan and the gym, that's all I cared about," as he laughed. "But really, I would sneak into the gym and play ball with Cuttino Mobley and Tyson Wheeler and then Lamar Odom and these other guys." "Back in Providence," he added, "we just had to deal with a lot of stuff that I didn't have to deal with when I was down at URI with you guys."

Gene Kelly's experience illustrates how the campus of the University of Rhode Island provided a form of escape for students from the realities of life in Providence and other cities in the state. Although Gene was not a student at the University, he was not alone. TD students, from the first class in 1968 to the current classes, have provided shelter for friends and family members at the University.

For Gene Kelly, Matt Buchanan, and others, the metaphor of the "underground railroad" was not an exaggeration. For young Black men, particularly from the housing projects where Gene and Matt had grown up, incarceration was far more likely than not. "Most of the brothers we grew up with were locked up at some point," said Matt. Their experiences are reflected in the research on the rise of incarceration rates for the cohort of Black men born in the mid- to late 1970s in the United States.

In 2009, Pettit, Sykes, and Western examined a cohort of Americans born between 1945 and 1949 and a second cohort born between 1975 and 1979 and calculated the chances of imprisonment by the age of 34 for members of these cohorts.[14] The researchers found that of the Black males born between 1945 and 1949, 1 in 10 had been in prison by the age of 34. For Black males born between 1975 and 1979, Matt and Gene's cohort, the chances of imprisonment increased to 1 in 4 by the time they reached the age of 34. For high school dropouts, the numbers are stark. Among Black males born between 1945 and 1949 who never completed high school, 14.7 percent had a prison record by age 34. Conversely, 68 percent of Black males born between 1975 and 1979 who dropped out of high school had a prison record by age 34.

In very significant ways, the University, which was only 30 miles south of Providence, provided an escape from the criminal justice system for many. Today, Gene Kelly works with young people in Providence, providing social services, education, and employment opportunities to young people. "I didn't attend URI but while I was down there I was able to buy time and get things together. I don't think things would have turned out the same if I didn't have that time."

DECLINING SUPPORT FOR HIGHER EDUCATION

By 1980, the program had weathered some challenges and continued to grow by expanding college access opportunities to the state's newest arrivals. The new decade, however, would also usher in a new president of the United States, who would lead a national conservative movement that would have significant political and economic implications for higher education, particularly for the poor and historically marginalized.

Although the Supreme Court decision in *Regents of the University of California v. Bakke* in 1978 did not end the use of race as a factor in college admissions, the battle against affirmative action policies gained momentum in the states during the 1980s.[15] However, challenges to affirmative action represented only one aspect of the growing battle over college access. In the 1980s, college affordability became an issue of significant concern for many.

By the 1980s, federal spending on higher education began to decrease from its highest levels in the late 1970s.[16] Importantly, the federal Pell Grants, which provided substantive support for college expenses to low-income students, were no longer keeping up with college expenses beginning in the 1980s. As sociologist Sara Goldrick-Rab notes, "Spending on the Pell program has lagged behind growth in the number of recipients for decades. These trends, along with rising college costs, have resulted in the significant erosion of the Pell purchasing power."[17]

In addition to decreasing federal support for higher education, another dynamic affecting college access was the emergence of for-profit colleges. In the 1980s, for-profit colleges began to receive government support for their expansion.[18] The expansion of for-profit colleges was facilitated by a strategic targeting of low-income students and students of color. Although the for-profit college industry offered opportunities to earn a college degree, its expansion has been highly problematic. As Tressie McMillan Cottom has argued, rather than lessening inequality through higher education, for-profit colleges "rely on persistent inequalities as a business model."[19]

Although federal resources for higher education began to decrease in the 1980s and the for-profit college sector began to gain support during the same period, perhaps the greatest factor affecting college access was the withdrawal of state support for higher education. In the 1980s, state funding for higher education began to decline.[20] As state funding decreased, state colleges and universities began to increasingly rely on tuition as their major source of income. Between 1980 and 2010, the average public 4-year tuition increased by 244 percent.[21] Moreover, by the early 1980s, students began to rely on loans more than grants to support their college education.[22] As Suzanne Mettler has argued, "In effect, public higher education has become increasingly privatized as students and their families have been left to shoulder the increased costs."[23]

The changing landscape of higher education created significant challenges for students of color in the 1980s and the decades that followed. As I will argue in later chapters, these conditions were part of a political response to the emergence of college access opportunities for Black students and other students of color. However, for the time being, it is important to mention the changing landscape of higher education in order to provide a context for understanding the conditions that shaped the realities for the TD Program and its students in the 1980s and into the 1990s.

The state of Rhode Island, like other states, began disinvesting in public higher education in the late 1980s and early 1990s. In fact, by 1992, Rhode Island ranked 47th in the nation in state support for higher education.[24] The state's cuts led the University of Rhode Island to increasingly rely on tuition to sustain the University. As tuition became the greatest source of income, out-of-state students, who paid the full freight of tuition, became increasingly important to the University. By 1989, the University began admitting more out-of-state students than in-state students.[25] Essentially, it stopped being a public university whose primary mission was to serve the residents of the state.

As the University was undergoing a transformation into an increasingly private university, the TD Program also went through a period of transition in the 1980s. Rev. Hardge, who joined the program in 1969 as an assistant director and shortly thereafter became the director, decided to retire in 1980. After leaving the program, Hardge went to work for the Opportunities Industrialization Center of Rhode Island, a job training and placement agency that he helped found along with Cliff Monteiro, Charles "Moe" Adams, and Michael Van Leesten in 1967.[26] After his departure, Leo DiMaio assumed the position as director of the program. Mr. D, became the program's "charismatic director" who led the program "with the discipline of a warden and the affection of a grandfather."[27]

In addition, Frank and Sharon Forleo, who were permanent employees of the program but in a part-time capacity, became full-time advisors in 1983 and 1984, respectively. The University had not provided full-time advising positions for the program; however, DiMaio was able to work out an agreement with the Athletics Department to hire Frank and Sharon full time. The football and basketball programs had several part-time positions for their advising and tutoring programs they had begun to develop in the early 1980s. The coaches agreed to combine their part-time positions with the TD Program and created full-time advising positions that both would share. The arrangement only lasted a couple of years because Athletics and TD would eventually need full-time advisors for each of their respective programs. However, TD remained connected with the basketball and football programs and student-athletes would rely on advising support from TD in the years that followed. In fact, TD would also become a support system to many students of color on campus, even if they were not part of the program. In later years, the program would create a scholarship to provide financial assistance, in addition to advising, to students who needed the support but were not part of the program.

Throughout the 1980s, as government support for higher education began to decrease and support for college access programs decreased as well, the TD Program was in a precarious state. However, throughout this period, the program's student enrollment remained steady. From the early to mid-1980s, roughly 150 students were admitted to the program each year. The program's grant, a key source of financial aid for students, while tenuous, was combined with the Pell Grant and helped cover tuition, room, and board for most of the students.

As the decade came to a close, the program and the University would experience significant changes. A hostile campus climate for students of color would lead to the largest student action since 1971. The students' mobilization and demands coincided with a transition of leadership at the University. Both would have significant consequences for the trajectory of the program.

BLACK STUDENT LEADERSHIP GROUP

By the late 1980s and early 1990s, institutional racism on the campus of the University started reaching a boiling point for Black students and other students of color. In November of 1991, URI staff members wrote a report after attending a conference in the W. Alton Jones campus of the University, which listed a number of issues concerning race on campus, including "the absence of any significant multicultural presence at the university" and a "lack of rigorous action and compliance by the affirmative-action office."[28] In February of 1992, the US Labor Department, which had received a complaint from concerned staff members at the University, issued a report concluding that the University "had fallen short of properly implementing its affirmative-action program," which contributed to the "lack of a racially and culturally diverse campus."[29] Tensions with the campus police were of particular concern. In September of 1992, a report commissioned by the University to study race concerns on campus stated "that racism prevails on the campus, particularly in the school's police department" which was described as an "agency that was out of control."[30]

That fall, the Black students on campus, whose frustration had been festering for years, decided that they had enough. That October, the university library inscribed a quote from Malcom X's *Autobiography* on the top far right corner of the library's entrance which stated:

MY ALMA MATTER WAS BOOKS

A GOOD LIBRARY . . .

I COULD SPEND THE REST OF

MY LIFE READING

JUST SATISFYING MY CURIOSITY

The library inscription angered the Black students because it did not include the full Malcolm X quote. The full quote read: "I told the Englishmen that my alma mater was books, a good library. Every time I catch a plane, I have with me a book that I want to read. And that's a lot of books. If I weren't out there every day battling the white man, I could spend the rest of my life reading, just satisfying my curiosity." By omitting "If I weren't out here everyday fighting the white man," students felt the inscription was "deliberately sanitized" by the University, which added to the student's frustration on campus.[31]

In addition to the tensions on campus, police tensions across the country were also reaching a boiling point. In March of 1991, White police officers in Los Angeles were videotaped beating Rodney King. When three of the four officers were acquitted of assault and use of excessive force on April 29, 1992, the city of Los Angeles erupted in a deadly uprising. These events of police brutality across the country and the building up of racial tensions on the campus of the University of Rhode Island led the students to organize a conference at the W. Alton Jones Campus on November 1, 1992. "We coordinated a retreat to get away and vent," said Malcom Anderson, who was the president of the Black student organization on campus, Uhuru Sasa, formerly the URI Afro-American Society, and a leader of the Black Student Leadership Group (BSLG), which organized the retreat. "Our job," he added, "as a core group included research, maximizing the strengths of group members, and crafting a 14-point plan directed toward the administration. We returned to campus focused and unified."[32]

The students decided that they would take over a university building to get attention from university officials. On November 10, 300 students took over Taft Hall, where the TD Program had its offices. The students, mostly Black, but who included members of the Narragansett Native Nation and Latinos as well, renamed the building Malcolm X Hall and issued a list of 14 demands that they wanted the University to agree to by noon the next day. Among the demands were the creation of an African American Studies major as well as a Native American Studies major. Sye Johnson, one of the student leaders, said, "As a Narragansett, this is my land that my people cultivated and died for, that I have no voice on."[33] Other demands included increasing Black student enrollment, increasing scholarships for students of color, hiring counselors of color, hiring an affirmative action officer, and renovating and renaming the multicultural center.

As the administration received the demands, it immediately became one of the biggest challenges of Robert Carothers's young presidency. Carothers had just started his tenure as president of the University in July of 1991. At the time of the takeover, Carothers was in New Orleans on a business trip and had to issue a response remotely. However, unlike former President Werner Baum, who dismissively responded to Black student demands two decades earlier and allowed the campus police, South Kingstown police, and the state police to remove the student protestors in 1971 by force, Carothers ordered university officials to leave the students alone and not respond until he returned from his trip.

In his absence, University Vice President John McCray, an African American, represented the administration. In response to questions about removing the students from the building, Dr. McCray said "there were no plans to make the students leave. I believe the students have behaved themselves in a polite and responsible manner. We are in sympathy with their concerns in the increasing incidents of racism not only in this community but worldwide."[34] Then, when asked about the student demands, McCray responded by calling the demands "reasonable" and added, "Obviously, not all these things can be done by Thursday. But if they hold the administration's feet to the fire, that's good too."[35]

The next day, President Carothers met with the students in Taft Hall (see Figure 4.1). The room was filled to capacity with nearly 200 individuals crammed into the meeting room on the first floor. Joining Carothers was McCray who stood behind his left shoulder and around the table were Malcolm Anderson and other current and former TD students, including

Earl Smith, Charles Watson, Michelle Fontes, and Laitin Yussuf. In addition to TD students, the program's staff, including Frank and Sharon Forleo, were involved in organizing, strategizing, and advising the Black Student Leadership Group. Ed Givens, a former TD student who joined the staff as an academic advisor, took on a leadership role as well. He was critical of the University's lack of responsiveness leading up to the takeover and agreed with "the overt racism and institutional racism that's going on on this campus." "The students want programs," he added, but "so far it's all been lip service."[36]

When the meeting started and Carothers began responding to the demands, he said, "Malcolm, I am proud of the leadership you and your colleagues have shown in advancing the agenda to eliminate racism and bigotry in this nation, this state and on the campuses of the University of Rhode Island." Once again, Carothers had demonstrated that he was going to take a different approach to the student demands than Baum did in 1971. He then added, "There is no issue more critical to our future as a people."[37]

Figure 4.1 Black Student Leadership Group (1992). (Credit: University of Rhode Island Archives)

Following Carothers's statement, Malcom Anderson responded. He said in his response to Carothers, "The state of Rhode Island is in the process of changing. A commitment has to be made from the top. I don't know that the commitment is ready to be made. How long do we have to wait for these changes? You seem to me like you're sincere about what you're saying. I don't know. Only time will tell."[38]

In the weeks and months that followed, the University responded by meeting some of the student demands, but not all. The University hired a new affirmative action officer, addressed concerns with the campus police department by firing a police officer who was known to harass students of color, created an African American Studies major, and built a new multicultural center on campus. During Carothers's years, TD experienced the largest increases in student enrollment in the program's history. Between 1991, the year Carothers was hired as president, and 2009, the year he retired, program enrollment increased from 299 to 1,173 enrolled students (see fig. 4.2).

However, while TD enrollments increased, the demand of accepting 20 percent students of color annually was never met. Although Carothers had proposed instituting student quotas to increase student of color enrollment, and the faculty senate approved the measure, the quota proposal was never realized.

Additionally, the University never created a Native American Studies major and Taft Hall was not changed to Malcom X Hall. Instead, the University named the room on the first floor of Taft Hall, where the

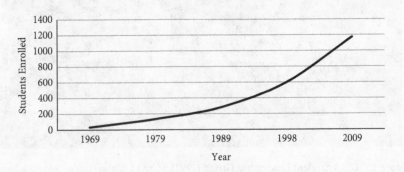

Figure 4.2 Talent Development student enrollment (1969–2008).

meeting between Carothers and the BSLG took place, the Malcolm X Reading Room. The University did not hire counselors of color in the University's counseling office or the office of career services immediately, which led to student criticism. However, those demands never went away and the University eventually hired counselors of color in the Counseling Center, including hiring a Black director of the Counseling Center before the end of Carothers's tenure.

Although the University was not able to deliver on all of the student demands, many of the demands were met. Perhaps the most important achievement of the BSLG could not have been measured at the time of their demands. As a result of their actions, which took place only a year into Carothers's presidency, the Black students set a tone and forged a relationship with the president, even if imperfect, based on demands for better opportunities and campus climate for current and future Black, Latino, Asian, and Native American students.

It is hard to say how Carothers would have responded to issues of race on campus if it had not been for the actions of the BSLG. When he first arrived on campus, he mentioned that he learned from his mother to have

Figure 4.3 Harold Langlois. (Credit: Dave Salerno)

Figure 4.4 Arthur L. Hardge. (Credit: University of Rhode Island Archives)

"a very strong, passionate sense of justice." "I think one of the reasons I work in public education," he added, "is that I have always felt the need to create opportunities for people—to create a more just world, where social class and wealth don't dictate the parameters of aspiration and achievement." Indeed, over time, Carothers became the most consequential URI president in TD's history. In addition to increasing student enrollment, Carothers also increased the amount of the University's grant for TD students. In future years, he would be known to say that his best investment was in the TD Program.

It may have been that Carothers was intent on doing his best to address issues of race and social justice on campus but there is also no denying that the University, the state legislature, state board of education, and other political institutions did not share his same views on racial justice. Therefore, without the demands from the students, it is highly unlikely that the University would have addressed the student concerns.

Equally as important, with the hindsight of history, we now know that the emergence of neoliberal policies in the 1990s seriously threatened and even ended college access programs and policies for students of color in states across the country. In the 1990s, the SEEK program in the City University of New York (CUNY) system, open admissions in the CUNY system, and affirmative action in California's public institutions of higher education were attacked or eliminated.[39] The state's disinvestment in public higher education did threaten the TD Program; however, student activism in the early 1990s, like the student activism in the early 1970s, led the University to expand rather than cut support for the program.

Figure 4.5 Leo DiMaio. (Credit: University of Rhode Island Archives)

TRANSITION IN LEADERSHIP

The program's leadership also played an instrumental role in the expansion of the program. Leo DiMaio kept the program together, and growing, as the director since the departure of Rev. Hardge in 1980. His deep contacts with state government officials and within the University also protected the program from internal and external threats. He was joined in this effort by Sharon Forleo, Frank Forleo, Ed Givens, and Earl Smith, who had joined the staff in the early 1990s. By the mid-1990s, Gerald Williams, a former TD student also joined the staff.

But by the late 1990s, there would be another period of leadership transition. DiMaio decided to retire in 1999. For nearly two decades, DiMaio had been the public face of the program. Following his departure, it was unclear who the next director of the program was going to be.

To many, Sharon Forleo or Frank Forleo seemed the obvious candidates to replace DiMaio. Frank had stepped in as interim director after DiMaio retired. Although he was considered a successful director of the program in the transition period, he did not have a master's degree which made him ineligible to apply for the permanent directorship. At the same time, Sharon was not interested in serving as director. Since the two most likely candidates were either ineligible or uninterested, it seemed like the new director would be coming from outside the program. However, Gerald Williams, who had been with the program since 1996 as an academic advisor, decided to apply for the directorship.

"We couldn't let someone from outside come in and run the program," said Williams. "The University has always had a certain vision for TD and we have never allowed that. We have kept our own identity. I didn't want to be the director but we needed somebody to step up. We needed to keep our identity."[40] As the application deadline approached, Williams applied for the position. There were many people who were surprised and some who did not think he was ready for the position. Sharon Forleo was among those who had their doubts. "I didn't think Gerald was ready," said Sharon. "He was young and he hadn't been with the program for very long at this time," she added.

Figure 4.6 Frank Forleo and Sharon Forleo.

Figure 4.7 Gerald Williams. (Credit: Dave Salerno)

Figure 4.8 Brothers United for Action rally. (Credit: Azikiwe Husband)

Indeed, Williams was only 36 years old at the time, and had only been with the program for 3 years by the time he applied. He had not been an assistant or associate director and did not have any experience managing a program budget, which was of great concern to President Carothers. Despite his lack of experience in leadership positions, Williams mobilized a powerful coalition in support of his candidacy.

From outside the University, he counted on the support of Dennis Langley, who was the president of the Urban League of Rhode Island at the time. He was also supported by Brenda Dann-Messier, a mentor and former director of a program where Williams had worked several years before joining TD. Dann-Messier was a well-respected education leader in Rhode Island, who would eventually serve as US Assistant Secretary of Education and Commissioner of Postsecondary Education in Rhode Island.

Within the University, Williams was supported by TD students, including the group Brothers United for Action (BUA) which he mentored.

BUA, like the students in 1971 and BSLG in 1992, emerged in the late 1990s to challenge racist policies at the University. Although the campus became aware of the group after they organized one of the largest demonstrations in the history of the University after a publication of a racist cartoon in the campus newspaper, *The Good Five Cent Cigar*, Williams had been mentoring and advising the group well before the incident. When Williams was named one of the finalists for the position, and the University held public meetings with the candidates, students filled the room to demonstrate their support for his candidacy. However, the most important ally in the application process was Vice President John McCrary.

Dr. McCray, who had been at the University since 1990 and had been President Carothers's point person during the BSLG demands, supported Williams. When Carothers expressed concerns with Williams's leadership and budgetary inexperience, McCray agreed to mentor Williams. "If it wasn't for Dr. McCray's support, I would not have gotten the position. He gave me a chance when others didn't." Indeed, McCray's support proved crucial and once Williams was selected as the new director, he would meet with McCray once a week, where McCray provided the mentorship he had promised.

The alliance that Williams created with McCray and other key officials within and outside the University, took many by surprise. The seemingly quiet Williams had been working out of the spotlight to create the relationships he needed to achieve his goal. This approach would characterize Williams's experience as a leader of the program for more than two decades. His unassuming character has often led many to underestimate his strategizing ability and intentions, including myself.

I met "G" my senior year at Central High School. He worked at Central as a counselor for Educational Talent Search (ETS), part of the federal TRIO program, designed to help students from underserved populations gain college admission. "Why are you always walking these hallways? Don't you have class?" He asked me one day. My family had moved to Providence from Union City, New Jersey, the summer before my senior year in high school. I enrolled at Central and my first-quarter schedule did not include a sixth-period class, the last period of the day.

My guidance counselor told me that they didn't have a class to put me in during sixth period because I had already taken the classes that were available. The other classes were full. Instead of having a full schedule of classes, I was free during the last period of the day and I would walk the hallways until I could take the bus back home at the end of the school day.

When I explained that I was new to the school, was a senior, and didn't have a class during sixth period, he asked me if I had registered to take the Scholastic Aptitude Test (SAT). When I replied that I had not, he asked me to walk with him to his office where we filled out and submitted the SAT registration form with a fee waiver he provided. As luck would have it, it was the last day to register for the October test. If I had missed that deadline, I would have missed the opportunity to apply to some colleges, including the TD Program at the University of Rhode Island. After that day, I would spend the last period of the day, during that quarter, getting help from G and his colleague Brian Scott, with college applications and a college essay. They also encouraged me to attend college recruitment visits. That is how I ended up in the Central High School auditorium on a fall day in 1993, listening to Leo DiMaio and Frank Forleo talk to a room full of students about the TD Program.

That was the important role programs like ETS played in my life and the life of many others. My guidance counselor barely knew me. We never had a conversation about my aspirations. It was not until I became a college admissions officer years later that I learned about the gatekeeping role of high school guidance counselors. In affluent schools, guidance counselors ensure that their students are on a pathway to college. That was not my experience or the experience of so many others. My spouse, Lisa Abreu, who also attended Central High School, remembers her guidance counselor telling her that she should attend the community college because she was not academically prepared to be at a 4-year college. Lisa, who was also part of ETS, received college application guidance from the program. She attended the University of Rhode Island with the help of TD. In fact, G was her academic advisor in the program. Today, she is a director of Teacher Education Advisement at a university.

My first encounter with G's strategic machinations occurred when I reached out to him to get advice about a dilemma I was experiencing as an admissions officer at Rhode Island College. After graduating from the University of Rhode Island, I joined the admissions staff at Rhode Island College and my main responsibility was to recruit and admit students from the urban high schools in Rhode Island, including through the Preparatory Enrollment Program (PEP), a special admissions program similar to TD. Like TD, PEP was created in the 1960s and was designed to admit first-generation, low-income students from Rhode Island who did not have the college admissions requirements to get accepted through the regular admissions process. Unlike TD, which was accepting classes of more than 500 students by the early 2000s, Prep was only accepting roughly 40 to 50 students per year.

I had a conversation with Associate Director of Admissions Deborah Johnson about creating an initiative to increase the number of PEP students, and she supported the plan. I worked with the staff at PEP, Joe Costa and Julia Nesbitt, and during the first 3 years, we doubled the number of students who entered the program. However, by year 4, I was informed that we could no longer continue growing the program and, in fact, the program could only accept around 50 students, the number the program had been accepting at the time I joined the College. The program, which covered all of the student expenses (tuition, room, and board) for the first two years, and a substantial amount the following two years, was becoming too expensive for the College.

I had stayed in touch with G after graduating from URI and would often see him at recruitment events at Central, Classical, Hope, and Mt. Pleasant high schools in Providence. When I learned about Rhode Island College's decision to stop growing PEP, I reached out to G to get his advice. As the director of TD, I thought he could offer some guidance on how to navigate the political obstacles within the College. "Yes, let's meet," he said. "I'm going to be at a meeting at CCRI (the Community College) next week. Meet me then."

When we met the following week, I was surprised to learn that he had no interest in helping me think about how to deal with the challenges at

RIC. He said, "Come work for TD." After initially being startled that he had no interest in discussing the "reason" for the meeting, I became excited about the possibility of joining the TD staff. Despite the challenges, I enjoyed my work at RIC. However, I was excited about the opportunity to recruit and advise students for a program that had helped me. "But I have to let you know," he said, "you would get paid less than you are getting paid now and you're not going to have any benefits for a year." He added that his plan was to hire me on a temporary basis for one year and "when the position opens up a year from now, you would have the experience to be a competitive applicant."

I said, "Let me get this right. I would lose health benefits, get paid less, and then there is no guarantee that I would get the job when it opens up a year from now?" He said, "Yeah, that's right," as he laughed. "I can't guarantee you the job but you have to trust me." I did trust him and joined the program as a temporary academic advisor. A year later, when the permanent position became available, I was indeed the most qualified applicant for the position.

I was part of a cohort of former TD students hired by Williams, which included Karoline Oliveira and Marc Hardge, the son of the beloved former director, Rev. Arthur Hardge. We joined Joanna Ravello, a TD graduate who had been working with the program as a graduate student in the late 1990s and then became a full-time academic advisor. Joanna, Karoline, and Marc were all part of the Black Student Leadership Group in the early 1990s. The new hires were part of Williams's vision of "keeping the identity of the program." The new cohort of former TD students joined Williams, Sharon Forleo, Frank Forleo, Ed Givens, and Ted Shear. Ted, who worked as an academic advisor and managed the program's data, did not have any connection to the program until he became a computer skills instructor for the summer program in 1995.

In addition to cultivating relationships with McCray and Carothers, Williams also built strong relationships with the deans of Admissions, Financial Aid, and Enrollment Management, and Thomas Dougan, who replaced McCray as the Vice President for Student Affairs. The TD Program fell under the Division of Student Affairs, which meant that

Dougan approved the program's budget. Additionally, any threats the program encountered, from the president's office, state legislature, or elsewhere, would make its way through Dougan's office, where he would share the information with Williams and thwart any potentially problematic concern.

With Dougan's support and the support of President Carothers, the program was on solid footing. Gerald Williams, the unlikely director, who many did not envision stepping in to lead the program in 2000, had steered the program through difficult challenges. Among his biggest achievements has been the growth of the program as well as increasing financial support for students. Despite budget cutbacks at the University, in 2011, Williams was able to get the University to commit to providing full-tuition scholarships to low-income students in the program. As Williams entered his 15th year as director, the program would experience other changes and challenges. Frank Forleo and Sharon Forleo decided to retire after working 40 years with the program. Joanna Ravello and Karoline Oliveira, also left the program to lead other offices on campus.[41] Thomas Dougan also retired in 2015.

In July of 2016, the University hired Kathy Collins as the new Vice President for Student Affairs. In the fall of 2016, the University commissioned a comprehensive study of the TD Program. The comprehensive study of the program represented a potential threat. Historically, the program would count on relationships with administration to prevent any significant threat from escalating. However, the University's president, David Dooley, who succeeded Carothers in 2009, did not have a strong connection to the program or Williams. Collins, the new Vice President for Student Affairs came from outside the University and also did not have any connection to the program.

Although there were reasons for concern as to the motivations of the University for commissioning the study, the six-member committee included three TD alums, Anna Cano Morales, Victor Capellan, and William Trezvant.[42] The presence of the TD alums, who had remained connected to the program in different capacities, provided some assurances that the program's interests were represented within the committee. The final report, while making recommendations for changes to several aspects of the program, did not recommend changes that were perceived as seriously endangering the future of the program.

Following the release of the study, Vice President Collins stated, "I want to assure the entire campus community that this process was never about eliminating TD from the University. Rather, it was and is an opportunity to strengthen and improve a program that has helped so many of our students."[43] University of Rhode Island President David Dooley added:

> The University of Rhode Island is strongly committed to the Talent Development Program. Talent Development has provided access to public higher education for almost 50 years for thousands of students from disadvantaged backgrounds. The comprehensive review of Talent Development provides us with a pathway forward to improve the outcomes for our Talent Development community. We will continue to support our students, faculty, and staff that are so dedicated to this program and look forward to better integrating their ideas and work across the university community.[44]

Through the process of conducting the comprehensive study, Dooley and other administration officials became more familiar with the program's deep roots in the University and the broader community. Moreover, one year after the publication of the report, the program celebrated its 50th anniversary. In October 2018, the program held an event to celebrate the anniversary and program alums from the first class of 1968 through its current students attended the reunion. The Omni Hotel in downtown Providence was filled with different generations of students and their families that evening as they shared stories about their time at the University and their ability to earn a college degree because of the TD Program.

Weeks after the anniversary event, President Dooley had a conversation with Williams and said, "Hey man, that reunion is still on my mind. It is one of the best things I have seen in my entire career." The president, who had arrived at the University with little understanding of the program, and perhaps some skepticism, gained a different perspective on the purpose of the program.

As the program enters its 53rd year at the time of this writing, it continues to evolve. The results of the comprehensive study have led the program to implement changes on a range of issues from admissions to advisement. The TD staff is now mostly comprised of program alums. In 2020, the COVID-19 pandemic had a profound effect on the program. For the first time since 1968, TD students were not roaming the campus of the University of Rhode Island during a summer program. New students participated in the summer prematriculation program remotely. In the fall, the face-to-face advisement that has been required of students was done remotely as well. As it has done from the beginning, the program has adapted to meet the needs of the students as they arise. Additionally, as challenges emerge, the program has continued to count on, and indeed cultivate, student mobilization.

Although the program has been able to fight off challenges and to grow in the face of these challenges, it has not been able to overcome one persistent problem. Certain majors, including business, nursing, engineering, and education, have been increasingly difficult for students to gain access to. The dominant narrative is that students have choices of major and their decisions reflect their interests. However, the barriers to the most selective majors are not a result of student interests. The barriers are part of a systematic response to the expansion of college opportunities to students from historically underserved populations. As the next chapter will discuss, at URI, entrance into the majors became increasingly competitive in the 1970s and by the 1990s, highly competitive. Although TD was expanding access to marginalized communities into the University, the University was implementing policies that restricted access to TD students to certain majors. And URI was not alone. Restricting access to particular majors was a national response.

Reproducing Restriction to College Access

Emergence of Hidden Forms of Restriction

The Myth of "Major of Choice"

Over its 50 years, the Talent Development (TD) Program has been able to weather challenges that threatened the survival of the program and the opportunities it provides to students who, without the program, would not have gained admission to the University. The threats have come from various directions and levels. In the early 1970s, the University, facing a budget shortfall from the state, attempted to cut back the program. Ultimately, the University reversed course following student protests. Years later, the University would also rely on decreasing retention rates to threaten the program, but the program survived those challenges as well.

In the 1980s, the stagnation of the Pell Grant awards presented a significant challenge to the TD students, who overwhelmingly relied on financial aid to attend the University. Additionally, the national debates about affirmative action created a climate against special efforts to recruit and retain students of historically underrepresented groups on college campuses. These challenges created a cloud that always lingered above the program. However, as the amount of the federal Pell Grants decreased, the program was able to increase the amount of financial aid that the students received from the University. Moreover, the program was able to overcome the negative climate challenge as well. As previous chapters have shown,

Developing Scholars. Domingo Morel, Oxford University Press. © Oxford University Press 2023.
DOI: 10.1093/oso/9780197636992.003.0006

protest, student mobilization, community presence, and relationships between program officials and state leaders and university officials have provided the political conditions that have allowed the program to survive
and, in some regards, thrive.

Yet despite the program's success in recruiting students who do not meet
the University's admissions criteria, and its ability to provide the academic
and social support students need to graduate, there has been one persistent challenge the program has not been able to overcome. Over time, TD
students have increasingly had difficulties graduating with degrees in, for
example, education, engineering, and nursing. For instance, a review of
TD student enrollment data between 2005 and 2015 shows that among
students who declared nursing as a major at the time of enrollment, only
34 percent graduated with a degree in nursing (see fig. 5.1). The education
major is particularly alarming. Among students who declared elementary
or secondary education as a major, only 8 percent graduated with a degree
in elementary or secondary education. The data also show that 47 percent
of students who declared engineering at the time of enrollment graduated
with an engineering degree. By comparison, an analysis of the 2012 cohort of first-time, full-time undergraduate students at the University of
Rhode Island showed that 68.7 percent of students who declared nursing,
54.4 percent of students who declared elementary and secondary education, and 51.5 percent who declared engineering at time of enrollment
graduated with the same major within 6 years of enrollment.[1]

RESTRICTING PATHWAYS TO MAJORS

While TD students have had difficulties graduating with degrees in
nursing and education, the challenge is not unique to students of color
at the University of Rhode Island. In fact, there is a growing gap between
White students and students of color graduating with these majors across
the country. In a 2018 study, the Center for American Progress found that
in addition to race inequities in college attendance and college completion
rates between students of color and White students, there are also wide

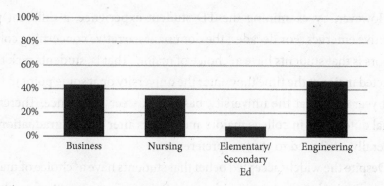

Figure 5.1 Talent Development students who declare business, nursing, education and engineering and graduate with their declared major (2005–2017).

racial gaps in the fields of study.[2] Using national data on college students between 2013 and 2015, the study found that Black and Latino students were less likely to earn bachelor's degrees in engineering and education. If Black and Latino students "were as likely to major in engineering as White students, this country would have produced 20,000 more engineers from 2013 through 2015" the report found. Additionally, there would have been "30,000 more teachers of color if students of color were represented equally among education graduates."

Similarly, a study by Georgetown University's Center on Education and the Workforce found that Black college graduates are underrepresented in the fields of engineering, business, and education.[3] According to the study, Black graduates "account for only 8 percent of general engineering majors, 7 percent of mathematics majors, and only 5 percent of computer engineering majors. They are similarly underrepresented in business: only 7 percent of finance and marketing majors are African American."

The field of education merits particular attention. In 2015, US colleges and universities conferred 91,596 bachelor's degrees in education. Whites represented 71,691 of the conferred degrees while Blacks and Latinos only represented 7,264 and 7,225 of the conferred degrees in education, respectively.[4] The gap in education degrees between students of color and White students has been attributed to several factors, including increasing college major options for students of color, particularly after the 1960s.

However, by examining the TD student experience, a different perspective emerges. For decades, the dominant narrative concerning college majors is that students have a "choice of major." That is, students pick their selected major at the time they enter the university or at some point in their first year or two at the university, based on career preference. Therefore, racial differences in college majors and careers after college graduation are generally attributed to student preferences.

Despite the widely accepted belief that students have a "choice of major," the reality is that for many students, certain majors are out of reach. As I will argue in this chapter, racial differences in college majors are not just a matter of choice. In the late 1960s, and the decades that followed, colleges have adapted to increasing student enrollments by altering access to particular majors. The emergence of *secondary admissions processes*, which included higher grade point average (GPA) requirements and/or higher standardized test scores, to enter particular majors became a barrier to entrance. For students who gained admission to the university through a special program, like TD, because they lacked the GPA or Scholastic Aptitude Test (SAT) score to enter the university through regular admissions, these secondary admissions requirements had a profound effect on access to selected majors, like business, nursing, engineering, and education.

In this chapter, I show how changing requirements at the University prevented TD students from entering these majors. Then, relying on an original national database of selected college majors (business, education, engineering, and nursing), I show that most state colleges and universities have adopted some GPA requirement to enter at least one of the selected majors. Additionally, I show how special college access programs and increases in Black and Latino student enrollment are associated with state colleges and universities increasing GPA requirements to enter selected majors.

Finally, this chapter also demonstrates that it is not just the emergence of secondary admissions processes but changing certification and licensing standards that have prevented students of color from entering certain professions as well. The restriction of pathways to selected majors and, by extension, career trajectories suggests that "choice of major" is a myth to many students. Indeed, the emergence of these restrictions represents a form of layering, or a hidden form of policy retrenchment, in response to the success of college expansion for students of underrepresented groups. An examination of the evolution of teacher preparation requirements helps demonstrate how the profession has become increasingly inaccessible to Black students and other students of color.

TEACHER EDUCATION

Throughout the early to mid-20th century, teaching was the most popular profession for Black college graduates.[5] Although teaching had historically represented one of the few professions available to Black Americans, teaching in the Black community was always viewed as much more than a profession. As sociologist Charles Payne has noted, "Education for African Americans has always had particular political and moral resonances."[6] Scholar Jarvis Givens has written that "Black education was a fugitive project from its inception—outlawed and defined as a criminal act regarding the slave population in the southern states and, at times, too, an object of suspicion and violent resistance in the North."[7] "Ever since Reconstruction," wrote Adam Fairclough, "black teachers have acted as community leaders, interracial diplomats, and builders of black institutions."[8] Ella Baker, the organizer who many activists of the 1960s relied on for "strategic and analytical insights and guidance," was a "movement teacher," wrote Barbara Ransby.[9]

The importance of the Black teacher in the Black community is what inspired several students in TD's first class of 1968 to pursue a degree in education. "I knew I wanted to be a teacher" said Deborah Bush, who graduated with a degree in education and taught for more than 40 years in the Providence public schools. Donna-jean Wosencroft, who was also part of the first class of 1968, also knew she wanted to be a teacher. For Bush and Wosencroft, the path to becoming a teacher was challenging. "We had some racist professors in some classes who thought that we didn't belong at the University," said Bush. However, their path to becoming a teacher did not involve multiple layers of admissions processes at the University that future students would encounter.

Although teaching was a vehicle to enter the middle class for Black Americans, by the 1970s, the number of Black teachers started to decline. Scholars have pointed to several factors to explain the decrease in Black teachers after the 1970s. First, the overall number of conferred bachelor's degrees in education decreased in the 1970s after a decade of growth in the 1960s. Between 1960 and 1970, the number of conferred bachelor's degrees in education increased from roughly 89,000 in 1960 to 176,614 in 1970 (see fig. 5.2). The expansion of higher education opportunities for histor-ically marginalized groups, including women, helps explain the increase of the 1960s. By the 1970s, about one third of women enrolled in colleges and universities in the United States were education majors.[10] However, between 1970 and 1980, the number of conferred degrees decreased to roughly 108,000. As the children of the baby boomers began to graduate from high school, the teaching labor market began to change.[11] In the 1980s, new hires for teachers decreased from a high in the late 1970s.[12]

In addition to the changing teacher labor market, desegregation also af-fected the Black teaching profession. Following the end of legal segregation of the schools, White teachers began to displace Black teachers, particu-larly in the South.[13] Estimates show that more than 35,000 Black teachers lost their jobs as a result of desegregation.[14] A study of 781 southern school

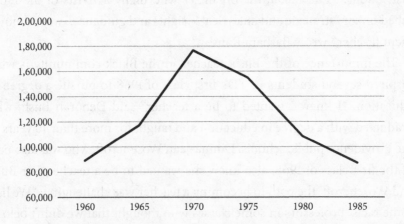

Figure 5.2 Conferred bachelor's degrees in education (1960–1985).

districts estimates that integration led to a 31.8 percent reduction in Black teachers between 1964 and 1972.[15]

A third factor that affected the Black teaching profession in the 1970s was choice of profession. Although teaching provided Black Americans one of the few avenues into the middle class throughout the early to mid-20th century, scholars note that the expansion of higher education opportunities as well as antidiscrimination policies in the 1960s opened opportunities to other professions that were previously out of reach to Black students.[16]

However, whereas desegregation and the opening of new professional opportunities and career choices contributed to the decline of Black teachers in the 1970s, these factors do not fully explain this decline. In the 1970s and 1980s, the process of becoming a teacher was made more difficult by the emergence of policies that prevented Black students from entering the profession. The rise of teaching accreditation standards in states, testing, and secondary admissions processes to enter teaching preparation programs at colleges and universities had a significant effect on Black Americans in the teaching profession.

In the mid-20th century, education associations began accrediting teaching preparation institutions and teachers. The aim was to profession-alize the field of education in the same way that law and medicine had professionalized their fields.[17] By the 1970s and early 1980s, concerns with the state of public education in the United States led to efforts to improve the "quality" of teachers throughout the country. Concerns with math and science education, declining SAT scores among Americans, and declining US competitiveness in the world as a result of poor education perfor-mance were among the justifications politicians and reformers provided for increasing teaching standards.[18] The quality of urban schools, which had become majority Black and Latino in many cities by the 1970s, gained particular attention.

As the national and states' governments dedicated increasing attention to improving education through quality control measures, the changing teacher preparation standards had a profound effect on the future of the Black teaching force. By the early 1980s, scholars and academic journals, focused on Black education, dedicated increasing attention to the effects of accreditation, competency, and preadmissions requirements for Black teachers. In the 1980s, *The Journal of Negro Education* devoted several summer editions to writings and empirical research on teacher assessment and student testing in general.[19] Much of this research and writing attempted to counter the dominant policy response to the *A Nation at Risk* report, which describe the apparent decline of student achievement across the United States.

In addition to scholars, organizations like the National Association for the Advancement of Colored People (NAACP) and Black teachers' organizations also raised concerns about dwindling Black teachers as a result of testing and accreditation standards. Beverly Cole, the Secretary of Education for the NAACP, authored several articles in the early 1980s, describing concerns about the disappearance of Black teachers. Cole highlights the emergence of admissions requirements to enter teacher training programs at colleges and universities and increasing preadmission tests and teacher competency exams as major reasons for the drop in Black teachers. For instance, as a result of changes in certification standards in Florida, approximately 2,000 Black teachers out of 5,500 prospective Black teachers were certified by the state in 1981.[20] Around the same period, Texas implemented a preadmission test at colleges and universities for prospective teachers. By 1985, only 203 of 900 Black students, and 732 of 2,136 Latinos had passed the exam.[21] Roughly two thirds of Blacks and Latinos who intended on becoming teachers in Texas in the early 1980s were not able to pursue a degree in education as a result of the preadmission exam.

As states increasingly adopted accreditation, certification, and preadmission requirements, the number of teachers of color, particularly Black teachers, declined. According to the Department of Education's Office of Civil Rights, between 1976 and 1983, the percentage of students of color earning a bachelor's degree in education decreased by 52 percent.[22] These figures suggest that it was not only the effects of segregation and increasing career choices for Black students in the 1960s that led to decreases in Black teachers and other teachers of color. State standards and university requirements, particularly secondary admissions requirements, created a barrier to the teaching profession.

SECONDARY ADMISSIONS REQUIREMENTS AT THE UNIVERSITY OF RHODE ISLAND

At the University of Rhode Island, similar secondary admissions processes emerged in education, as well as other majors like business administration and nursing in the 1970s. Prior to 1972, students admitted to the university were able to begin working toward earning a degree in their major of choice. However, in 1972, the University created "University College" as the point of entry for all first-year students. Students admitted to the University now had a transition period before entering their "major." The University College staff was "drawn from the faculties of each of the undergraduate colleges" and was "responsible for providing precise information about the academic programs and requirements of the colleges as well as of the University, about requirements for professional certification and for admission to graduate and professional schools."[23]

Around the same time that the university created University College, a number of majors began adding, and then increasing, GPA requirements to gain admissions into their programs. In 1974, the College of Nursing and the College of Business Administration added a 2.0 GPA requirement for students transferring from University College into their majors. In 1976, business increased its GPA requirement to a 2.2, and for the first time, the University included language in its course catalog about the limited seats in particular programs (business and education). Over time, nursing and business continued to increase their GPA requirements. By 2007, the School of Business required a 3.0 GPA in foundational courses for students transferring from University College after sophomore year. By 2011, the School of Nursing required a 3.0 GPA for students to enter their program (see fig. 5.3).

The education major implemented a similar policy. In 1986, students entering the education program were required to have a 2.5 GPA to

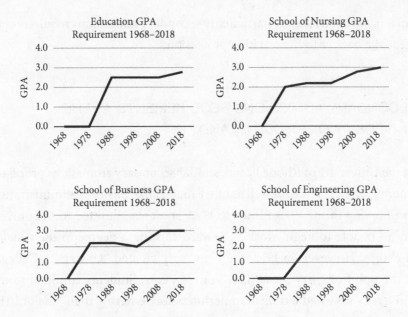

Figure 5.3 University of Rhode Island GPA requirements to enter nursing, business, engineering, and education majors (1968–2018).

transfer from University College. In 1998, the education program implemented an entire secondary admissions process for prospective students. In order to enter the education major, students had to apply and submit faculty recommendations, a personal statement, and standardized test scores (SATs), and they were required to have 2.5 GPA in foundational courses. In 2005, the education program changed its standardized test scores requirement to include passing scores on the Praxis I Pre-Professional Skills Test (PPST), a teacher certification exam administered by the Educational Testing Service (ETS), the same organization that administers the SAT. The required scores to gain admission into the education program were: Reading 172, Writing 171, and Math 171. In lieu of the PPST, students could also gain admission by scoring an 1100 on the SAT.

For students who entered the university with the support of the TD Program, because they did not have the SAT or GPA requirements to enter through regular admissions, the requirements to enter the education program were out of reach. The majority of students did not score an 1100 on the SATs; if they had, they would have gained admission to the University without the program. Furthermore, the Praxis test scores, similar to the SATs, have also proven problematic for students of color. A 2011 study by ETS found "significant differences in average scores between test takers of different racial/ethnic subgroups." "The largest differences," wrote the authors, "exist for African-American test takers, with passing rates that are lower than White test takers by 35% or more." The authors conclude that the gaps in scores between racial/ethnic subgroups "were consistent" with the gaps "from similar tests of academic skills, such as the SAT and ACT."[24]

As the education program was implementing these secondary admissions policies, the pathway to a degree in education was restricted for TD students. The profession that had provided Black students a path to the middle class for decades was now out of reach to many students. Although elementary and secondary education has been one of the most popular majors among TD students at time of enrollment (see table 5.1), more than 90 percent of students who declare education as a major do not graduate with a degree in education.

The changing admission requirements for the other majors had an effect on TD students as well. The increasing GPA requirements to enter the Schools of Business, Nursing, and Pharmacy presented significant obstacles for the students in the program. Since 1968, the program's philosophy had been that with adequate support, students could be successful college students. However, the program, like other similar

Table 5.1 TOP 5 MAJOR CHOICES FOR TD STUDENTS AT TIME OF ENROLLMENT (2005–2017)

Major	Number	Percentage of Total Declared Majors
Business	267	14%
Psychology	210	11%
Nursing	200	10%
Biology	185	10%
Education (Elementary and Secondary)	107	6%

programs across the country, understood that the process of helping transition students requires time, since the students are arriving to the University without the same high school preparation as other students. By requiring students to have a 3.0 GPA after their first year in foundational courses, the logic of "development" that the program offers is undermined. In many instances, students in the program need the first two years to adjust to the rigors of the academic demands of the University. However, for many of the more selective majors, including business and nursing, that two-year window of development is not available to students. As a result, even when students declare their interest in business or nursing as a major, most students in the program graduate with a different degree.

These secondary admissions processes at the University of Rhode Island were implemented by faculty and the faculty senate in response to a confluence of pressures. Accreditation organizations, which increased their standards for certification, put pressure on universities, like the University of Rhode Island, to change their requirements. Additionally, state government, through certification and licensure requirements, like teacher certification, for instance, also influenced the emergence of secondary admissions processes. Equally as important, concerns with prestige and the appearance of highly competitive programs and majors also influenced faculty to implement secondary admissions policies. In the pursuit of a competitive advantage against other institutions, URI, like other colleges and universities, touts the competitiveness or selectivity of their programs in the battle over prestige and rankings.

EXAMINING GPA REQUIREMENTS
ACROSS UNIVERSITIES

An examination of the University of Rhode Island shows how certain majors, particularly business, education, and nursing, became more selective over time by increasing GPA requirements to enter the major. The GPA requirements were part of the secondary admissions processes

Table 5.2 PERCENT OF PUBLIC COLLEGES OR UNIVERSITIES WITH SOME GPA REQUIREMENT TO ENTER BUSINESS, EDUCATION, ENGINEERING, OR NURSING MAJOR, 2019

	Number	Percent
No GPA Requirement	46	9.29
Some GPA Requirement	449	90.71

that began emerging in the 1970s and have presented a barrier to many students of color at the University.

Are secondary admissions processes unique to the University of Rhode Island? Do other universities require GPA requirements to enter particular majors like business, education, engineering, and nursing? If so, what factors help explain variation in GPA requirements across universities?

To answer these questions, I constructed an original dataset of GPA requirements for business, education, engineering, and nursing majors at every 4-year, public college and university in every state in the United States.[25] The list of colleges and universities were accessed from the National Center for Education Statistics' Integrated Postsecondary Education Data System.[26] The data for college majors were collected in 2019 from college and university websites, through course catalogs and/or department websites. Based on the limits of data availability over time, this analysis is meant to provide a cross-sectional snapshot of the factors associated with GPA requirements as of 2019.

The results of the data collection show that an overwhelming majority of colleges and universities have some GPA requirement to enter at least one of the selected majors. As of 2019, nearly 91 percent of all public colleges and universities had some GPA requirement to enter at least one of the selected majors (see table 5.2).

The results also show that more than 78 percent (78.38 percent) of public colleges and universities had some GPA requirement of 2.75 or higher (on a 0–4.0 scale) to enter at least one of the selected majors (see table 5.3). Finally, nearly half of all public colleges and universities (47.27 percent) had some GPA requirement of 3.0 or higher to enter at least one of the selected majors (see table 5.4).

Table 5.3 PERCENT OF PUBLIC COLLEGES OR UNIVERSITIES WITH SOME
GPA REQUIREMENT OF 2.75 OR HIGHER TO ENTER BUSINESS, EDUCATION,
ENGINEERING, OR NURSING MAJOR, 2019

	Number	Percent
No GPA Requirement of 2.75 or Higher	107	21.64
GPA Requirement of 2.75 or Higher	388	78.38

Table 5.4 PERCENT OF PUBLIC COLLEGES OR UNIVERSITIES WITH SOME
GPA REQUIREMENT OF 3.0 OR HIGHER TO ENTER BUSINESS, EDUCATION,
ENGINEERING, OR NURSING MAJOR, 2019

	Number	Percent
No GPA Requirement of 3.0 or Higher	261	52.72
GPA Requirement of 3.0 or Higher	234	47.27

The findings show that most colleges and universities have some
GPA requirements to enter at least one of the selected majors. To examine which factors may explain variation of GPA requirements across
colleges and universities, I rely on the University of Rhode Island case
study as well as political science scholarship that examines variation in
higher education outcomes like higher education spending by state.
To test whether special college access programs are associated with
differences in GPA requirements, I include a college access program variable (coded 0 = no program, 1 = university has a college access program
as of 2019) in the models. The models also include the following inde-
pendent variables: instate tuition; percent of students who apply to the
University who are admitted; total undergraduate population; percent of
undergraduate Black, Latino, and White student population; percent of
women enrolled at the University; and the percentage of enrolled students
who receive Pell Grants (see table 5.5).

The models include several state-level variables. I use full-time equiv-
alent (FTE) students enrolled at a state's public universities ("State Net
Public FTE Enrollment") and to assess state spending on higher education, the amount of state funding appropriated per FTE student in public

Table 5.5 DESCRIPTIVE STATISTICS: INDEPENDENT VARIABLES

Variable	Obs	Mean	Std. Dev.	Min	Max
Special College Access Program	507	0.323	0.468	0	1
Instate Tuition	469	25697.03	4562.623	5050	39595
% Admitted	507	0.669	0.242	0	1
% Black Students	507	0.095	0.091	0	0.74
% Latino Students	507	0.141	0.149	0	0.95
% White Students	507	0.591	0.204	0.02	0.92
% Women Enrollment	507	0.551	0.090	0.11	0.88
Undergraduate Enrollment	507	11606.04	10162.46	3944	58821
% Pell Grant Recipients	507	0.394	0.148	0	0.87
State Net Public FTE Enrollment	507	381027.3	386271.8	18456	1566376
State Educational Appropriations per FTE	507	7303.098	2518.213	2958.95	16391.41
State Population	507	1.13	1.02	578759	3.95
% White of State Population	507	0.646	0.152	0.217	0.93
% Black of State Population	507	0.129	0.085	0.006	0.378
% Latino of State Population	507	0.149	0.120	0.017	0.493
State Board of Higher Education Governing Power	507	0.508	0.523	0	1
# of Members on State Board of Higher Education	507	13.667	6.469	0	29
State Board of Higher Education Elected	507	0.029	0.169	0	1
# of Education Interest Groups in State	507	142.163	123.152	11	483
Union Density	507	12.014	6.205	3	25.3
Democratic Control of State Government	507	0.496	0.321	0	1

universities. To control for state population, I use total state population and percent Black, Latino, and White of state population.

The models also test for various political factors. Research has shown that party control of government has been associated with higher education spending at the state level.[27] To examine whether party control of state government is associated with differences in GPA requirement, I use the Ranney Party Control Measure for a 4-year moving average of state party control (coded 0 = unified Republican control, 1 = unified Democratic control, 0.5 = neither). As public institutions, state colleges and universities are governed by state boards of higher education, and research has shown that state boards of higher education can have an influential role in higher education policy.[28] The models include three state boards of higher education variables: "State Board of Higher Education Governing Power" (coded 0 if the board is only a coordinating board and 1 if the board has governance authority), number of members on the state board of higher education, and whether the members of the state board of higher education are elected (coded 0 for appointed and 1 for elected).

Finally, scholars have shown that interest groups also play an influential role in shaping higher education policy.[29] To test whether interest groups may have an effect on GPA requirements, the models include the number of registered education interest groups in the state. The models also include a union density variable (proportion of (nonagricultural) workforce represented by a union in the state).

Before I conducted analyses of the factors associated with changes in GPA requirement for each major, I first ran a test using the cumulative GPA across the 4 selected majors: business, education, engineering, and nursing. The dependent variable, "Combined GPA," is a continuous variable that adds all the minimum GPA requirements for each of the selected majors at each college or university (see table 5.6 for descriptive summary).

Table 5.6 DESCRIPTIVE STATISTICS: COMBINED GPA

Variable	Mean	Std. Dev.	Min	Max
Combined GPA	5.66	3.14	0	14.53

The results of the ordinary least squares (OLS) model show that special college access programs are associated with a positive and statistically significant relationship with higher GPA requirements. The presence of a college access program at a public college or university is associated with a 0.77 increase in the combined GPA, holding all else equal. Additionally, the results show a statistically significant relationship between Black student enrollment as well as Latino student enrollment and GPA requirements. That is, increasing percentages of Black and Latino student enrollment are associated with higher cumulative GPA requirements as well (see table 5.7). The results also show a statistically significant relationship between increases in the percentage of women enrolled at a public institution and higher combined GPAs.

To better interpret the association between Black and Latino student enrollment and increases in combined GPA requirements, I ran predicted probabilities. Figures 5.4 and 5.5 show the predicted probability of increases in Black and Latino percent of the overall enrollment at a public college and university and their association with increases in combined GPA requirements, holding all else equal. As figure 5.4 shows, a 10-point increase in Black student percentage of total enrollment is associated with a roughly 1-point increase in the combined GPA requirements among the selected majors. Figure 5.5 shows that a 10-point increase in Latino student percentage of total enrollment is associated with a roughly 0.5-point increase in combined GPA requirements.

The results of the OLS model also show that increases in undergraduate enrollments are associated with increases in cumulative GPA requirements, while increases in the percentage of students who receive the Pell Grant are associated with decreases in the cumulative GPA requirements. Overall, the results of the combined GPA model suggest that the presence of a special college access program and increases in the overall percentage of Black, Latino, and women enrolled at public colleges and universities are associated with increases in GPA requirements for business, education, engineering, and nursing majors.

I then conducted a series of tests to analyze the factors that may be associated with increased GPA requirements for each selected major

Table 5.7 COMBINED GPA REQUIREMENTS FOR SELECTED MAJORS, 2019

	Coefficients	Standard Errors
Special College Access Program	0.765**	0.33
Instate Tuition	-0.00001	0.00003
% Admitted	0.536	0.63
% Black Students	8.07***	2.91
% Latino Students	4.39*	2.33
% White Students	1.30	1.85
% Women Enrollment	5.97***	1.72
Undergraduate Enrollment	0.01***	0.001
% Pell Grant Recipients	-5.19***	1.70
State Net Public FTE Enrollment	-0.0001***	3.21
State Educational Appropriations per FTE	-0.0001	0.0001
State Population	4.55	1.37
% White of State Population	1.94	3.57
% Black of State Population	0.38*	4.18
% Latino of State Population	-0.53	4.54
State Board of Higher Education Governing Power	-0.05	0.44
# of Members on State Board of Higher Education	-0.08	0.03
State Board of Higher Education Elected	-0.58	0.85
# of Education Interest Groups in State	-0.007	0.002
Union Density	0.07	0.05
Democratic Control of State Government	-0.86	0.63
Constant	2.53	2.52
R^2	0.28	
N	461	

Note: Ordinary Least Squares (OLS).

$*p < 0.10$, $**p < 0.05$, $***p < 0.01$

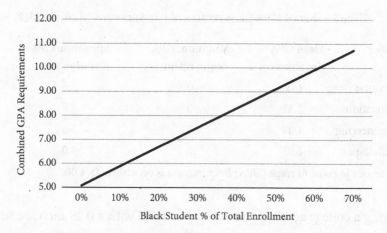

Figure 5.4 Predicting combined GPA requirements for selected majors by black student enrollment.

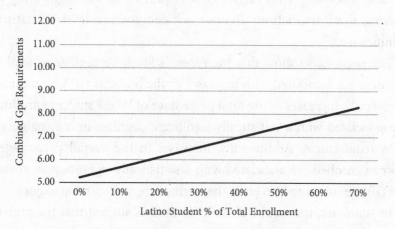

Figure 5.5 Predicting combined GPA requirements for selected majors by Latino student enrollment.

(business, education, engineering, and nursing). I ran a regression model for each major as the dependent variable (dependent variable coded on a 0–4.0 scale; see table 5.8 for descriptive summary for each dependent variable).

The results of the OLS models show that the presence of a college access program is associated with a statistically significant increase in the GPA requirements for the business and education majors (see table 5.9).

Table 5.8 Mean GPA Requirements for Selected Majors, 2019

Major	Mean GPA Requirement	Minimum GPA Requirement	Maximum GPA Requirement
Business	1.19	0	3.6
Education	2.32	0	3.8
Engineering	1.09	0	3.8
Nursing	2.57	0	4.0

Note: Grade Point Average (GPA) Requirement is on scale of 0–4.00.

Having a college access program is associated with a 0.29 increase in the business GPA requirement and a 0.39 increase in the GPA requirement to enter the education major. Although special college access programs are also associated with higher GPA requirements for engineering and nursing, these associations do not reach conventional levels of statistical significance.

The results also show that increases in Black percentage of total enrollment are associated with increases in the business GPA requirement. Conversely, increases in the total percentage of White student enrollment are associated with a statistically significant decrease in the engineering GPA requirement. Additionally, increases in the overall percentage of women enrolled are associated with a statistically significant increase in the GPA requirements to enter the engineering and nursing majors.

In summary, the results of the OLS models suggest that the presence of a special college access program is associated with increases in the combined GPA requirements to enter the selected majors and specifically the business and education majors. Likewise, increases in the percentage of Black and Latino students at public colleges and universities are also associated with higher combined GPA requirements. The analysis from the TD Program at the University of Rhode Island as well as the investigation of GPA requirements at public colleges and universities throughout the United States demonstrate that for many students, particularly students of color, barriers to access to higher education still exist. These findings suggest that as communities successfully challenged barriers to access

Table 5.9 Business, Education, Engineering, and Nursing Majors GPA Regression Models

Dependent Variables

Independent Variables	Business GPA	Education GPA	Engineering GPA	Nursing GPA
College Access Program	.287** (0.144)	.389*** (0.124)	0.121 (0.182)	0.050 (0.128)
Instate Tuition	-0.00004** (0.0002)	-0.00002 (0.00002)	0.00001 (0.00002)	0.00001 (0.00001)
% Admitted	-0.062 (0.285)	-0.054 (0.237)	.463 (0.410)	.045 (.254)
% Black Students	3.52*** (1.27)	0.027 (1.11)	1.07 (1.73)	-.465 (1.16)
% Latino Students	1.46 (1.03)	0.894 (0.917)	.658 (1.41)	.214 (.956)
% White Students	0.216 (0.823)	.497 (0.736)	-2.02* (1.07)	-.792 (0.784)
% Women Enrollment	0.272 (0.788)	-0.069 (0.790)	1.71* (0.962)	1.66** (0.820)
Undergraduate Enrollment	0.003*** (0.0007)	0.0007 (0.0006)	0.0004 (0.0008)	0.0003 (0.0006)
% Pell Grant Recipients	-3.11*** (0.741)	0.006 (0.655)	-2.73** (1.02)	-1.29* (0.663)
State Net Public FTE Enrollment	-1.40 (1.40)	-6.03*** (1.25)	-5.30 (1.69)	-9.24 (1.19)
State Educational Appropriations per FTE	-0.0004 (0.0003)	0.00002 (0.00002)	8.55 (0.00004)	0.00003 (0.00003)
State Population	3.66 (5.95)	2.56*** (5.24)	1.96 (7.26)	7.39 (5.08)
% White of State Population	1.07 (1.55)	-0.098 (1.49)	2.20 (2.16)	1.92 (1.33)
% Black of State Population	0.311 (1.84)	0.161 (1.68)	1.41 (2.42)	1.77 (1.57)
% Latino of State Population	3.04 (1.98)	-1.72 (1.81)	0.356 (2.65)	-0.607 (1.68)

(continued)

Table 5.9 CONTINUED

Dependent Variables				
State Board Governing Power	-0.260 (0.188)	0.182 (0.159)	-0.050 (0.257)	0.064 (0.168)
# of Members on State Board	0.015 (0.015)	-0.036*** (0.012)	-0.011 (0.019)	-0.011 (0.013)
State Board Elected	-0.476 (0.361)	-0.413 (0.298)	0.071 (0.480)	-0.170 (0.328)
# of Education Interest Groups in State	-0.0009 (0.001)	-0.004*** (0.001)	0.001 (0.002)	-0.001 (0.001)
Union Density	0.081*** (0.020)	0.014 (0.017)	0.003 (0.025)	0.010 (0.017)
Democratic Control of State Government	-0.618** (0.272)	-0.039 (0.227)	-0.655* (0.340)	0.008 (0.237)
Constant	0.726 (1.53)	2.69* (1.48)	-0.090 (2.16)	1.21 (1.38)
R^2	0.220	0.140	0.123	0.090
N	443	394	316	347

Note: Ordinary least squares (standard errors in parentheses).

*$p < 0.10$, **$p < 0.05$, ***$p < 0.01$

to colleges and universities, many institutions began erecting secondary admissions processes to restrict access to specific majors and professions.

The results of the examination in this chapter provoke further questions. Why have public universities implemented secondary admissions processes and why are increasing enrollments of students of color and women associated with these policies? What are the political factors that help explain the emergence of these policies? The next chapter examines these questions and raises additional questions about the function of higher education and its promise as a vehicle for addressing inequality in the United States.

Shifting the Politics of College Access from the Public to Private Sphere

The previous chapter showed how the University of Rhode Island began implementing secondary admissions processes in the 1970s. Prior to 1972, students admitted to the University did not have to meet additional admissions criteria to enter their major of choice. However, by the 1970s, programs like business, education, engineering, and nursing, began requiring students to meet certain grade point average (GPA) thresholds before gaining admissions to their programs. Business and nursing would eventually require a 3.0 GPA for students. The education major required an entire secondary admissions process that consisted of a 2.5 GPA in foundational courses, standardized test scores, and letters of recommendation.

An analysis of GPA requirements across state colleges and universities in the United States showed that the University of Rhode Island is not unique in adopting GPA thresholds to enter the business, education, engineering, and nursing majors. The results of the study showed that more than 90 percent of public institutions have some GPA requirement in at least one of the selected majors. Additionally, the results show that the variables most strongly associated with increasing GPA requirements are increasing percentages of students of color and women enrolled at an institution.

Developing Scholars. Domingo Morel, Oxford University Press. © Oxford University Press 2023.
DOI: 10.1093/oso/9780197636992.003.0007

Why are women and students of color, particularly Black students, associated with increasing GPA requirements to enter the selected majors? To begin answering this question it is important to note that GPA requirements are only one of several factors associated with changing requirements to enter majors and their respective professions. As the previous chapter demonstrated, in addition to GPA requirements, some majors require a minimum score on a standardized test for admission into the program. Additionally, some majors require students to gain certification before entering their profession, and that process may include passing a national exam.

The process of investigating why the growth of underrepresented groups is associated with increasing standards to enter majors and their respective professions points the examination in the direction of state governments. State governments play a significant role in determining standards to practice in the professions. Moreover, an examination of the role of state governments demonstrates how state credentialing policies have led to the exclusion or displacement of African Americans from certain professions. In the field of teacher education, for instance, states have the ability to implement policies that affect teacher preparation programs and teacher certification. As this chapter will show, in the South, teacher "competency" measures were adopted by state governments working with local school districts to displace Black teachers and eventually limit the entrance of aspiring Black teachers into the profession.

At the same time, an investigation into the connection between the emergence of secondary admissions processes and historically underrepresented groups in higher education also reveals a layer of political influence among groups that has not received sufficient scrutiny in the debates concerning college access in the United States: private foundations and professional associations. Private foundations have played a significant role in establishing standards and promoting reforms for licensure and certification in the professions. Likewise, professional associations influence higher education policies by setting standards for programs to gain accreditation and for students in these programs to become certified to enter the profession.

However, since debates about "college access" have generally focused on concerns about the process of gaining admission to a college or university, the process of gaining admission to majors and to their respective professions has been largely ignored as an aspect of college access. As a result, the historical role of foundations and the ongoing influence of professional associations in influencing higher education policy, and particularly shaping who gets into the majors and the professions, have been less examined as critical components of college access. Moreover, as this chapter will demonstrate, various professional associations have a history of racism and exclusion, and I argue that their continued role as gatekeepers to today's professions are a continuation of their racist and exclusionary past.

By examining the role of private foundations and professional associations, we begin to better understand why despite the vast expansion of higher education opportunities, particularly for students of color, we do not see students of color gaining access to professions that have historically provided a path to upward social mobility. Indeed, I argue that the political mobilization that led to the expansion of opportunity to previously excluded groups produced a political response to restrict access in a method that has been largely hidden from public scrutiny. In other words, as communities successfully challenged barriers to college access, the political venue of denying access shifted from public officials to private credentialing organizations.

These *credential cartels*—the partnership between private foundations and professional organizations in establishing and modifying standards for entrance into majors and the professions—are a major political force in determining college access policy. Furthermore, by examining their political influence, another question emerges. If the credential cartels, working in conjunction with state governments, are preventing students from historically underserved populations from entering the marketplace, how can higher education serve as a vehicle for addressing inequality?

In this chapter, I examine the historical and contemporary role of private foundations and professional associations in influencing college access and attempt to draw a link between state colleges and universities, the professional associations, and the economic structure that relies on gate-keeping. I argue that the current arrangements are incapable of addressing inequality and that a serious effort at addressing inequality through higher education will require a different approach. I discuss this approach in the following chapter. But first, I examine the role of credentialing as a mechanism of restricting opportunity among students of color and begin with the field of teacher education.

RACE AND CREDENTIALING IN THE TEACHING PROFESSION

As the previous chapter demonstrated, the education major and requirements to become a teacher have undergone significant changes over the past 50 years. Throughout this same period, the number of teachers of color in the United States, particularly Black teachers, has decreased significantly as well. The changing requirements to enter the education major, graduate with a degree in education, and gain the adequate certification to teach were necessary, according to education associations and reformers, to improve the teaching profession and American education.[1]

However, research on preadmission teaching preparation requirements suggests that these increased requirements have not led to the improved quality of teaching as their advocates predicted. As the previous chapter showed, over time, teaching preparation programs began requiring prospective students to meet a certain standardized test score, through the Scholastic Aptitude Test (SAT) or Praxis I/Praxis Core to enter the program. In one study, Henry et al. examined how teacher preparation program requirements, including high school class rank, SAT scores, or Praxis I scores may affect student academic performance.[2] The researchers found that when controlling for a number of factors, SAT scores and Praxis I scores were not associated with improving student math or reading test scores. Moreover, the study found that high school class rank was negatively associated with student test scores. This study joins other studies that have also concluded that standardized test scores are inadequate measurement instruments for assessing teacher potential.[3]

Although the scholarship has failed to provide convincing evidence that increasing admissions criteria for teacher preparation programs at colleges and universities, like high school class rank and standardized test scores, lead to improved student outcomes, we do have strong evidence that these admissions requirements are preventing potential teachers of color from entering the profession. Additionally, these exclusionary admissions standards persist despite a growing body of research showing that teachers of color improve educational outcomes for students of color.[4]

In the face of this evidence, it may seem puzzling that these requirements endure. However, while the empirical evidence on the link between teacher education requirements and teacher performance may not provide a convincing justification for these standards, an historical perspective on the role of race, credentials, private foundations, and professional organizations helps explain why these requirements persist despite evidence of their futility.

The previous chapter focused on how preadmission requirements have prevented aspiring teachers of color from entering teaching preparation programs. However, preadmissions standards represent only one aspect of the barrier to the teaching profession. To enter the teaching profession, prospective teachers have to become certified, which requires students to pass an exam. Although the certification exam is determined by state policy, the process of adopting state examination requirements for certification has been influenced by professional organizations, including accrediting organizations. The adoption and expansion of these teaching certification examinations are rooted in a history of racial exclusion.

National Teacher Examinations

In the 1930s, the American Council on Education, through its Cooperative Test Service, developed a teaching examination program to encourage school superintendents to adopt some testing requirement in the process of "teacher selection."[5] According to Ben Wood, the director of the Cooperative Test Service, and one of the most forceful advocates of teacher testing, "the only possible hope for our children lies in having them educated, so far as possible, by persons who are themselves educated."[6] Wood also argued that after years of having a surplus of teachers due to the layoffs of the Great Depression, a teacher test "would allow superintendents to weed out incompetents and restrict employment to educated persons."[7] The Carnegie Foundation, which was interested in developing a test to measure teacher competency, funded the Cooperative Test Service. With the financial support from the Carnegie Foundation, Wood was able to create and launch the National Teacher Examinations (NTE) in 1940.

Although the NTE was not widely adopted in its early years, Wood found the opportunity to expand the NTE when Southern states asked for his support in their fight against the National Association for the Advancement of Colored People (NAACP), which had been waging court battles for equal pay for Black teachers in the South. Under the leadership of Thurgood Marshall, the NAACP had filed lawsuits in the South in the mid- to late 1930s, arguing that there was no legal justification for Black teachers to earn, on average, 61 percent of what White teachers earned throughout the South.[8]

In 1940, the NAACP won a significant decision when the Fourth Circuit Court of Appeals ruled in *Alston v. School Board of Norfolk* that salary differences between Black and White teachers were unconstitutional because they were based on race.[9] As a result of the *Alston* decision, local school boards in the South could no longer legally maintain their system of unequal salary schedules for Black and White teachers. According to historian Scott Baker, the *Alston* decision allowed Ben Wood, who was frustrated with the lack of widespread adoption of the NTE, to work with Southern politicians to adopt the test as a legal method of justifying salary differences.[10] Wood knew, based on previous results of the exam, that White teachers were more likely to score higher on the NTE than Black teachers, therefore providing a "merit-based" justification for the wage differences.[11]

Throughout the early 1940s, Wood continued to work with Southern politicians to promote the use of the NTE, and in 1945, South Carolina became the first state to adopt the NTE as part of the process of certifying teachers. Then, following the *Brown v. Board of Education* decision in 1954, additional forms of teacher testing began to expand throughout the South. In a study of Black teachers in Louisiana, Butler documented how evaluations, testing, and "competency" were used to legally justify the displacement of Black teachers in the years following the *Brown* decision.[12] As White teachers began to displace Black teachers in the South, Black teachers filed discrimination lawsuits to protect their teaching jobs, arguing that their displacement was a violation of the equal protection clause in the Fourteenth Amendment. Although in one ruling, *Smith v. Board of Education of Morrilton School District* (1966), a federal judge ruled that the Fourteenth Amendment does not protect teachers' jobs, in *United States v. Jefferson County (Ala.) Board of Education* (1966), the Fifth Circuit—which covered almost the entire Deep South—ruled:

> In any instance where one or more teachers or other professional staff members are to be displaced as a result of desegregation, no staff vacancy in the school system should be filled through recruitment from outside the system unless no such displaced staff members is qualified to fill the vacancy.[13]

This ruling meant that districts that wanted to replace Black teachers with White teachers following desegregation had to do so by demonstrating that the Black teachers were not "qualified." Thus, with the 1966 Fifth Circuit decision, Southern states were able to use testing as method of measuring "competency" to justify the displacement of Black teachers. Alongside the *Alston* decision in 1940, which created a pathway for testing to be used to justify salary differences between White and Black teachers, based on "merit," the South had legal cover to adopt wage discrimination policies and displace Black teachers. In addition to legally sanctioning salary inequities and displacement, testing was also eventually used to prevent aspiring Black teachers from entering the profession.

In 1969, South Carolina, which was the first state to adopt the NTE as a requirement for teacher certification, increased the minimum passing score on the test. Following the policy change, Black teachers and other concerned groups argued that increasing score requirements were going to disproportionately affect Black prospective teachers. Among the groups raising concerns was the National Education Association (NEA), the largest teachers' union in the United States.

The support of Black teachers by the NEA was part of a transformation of the organization that had begun in the 1960s. Although the NEA made statements in support of Black teachers throughout its history, the organization was segregated, and Black teachers did not view the NEA as an organization that was interested in their professional development or success.[14] For instance, in 1926, the NEA created the Committee on Relations with Black Teachers; however, the committee chairs were White southerners who did not champion causes of interest for Black teachers.[15] But, by the 1960s, the association committed to integrating and advocating for teachers of color, and in 1967 and 1968 elected their first Latino and Black presidents in the organization's history.

In 1975, the NEA, the South Carolina Education Association, and Black teachers joined the US Department of Justice in a class action lawsuit against the state of South Carolina, arguing that increasing the score requirement on the NTE was explicitly discriminating against aspiring Black teachers. Indeed, research in the 1970s showed that the NTE was racially and culturally biased and Black test-takers were more likely to score lower than White test-takers.[16] However, in 1977, the Supreme Court ruled in *United States v. State of South Carolina* that a state may use a standardized test to hire and pay teachers.[17] Following the Court decision, other Southern states adopted the NTE for teacher certification. Between 1977 and 1983, the states of Arkansas, Louisiana, Mississippi, North Carolina, Tennessee, Virginia, and West Virginia required passing the NTE as a requirement for teacher certification.[18] By the late 1980s, all 14 states in the southeast of the United States had adopted the NTE.

Since the majority of Black teachers were in the South, the NTE had a devastating effect on the Black teaching force in the United States. Beverly

Cole of the NAACP, who had expressed concerns about the effects of testing on Black teachers, wrote, "It is very interesting to note that the southern states are in the vanguard of this movement. The southern states were the first to use minimum competency tests for new teachers and now all 14 states in the Southeast have such tests. . . . These are the states with the greatest number of minority students and the greatest number of minority teachers."[19]

Although the National Teacher Examination was ostensibly about improving the quality of teachers entering the profession, the test was used by the American Council on Education, the Carnegie Foundation, and local and state governments, to legally justify pay inequities between Black and White teachers, the displacement of Black teachers in the South, and, ultimately, denying prospective Black teachers an opportunity to enter the profession. By the early 1990s, more than half of American states had adopted the NTE as a requirement to certify teachers. In 1992, the Educational Testing Service (ETS), which administers the test, changed the NTEs to the Praxis.[20] As of 2021, 40 states use the Praxis for teacher certification.[21]

RESTRICTING ACCESS TO THE FIELDS OF MEDICINE, LAW, AND ENGINEERING

This chapter has primarily focused on credentialing in teacher education because teaching represents a professional field that has been historically accessible to African Americans but whose membership in the profession has declined significantly over the past four decades. Although scholars have argued that this decline is attributed to student choice and trends in the teaching market, I have argued that the teaching profession, through the implementation of secondary admissions processes, testing, and certification mechanisms, has deliberately excluded Black students and other students of color from entering. However, while the teaching profession represents one of the most blatant examples of systematic exclusion of people of color, it is not the only profession to engage in these practices.

The fields of medicine, law, engineering, and psychology, among others, have historically relied on credentialism to prevent Black people from entering the profession as well.

In the field of medicine, a focus on the profession's largest professional association, the American Medical Association (AMA), shows how the organization helped implement policies to restrict access to the profession, and how these policies affected Black membership in the profession. The AMA emerged in the mid-1800s, and by the early 1900s became a powerful organization whose influence transformed the science of medicine as well as the standards for the profession. By the 1930s, the organization was able to wield its influence to prevent doctors who were not part of the organization from gaining the necessary accreditation to practice medicine, particularly at local hospitals. The accreditation policy was used by the organization and local hospitals to discriminate against Black doctors and keep them from gaining membership in the organization. As Paul Starr, a scholar who has studied the history of the medical profession, has noted, "Black doctors, who were excluded from the local societies (of the AMA), could be kept out of hospital positions on those grounds."[22]

Perhaps the most significant effect on the development of Black doctors came in the partnership between the AMA and the Carnegie Foundation in the production of the Flexner Report in 1910. The Carnegie Foundation hired Abraham Flexner to lead an investigation of medical schools in the United States and Canada. The report, which advocated for medical school reforms, led to major changes in the training of doctors and the medical profession. A major consequence of the report was the closing of medical schools. Between 1900 and 1930, the number of medical schools in the United States decreased from 160 to 76.[23] Additionally, the report led to changes in the process of securing state licensure to practice medicine, which, following the publication of the report, was only provided to graduates from medical schools accredited by the AMA.[24]

The process of securing state licensure through an organization that discriminated against Black doctors and the closing of medical schools had significant consequences on African Americans in the medical profession. As Linda Dynan, who studied the effects of the Flexner Report on the health care of Black Americans, notes, "By 1923, medical education reform had contributed to reducing the number of medical schools that specialized in training black physicians from eight to just two."[25] As a result of these reforms, there were fewer Black physicians in 1950 than in 1900.[26]

The legal profession in the United States has a similar history of exclusion. Research has shown how the Bar exam was used to both deny accreditation for majority-minority law schools and systematically reduce the number of Black lawyers between the 1920s and the 1950s using Bar exam score cutoffs for admissions.[27] In the late 1920s and 1930s, members of underrepresented groups began to pursue the legal profession. To gain access to the law schools, Black applicants sued state law schools for discrimination. The successful lawsuits resulted in gradual integration in some states and the creation of separate state-run Black law schools in others. However, when the number of lawyers began to reduce the financial compensation of the previously White cadre of lawyers, the Bar "reduced the bar exam pass rates and tighten[ed] law school accreditations" by refusing to accredit schools with lower bar pass rates.[28]

These restrictive initiatives substantially reduced the number of Black lawyers and others from underrepresented groups by the 1930s. Between 1928 and 1932, three law schools that served Black students were shut down.[29] By the early 2000s, the Bar would deny accreditation to many law schools whose minimum Law School Admission Test (LSAT) score was below 143, aware that the average LSAT score for Black test-takers was a 142, compared to 152 for Whites.[30] As Shepherd (2003) has noted, many of the threats to deny accreditation have targeted historically Black law schools and law schools that predominantly serve students from underrepresented groups.

Similar to the fields of medicine, law, and education, the field of engineering has also implemented policies that have prevented Black students from entering the engineering profession. In *Race, Rigor, and Selectivity in U.S. Engineering*, Amy Slaton studied engineering programs in three states between the 1940s and 1990s.[31] Slaton points out that "merit" and changes in admissions policies, including a shift from formerly open admissions policies in engineering programs to more rigorous standards, have contributed to disparities between Blacks and Whites in the engineering profession. The changes in requirements over time, like the changes that have been documented in other academic programs, have contributed to decreases in Black students, and other students of color, in engineering programs and inevitably the engineering profession.

These examples of discriminatory policies in the fields of education, medicine, law, and engineering demonstrate that there are additional barriers in the college access process that merit further examination. Credential cartels, which have an influential role in the college access process, emerged as a political force at a time when the professions were seen to have a "surplus" of workers. The development and expansion of the NTEs by the American Council on Education and the Carnegie Foundation occurred at a time when there was a "surplus" of teachers following the Great Depression, and when desegregation created another form of "surplus," Black teachers had to be displaced to create opportunities for White teachers to teach in majority Black schools.

Similarly, the emergence of the AMA as a major political actor, and the Carnegie Foundation's support for the Flexner Report, occurred at a time when members of the medical profession grew concerned with the growing number of doctors in the profession. Likewise, the Bar Association increased test score requirements in response to concerns among its members that the growing number of lawyers was negatively affecting their finances. In each of these cases, racially biased testing was employed as a mechanism for reducing the "surplus" of workers. Not only did these methods disproportionately affect Black current and aspiring members of their respective professions, but the use of testing emerged at the time when Black membership in the professions was growing after successful mobilization and lawsuits to remove barriers to participation in the professions. In other words, the use of racially biased testing emerged as a mechanism to address a perceived problem of education inflation, following the expansion of education opportunities to previously excluded groups.

By the 1950s and 1960s, discriminatory admissions policies, including the use of SAT scores, were recognized by communities of color as barriers to college access. In response, communities organized and mobilized against these mechanisms of exclusion by demanding access for Black and Latino students to their universities through affirmative action policies, including the community-centered affirmative action college access programs. However, as communities were gaining ground in the struggle over access to college admissions, professional organizations assumed an important but often hidden role of restricting college access by closing opportunities to the professions.

Indeed, the mechanism of closure to the professions is consistent with a body of literature in sociology concerning the role of professional organizations. Sociologist Max Weber developed the concept of "social closure" to describe how organizations restrict competition from outside competitors seeking entry into their professions.[32] Scholar Raymond Murphy (1988) described Weber's definition of closure as "the process of subordination whereby one group monopolizes advantages by closing off opportunities to another group of outsiders beneath it which it defines as inferior or ineligible."[33]

Following Weber, other sociologists have further developed the concept of social closure by identifying and describing the mechanisms organizations employ to promote closure. In 1975, sociologist Randall Collins argued that the emergence of credentialism for job opportunities represented a method of social closure, to restrict access to outside competitors.[34] According to Collins, education credentialism legitimized restriction by promoting a logic of qualifications, while masking other forms of exclusion based on race and gender, for instance. Equally as important, Collins argued that "the rise in educational requirements for positions has been provoked by the increased supply of educated personnel rather than by new job-performance demands of those positions."[35] In other words, the increase in competition that was created by the opening of college access opportunities to previously excluded groups led to the rise of credentialism as an instrument of exclusion.

More recent research provides further evidence of the role of organizations in promoting social or occupational closure. Sociologist Kim Weeden (2002) builds on the scholarship by providing empirical evidence on how the mechanics of credentialism contribute to social closure. Relying on individual and occupational data in the 1990s, Weeden shows how licensing requirements, educational credentialing, and certification restrict the labor supply as well as occupational earnings in the United States.[36]

By incorporating the perspective of social closure, we are better able to understand the emergence of secondary admissions processes to enter majors and increasing certification standards to enter the professions. This perspective also may help explain why increasing percentages of women and students of color at public colleges and universities, the groups that benefited from the expansion of college access opportunities in the 1960s, are associated with higher GPA requirements to enter specific majors. The emergence of restrictive secondary admissions and certification policies was in response to the specific expansion of opportunities to these groups.

However, while the concept of social closure has been developed and studied by sociologists, the proliferation of social closure in the 1970s following the expansion of college access opportunities for previously excluded groups in the 1960s is political, and should be a focus of attention among political scientists as well. The process of legitimizing social closure through licensure and certification involves state legislative action. Furthermore, as the argument for discriminating against previously excluded groups was no longer tenable on account of race or gender, it produced a form of "layering," where the political terrain concerning college access shifted from public officials—admissions officers, college presidents, college board of trustees—to private organizations that used ostensibly "merit-based" measures to restrict access. The shifting of the political struggle to expand college access from the public to the private spheres in response to political pressures, indicates that the process of addressing or eliminating these hidden forms of restriction will also require political mobilization. These factors and conditions further substantiate the examination of college access and social closure as subjects of political analysis.

Additionally, by conceptualizing college access as consisting of both a front end (college admissions) and a back end (access to majors and professions), we are also better able to understand the limitations of higher education and its ability to address inequality. The use of racially biased mechanisms to reduce and limit the participation of certain groups from the workforce challenges the notion of higher education as a vehicle to alleviate inequality. As the history of professional organizations demonstrates, the expansion of opportunity to previously excluded groups has not been viewed as promising for the professions but as a form of inflation that had to be addressed by reducing the workforce. That the expansion of education opportunities led to a perception of education inflation that had to be addressed by restricting pathways to the professions is problematic, not only for higher education but for the promise of education as a whole. I return to this point in the final chapter.

Finally, by showing how credential cartels work with state governments to restrict access to new participants in the marketplace, these findings also challenge the claims of the dominant economic philosophy of the last four decades and raises further questions about the capacity of the existing economic system to adjust to expanding opportunities for historically marginalized populations.

NEOLIBERALISM AND THE CLOSING OF MARKETS

For decades, proponents of open markets have argued that economic expansion and individual prosperity are best achieved by limiting, and, in some instances, eliminating, government intervention in the economy. This economic theory, advanced by economists like Friedrich Hayek and Milton Friedman, among others, emerged as a response to Keynesian economics, the dominant economic model between the 1930s and 1950s. The Keynesian model, which argued for government intervention to stabilize and help grow the economy, was employed by the United States and other nations to emerge out of the Great Depression.[37] Utilizing the Keynesian approach, President Roosevelt promoted a "New Deal" for Americans who were struggling economically as a result of the Great Depression by using the government to invest in job creation.[38] However, despite the historic expansion of the American middle class and the unprecedented reduction of income and wealth inequality that the United States experienced in the 1940s and 1950s, by the 1960s, the work of Hayek and Friedman, began to challenge the Keynesian model.

The dominant argument, among scholars, is that the global economic recession of the 1970s, caused by an oil crisis, among other issues, created the opportunity for advocates of open markets, or neoliberals, to promote their economic theories. In Chile, Milton Friedman and the "Chicago Boys"—a group of Chilean economists trained by Friedman at the University of Chicago—designed and implemented the country's free market policies following a military coup in 1973.[39] Then, the elections of Margaret Thatcher in the United Kingdom and Ronald Reagan in the United States, both proponents of the neoliberal approach, completed the rupture with Keynesian economics and solidified the era of neoliberalism. The neoliberal era, as scholars have shown, would mark a period of government deregulation in the economy, an embrace of open markets, and the increasing privatization of public institutions.

However, while the dominant argument is that the emergence of neoliberalism in the 1970s was motivated by a logic of withdrawing the role of the state in the economy, a growing body of literature has emerged challenging this narrative. In his book on the rise of global neoliberalism, historian Quinn Slabodian argues that the neoliberals were not against state action in the markets.[40] In fact, the neoliberals viewed state action as necessary to shield capitalism from the threats that emerged between the 1940s and 1960s. These "threats," Quinn argues, were democracy and the decolonization movements that spread throughout the globe in the mid-20th century. Quinn writes that prominent liberals, like Hayek and Friedman, believed that "restricting political freedom, as commonly understood, was necessary under some circumstances to preserve economic freedom."[41]

From this perspective, the emergence of global neoliberalism was a response to the decolonization movements, which included socialist revolutions, to protect global capitalism. However, expanding democratic rights did not only threaten capitalism itself, it threatened the winners within the existing capitalist order. The democratic movements of the 1950s and 1960s opened opportunities to new competitors in the capitalist system. In the United States, this meant that millions of previously excluded individuals, women and people of color, were new participants not only in the political process but in the economy as well. The political movements that led to expanding college access opportunities to previously excluded groups also led to expanding economic opportunities. As the activists of the 1950s and 1960s understood, the struggle for political rights was also a struggle for economic justice.

The assumption by many, influenced by the arguments presented by proponents of open markets, was that the economy would adjust to the new participants and expand economic prosperity. However, this is not what happened in the United States. As college opportunities expanded, inequality also expanded. Rather than grow to expand economic prosperity, the economy adjusted to protect those who were already winners under the existing arrangements. And while free market enthusiasts would like to make the argument that these results were part of an organic reaction to changes in the economy, the reality is that the restriction of economic opportunities to marginalized groups was made possible by those in power using the state to protect their dominant position.

An important part of the logic that undergirds the assumption that the economy would expand opportunities is the widespread belief that higher education provides the vehicle to achieve upward social mobility and reduce inequality. However, the evidence presented throughout this book suggests that this is not empirically accurate. The political movements that led to expanding college access opportunities for Black students, Latinos, first-generation, and low-income students reveal the many layers of obstruction, facilitated by the state working with the private sector to prevent these marginalized groups from achieving upward social mobility. As this book has demonstrated, attacks against affirmative action, open admissions, special college access programs, cuts in financial aid, and disinvestment in state systems of higher education are all a result of state actions to limit the expansion of opportunities. Equally as important, through credentialism, states and credential cartels use admissions, licensing, and certification requirements to restrict access to members of marginalized groups, particularly Black students, to professions like education, medicine, law, and engineering.

Therefore, the state and private sector's collusion in the restriction of economic opportunities for marginalized populations is inconsistent with the theory of free markets and open competition. Through the examination of higher education, we can see that the task of the neoliberals was not to open markets but to close markets to the new participants. Contrary to the argument that neoliberals were primarily motivated to privatize public institutions in the pursuit of financial rewards, this examination suggests that the dismantling of public institutions like public education were not simply motivated by an interest in profits but by an interest in eliminating the source of competition. Since public education emerged as the most powerful political instrument in challenging inequality, public education itself had to be challenged. Neoliberalism emerged as a political project to disarm and subjugate the new participants in the political and economic arena.

In the United States, these neoliberal policies that have restricted college access and career pathways have not been limited to any particular political party. Concerns about college "deservedness" and "merit"—the parlance of neoliberal orthodoxy—cut across ideology and partisan identification. The demand for higher grade point averages for particular majors, as well as increasing licensure and certification requirements, has gained support from a wide range of constituencies, including faculty members who consider themselves "liberal." Therefore, the work of restricting college and career pathways is not exclusive to any political party.

However, while the power to restrict access to marginalized groups has not been exclusive to any political party, as people of color, particularly Black Americans, increasingly identified with the Democratic Party, the Republican Party increasingly became the party that utilized its power to restrict opportunities to Black people and other people of color. Researchers have shown that while both Democrats and Republicans at the state and national level have been responsible for the disinvestment in higher education, decreases in state appropriations for higher education have been mostly led by Republican state officials.[42]

At the same time, research by Taylor et al. has shown that Republican-controlled state governments are not always opposed to increasing state spending on higher education.[43] They show that in Republican-controlled states where Whites are overrepresented in the population (in relation to the average state), state appropriations for higher education actually increased. However, in Republican-controlled states with declining White overrepresentation, state appropriations for higher education were likely to decrease. Therefore, it is not just partisan politics that are shaping investments in higher education but *race and partisan politics* that help explain decreases in state appropriations. These findings provide further evidence of the salience of race in helping explain the barriers to college opportunities and career pipelines.

Through the examination of higher education, and particularly the expansion of college access to previously excluded groups, we see how the winners in the existing political and economic order have mobilized the state through the instrument of credential cartels to protect their status and restrict opportunities to historically marginalized people. Based on this analysis, it does not appear feasible to expect that under current conditions, higher education can serve as a vehicle of upward social mobility and reduce inequality. In order to meet this promise, democratic pressures would have to be asserted to mobilize the state away from the grip of neoliberalism and its objective of restricting opportunities to a more democratic direction, where expanding opportunities for all and a vision and commitment to developing scholars are a possibility.

A Developing Scholars Approach

In the early 20th century, W. E. B. DuBois wrote about and advocated for the development of institutions of higher education for Black people as a way to "guide" and "elevate" the masses and build a foundation for Black intellectual and economic development.[1] At a time when higher education opportunities were broadly limited, particularly among Black Americans, DuBois called for an expansion of opportunity for those best positioned at the moment to receive an education and become leaders of their communities. According to DuBois, "the Negro race, like all races, is going to be saved by its exceptional men."[2]

DuBois referred to this class of "exceptional men" as the "Talented Tenth." The Talented Tenth, an elite class of African Americans, would in his view, lead the masses of Black people out of the wretched conditions following the abolition of slavery, if provided the opportunity of higher education. Although DuBois's focus of expanding higher education opportunities was centered on the Talented Tenth, his argument was that through these "exceptions," a broader possibility is revealed about Black people. DuBois writes that "exceptional it is to be sure, but this is its chiefest promise; it shows the capability of Negro blood, the promise of black men."[3]

In the decades that followed, DuBois's vision of expanding higher education opportunities to Black elites would slowly materialize. By mid-century, the children of Black elites would be attending colleges and universities, including the most elite institutions of higher education

Developing Scholars. Domingo Morel, Oxford University Press. © Oxford University Press 2023.
DOI: 10.1093/oso/9780197636992.003.0008

in the country in greater numbers than when DuBois wrote about the Talented Tenth in 1903. However, this expansion of higher education opportunities did not result in the educational and economic development of the masses of Black people as DuBois had initially hoped for, if not predicted.

DuBois's belief that higher education could provide an opportunity out of impoverished conditions was shared by many, including leaders of the Civil Rights movement. As early as the 1940s, Black leaders were advocating for affirmative action policies to address the lack of employment opportunities for Black people. By the mid-1960s, the push for affirmative action expanded to higher education. Proponents argued that through affirmative action, high-achieving Black students who were prevented from entering colleges and universities for various reasons, including racially biased standardized test score requirements, could be offered opportunities to attend institutions of higher education and achieve upward mobility. Affirmative action offered a solution to high-achieving Black and other students of color to earn admissions to selective colleges and universities. It also offered a solution to elite institutions, and presidents of elite institutions, who were promoting the use of Scholastic Aptitude Tests (SATs) at the same time that they expressed an interest, at least rhetorically, in expanding college access opportunity to all students. The adoption of affirmative action policies at the elite institutions was a solution for the contemporary Talented Tenth.

Although thousands of students would benefit from affirmative action policies, by the late 1960s, a movement, mostly led by young students and community activists in cities across the country, pushed for a more *community-centered* approach to affirmative action. These activists were not satisfied with expanding college opportunities to a selected few; they demanded college access for all students. Rather than accepting traditional conceptions of "talent" as a form of exceptionalism, these activists viewed the ability to excel academically as an ability possessed by all. In their view, racial subjugation, not some natural gift or talent, was the reason Black students were not able to excel academically. By removing the barriers of subjugation—educational, social, political, and economic—all students could develop "talent." Within higher education, this meant that barriers to admissions, including SAT scores, grade point average (GPA) requirements, and class rank, were mechanisms of subjugation and had to be removed in order to provide historically oppressed people the right to flourish.

As previous chapters have demonstrated, in the 1960s, Black and Latinx students and community activists in Newark, New Jersey, New York City, and Providence, Rhode Island, demanded greater access to their public institutions of higher education. Communities made similar demands in other states, including California, Massachusetts, Florida, Illinois, and Pennsylvania. I argue that these programs represent a version of a radical affirmative action that has received less attention in the scholarship. Moreover, the book has also argued that contrary to conventional wisdom, the urban rebellions of the 1960s helped provide the political conditions that led to the creation of these programs. Despite the many political obstacles these programs encountered at their launch and throughout their early years by some state officials, members of their governing boards, and unsupportive faculty and administrators, these programs demonstrated success and offered opportunities to thousands of students who otherwise would not have an opportunity to attend their own state colleges and universities.

However, despite the success of these programs in creating college access opportunities for the "disadvantaged" students, only a few years after the programs were created, many of them would experience significant threats, and some would be eliminated altogether. Attacks on race-based admissions policies, federal cuts to financial aid, and state disinvestment in higher education contributed to the withdrawal of support for the special college access programs of the late 1960s. The elimination of these programs is consistent with a vast body of social movement scholarship.[4] According to the scholarship, once the threat of protest and civil unrest subsided, state officials no longer felt the political pressure or political incentives to continue supporting the programs. This is indeed what happened to many programs. By the 1970s, as the threat of violent protests diminished, support for these programs waned as well.

Yet, despite the elimination of many programs, some are still in existence and some have managed to grow through periods of significant political threats. I argue that the reason why the Talent Development (TD) Program was able to grow is because the program never ceased being a political movement. At every juncture, when the program faced existential threats like other programs encountered during the early threats of the 1970s, the wave of neoliberal policies of the late 1980s and early 1990s, and the massive disinvestment in higher education of the late 1990s, students mobilized in defense of the program. They took over university-administration buildings; faced violence from state, local, and university police; and, rather than accept the cut or elimination of the program, demanded its expansion. As a result of these student actions, the program has been able to survive. Additionally, savvy program leaders and staff have cultivated political relationships within the University and with the broader community to strengthen its political standing with university and state officials. In short, the program's ability to rely on inside politics and political protest when needed, have contributed to its success over the past 50 years. By showing how protest has been a critical component to the ongoing success of the program, these findings contribute to our understanding of how protest can be an important aspect of policy maintenance.

At the same time, while the program has been able to grow, the case study analysis revealed other challenges. Despite providing opportunities to thousands of students who otherwise would not have the opportunity to attend their state university, the results of the study show that since the 1970s, students in the TD Program have found it increasingly difficult to graduate with degrees in education, business, nursing, and engineering. An analysis of national graduation trends shows that this is not unique to students of color at the University of Rhode Island. National data show that Black and Latinx students were less likely to earn bachelor's degrees in engineering, business, and education.[5]

The dominant scholarship has suggested that the reason for the lack of students of color, particularly in education, a field that has historically provided a path to the middle class for African Americans, was a result of increased choices of professions available to Black students. According to this view, Black students were no longer restricted to the teaching profession, and had other options available beyond education. However, the argument in this book is that the "choice of major" explanation is a myth. As previous chapters have demonstrated, systematic barriers—secondary admissions processes and increasing certification standards—emerged in the 1970s in response to expansion of college access opportunities, particularly for Black students and other students of color, which prevented them from gaining access to particular majors and eventually to their respective professions. Moreover, the book demonstrates how the politics of college access shifted from the public to private sector, in an effort to shield college access restriction from public pressures. These findings help contribute to our understanding of how policies are retrenched through a form of layering, where credential cartels working with state governments circumvented the political movement for greater college access by creating hidden forms of restriction to college access.

Based on these findings, I argue that contrary to the belief of many, under existing conditions, higher education is incapable of serving as a vehicle for upward mobility and, therefore, incapable of serving as a tool to address growing concerns of inequality in the United States. However, just as the community activists created the conditions, through political mobilization, to expand opportunities to students who were not considered "college material," political mobilization can dismantle barriers that exist in college admissions, access to majors, and access to the professions and provide a path for addressing inequality.

TRANSFORMING HIGHER EDUCATION INTO A MECHANISM FOR ADDRESSING INEQUALITY

Over the past decade, scholars, activists, and practitioners have proposed an array of policy initiatives to address growing concerns with higher education and its ability to serve as a vehicle for upward mobility. Key among them, is a renewed investment in higher education at the state level. Since the 1980s, states have been disinvesting in higher education, which has had significant implications on how state colleges and universities can serve students. One of the most significant consequences is that as state funding decreased, state colleges and universities increasingly relied on tuition as a major source of income. Moreover, as tuition became the most important source of income, out-of-state students, including international students, who pay the full freight of tuition, have become increasingly important to colleges and universities.

Although state colleges and universities should serve out-of-state students and international students, their primary responsibility, as described in their state charters, should be to the students of their respective states. However, state cuts to higher education have led state colleges and universities to shift increasing focus to those who can pay tuition rather than to the students they were created to serve, in-state residents. The reliance on tuition has not only led to concerns over who state colleges and universities are serving, it also led to the major problem of college affordability.

Between 1980 and 2010, the average public 4-year tuition increased by 244 percent.[6] As a result, these increases in tuition prices led to a series of additional problems in higher education. At the same time that tuition began to increase, financial aid did not keep up with rising costs. As scholars like Sara Goldrick-Rab and others have noted, since the 1980s, the Pell Grants, the most substantive federal financial support program for low-income students, have decreased their purchasing power for students.[7]

Additionally, as college became increasingly difficult to afford and financial aid was not keeping up with costs, school loans became an increasing reality for college students. As of 2020, the total student loan debt in the United States was over $1.6 trillion and the average college graduate owed more than $30,000 in school loans.[8] The student loan debt crisis has disproportionately affected low-income students and students of color, who are less likely to have individual or community wealth and take on a disproportionate amount of student debt to finance their education.[9] Moreover, the difficulties of repaying college loans are also disproportionately experienced by students of color. Morgan and Steinbaum (2018) note "evidence that delinquency, default, and other forms of nonpayment are especially severe among Black Americans."[10] To address these major concerns, advocates have argued that it is not only important to increase state funding for higher education, but it is equally important to increase federal funding for Pell Grants and to initiate a process of student loan forgiveness.[11]

More recently, a movement to make all state colleges and universities tuition-free has gained momentum as well. The movement gained nationwide attention partly as a result of Senator Bernie Sanders, who pushed for tuition-free colleges and universities during his presidential campaigns in 2016 and 2020. Although half of US states offer free college tuition at their community colleges, proponents of free college tuition have argued for expanding free college tuition for all state colleges and universities.[12]

In addition to proposing solutions to address concerns with funding and affordability, a movement for ending the use of SATs in the admissions process has been gaining momentum as well. For decades, opponents of the SATs have argued that the test is biased and its use discriminates against low-income, Black and Latinx students. While most colleges and universities still have SAT requirements, a growing number have made SATs "optional" and in 2020, the University of California system voted to phase out the use of SAT requirement in the next 4 years.[13] Although the growing trend in "SAT optional" may seem like a step in making colleges more accessible and racially diverse, scholars caution that this may not be the case. In one recent study, scholars found adopting SAT-optional policies did not increase the number of low-income and underrepresented student enrollment.[14] It may be that since test "optional" policies still allow students to submit their scores, students who have higher scores submit them while students with lower scores do not submit them, and admissions offices may still favor the higher scores even if they are optional.

Finally, there is the widely debated and politically contested policy of affirmative action. Since the 1970s, affirmative action has faced enduring challenges in the courts and state capitols. Although the Supreme Court has not struck down affirmative action, as has been discussed throughout this book, the Court's decisions have left the policy vulnerable to future challenges. Additionally, several states have banned the use of race in admissions decisions at their public institutions, including California, Florida, Michigan, and Texas. In 2020, California voters rejected a ballot measure that would have reversed the state's affirmative action ban.

At the private, elite institutions, race can still be used in its admissions policies but that is under attack as well. Harvard's use of race in admissions was challenged by a group charging that its policies discriminate against Asian American applicants. In the fall of 2020, the case had made its way to the circuit court of appeals where the court upheld a district court opinion which ruled that Harvard's affirmative action policy is not unconstitutional and does not discriminate against Asian American students. However, that decision was appealed and the Supreme Court has agreed to hear the case. Based on the conservative make-up of the Supreme Court, some observers believe that the Court will strike down affirmative action.[15]

Collectively, these policy initiatives—increasing state support for higher education, increasing Pell Grants, student loan forgiveness, tuition-free college, abolishing SATs in admissions, and upholding and expanding affirmative action—would contribute significantly to removing barriers to higher education, particularly for students of color. Any effort at helping transform higher education into a vehicle for upward mobility must include these initiatives.

However, as the arguments and findings in this book have demonstrated, even if all of these policies are implemented and expanded, higher education will still fall short of addressing inequality. These measures, as important as they are, do not challenge the hidden layers of inequality in higher education that have been discussed in this book: secondary admissions processes and the credential cartels that obstruct pathways to careers. Indeed, by removing the barriers of front-end college access (college admissions) and addressing affordability, the findings in this book suggest that the back-end aspect of college access (pathways to the majors and professions) will become more restrictive. Therefore, a more comprehensive approach to transforming higher education must take into account these hidden layers of inequality and equally as important, the structure of the economy.

A POLITICAL STRATEGY FOR HIGHER EDUCATION

In order for higher education to fulfill its promise of serving as a vehicle for addressing inequality, communities must advance a political strategy that includes a commitment to a scholar development logic, the disarming of credential cartels, and creating a public sector economy that is capable of absorbing new participants and generates economic and employment opportunities to historically marginalized populations.

Part I. Access and Support

Programs like TD, Education Opportunity Fund (EOF), and Search for Education, Elevation, and Knowledge (SEEK) have a proven track record of admitting students who do not meet traditional admissions requirements and providing the support systems (advising, tutorial, financial, social, and emotional) to guide students through their undergraduate college experiences. These programs provide a model for the type of approach colleges and universities can adopt to expand opportunities to populations—Black, Latinx, Native Nations, low-income, first-generation, urban, and rural—that are underrepresented in attending and earning college degrees.

By emphasizing an approach to admitting and supporting students who come from underrepresented populations, who do not present the characteristics that traditional college admissions offices seek when admitting students, colleges and universities can depart from the traditional conventions of who can be a college student. At the same time, the work of providing the support students need is as equally important as establishing paths to admissions. Unlike the for-profit colleges, where the objective is to bring students through the doors, only to saddle them with debt and oftentimes no college degree, the mission of special college access programs like TD, EOF, and SEEK is to ensure that students are able to earn a college degree.

The programs achieve this success by ensuring that students have financial aid and academic support through advisement, tutoring, and developmental courses. Additionally, these programs offer social and emotional support that is not often discussed but of great importance to students. For instance, helping secure legal representation for students and their families when they must go to court for immigration, criminal, or civil issues, like preventing eviction. Oftentimes, these programs help provide food and shelter to students who do not have a place to live when the schools are on winter and summer break. They also work to provide financial aid to undocumented students who are not eligible for federal financial aid. These programs provide these and other forms of support on a day-to-day basis for their students.

Equally important, recruiters and advisors for these programs are often graduates of their respective programs and are embedded in their respective communities. The connection between the programs and communities not only establishes pipelines from the community to the University but provides a mechanism to check the University when it is deviating from its promise to these students and their communities.

Additionally, unlike the dominant conception of affirmative action policies, these community-centered affirmative action programs are not focused on recruiting and admitting the highest-achieving students in their respective high school classes, thereby creating pathways for students from communities that have been historically marginalized and excluded from attaining higher education. Moreover, these programs are not exclusively focused on providing opportunities to students of color. Poor White students, who are also excluded from accessing college opportunities, are also part of the targeted communities. Supporting existing special college access programs, reviving programs that are no longer in existence, and creating new programs where they have not existed will help address concerns with college access among historically underserved populations.

Part II. Disarming the Credential Cartels

In addition to supporting existing, reviving former, and creating new programs that provide college access and support services to students from underserved populations, an emphasis needs to be placed on challenging the credential cartels that prevent students from gaining access to particular professions like education, nursing, engineering, business, law, and medicine. For decades, the use of secondary admissions processes like standardized test scores, increased GPA requirements, and premajor test requirements have been accepted as the norm in many colleges and universities. Although these policies have been justified as legitimate because they are "merit-based," as this book has demonstrated, they are rooted in a history of racism and exclusion, and they continue to serve as a mechanism to restrict college access to students of color. Secondary admissions policies emerged in response to the expansion of higher education opportunities in the late 1960s, and particular policies, like increasing GPA requirements to enter particular majors, are associated with the increase in Black and Latinx students at a college or university.

Moreover, these policies persist despite evidence that these additional requirements to enter a major are not predictors of competency in these particular fields. The research is consistent in demonstrating that the best predictor for success in a profession is training, exposure, and experience, not standardized test scores or even high school GPA. Therefore, creating genuine opportunities for students will require the removal of secondary admissions processes like demanding higher SAT scores, higher GPAs, or class rank to enter a major after a student has already been admitted to a university.

In addition to removing the secondary admissions barriers, communities and their students need to push for professional certification and licensing requirements that reflect ability rather than wealth and privilege, as standardized tests, like the SATs, more accurately measure. The education, nursing, medical, business, and engineering professions need to ensure that practitioners are trained and are indeed qualified to be teachers, engineers, doctors, and nurses. However, the process of entering training programs and securing adequate licensing or certification has historically discriminated against Black students and other students of color. The professional organizations, like teacher preparation accreditation organizations, the American Medical Association, the Bar Association, and others, are incentivized to restrict opportunities rather than open doors for the historically marginalized. Without political pressure from those affected by these restrictive practices and policies, and those professing to be champions of equality and opportunity, like faculty members, university presidents, and practitioners, these invisible obstacles to the professions will endure. The process of credentialing has to be democratized and subjected to increased public scrutiny.

Finally, even if communities are successful in expanding opportunities for college access for students of underrepresented populations, creating support programs for these students, removing secondary admissions requirements, and creating certification and licensing standards that open doors and more accurately measure ability to perform in a profession, the American economy must be able to absorb the new participants in the labor market. However, the dominant economic philosophy of the last four decades and its emphasis on privatization and repudiation of government intervention is incapable of creating the economic opportunities for the new participants. To fulfill the promise of higher education, a political movement to increase access and remove barriers to the professions must be matched with a renewed focus on revitalizing the public sector as a mechanism for economic opportunities.

Part III. An Economy for the Public

As was discussed in the previous chapter, the 1970s ushered in an era of neoliberalism, where "free markets," government deregulation, and privatization of public institutions became the dominant economic philosophy. Although some scholars have argued that the emergence of neoliberalism was in response to global economic crises in the early 1970s, which created an opening for the free-market philosophies of economists like Hayek and

Friedman, I have argued that neoliberalism was not motivated by opening markets but rather closing markets to the new participants who entered the political and economic arena in the 1960s. Therefore, the existing economic structure has been constructed to restrict upward mobility rather than create economic opportunities for politically and economically marginalized people. As a result, higher education is not able to become a vehicle of upward mobility, as many have suggested.

These limitations demand the adoption of different economic approaches to creating opportunities. A good place to start is by examining the last period of significant upward mobility in the United States. Between the 1940s and 1960s, the United States experienced the largest expansion of the middle class and the lowest levels of wealth and income inequality. This was also the period of the largest expansion of higher education in the United States until the larger expansion efforts of the late 1960s. As economists and political scientists have shown, the expansion of the middle class and reduction in income and wealth inequality during this period was possible because of the role government played in the economy. Taxation policies, government investment in infrastructure, and education, particularly higher education, helped open the economy to the new participants of that era.

However, while government intervention helped expand economic opportunities to new participants, Black Americans and other marginalized groups were often excluded from these opportunities. Although wealth and income inequality decreased in America, Black people were not equal beneficiaries of these opportunities. Additionally, while higher education opportunities expanded for many Americans, including World War II veterans, Black Americans were not equal beneficiaries of these opportunities either. The political, economic, and social movements of the 1950s and 1960s, including the urban rebellions of the late 1960s that spurred the creation of special college access programs for Black and Latinx students, were intended to dismantle these enduring mechanisms of political and economic subjugation.

Therefore, although it is instructive to look at the post-World War II period as a model for a future path, the exclusion and racism of that that era are also instructive. A plan to create possibilities of political and economic opportunities for all Americans must incorporate race and racial justice at its center, not the periphery. In other words, if higher education is to fulfill its promise of creating opportunities for upward mobility, expanding opportunities for people of color, including those who do not meet traditional requirements for college admissions, must be an explicit objective.

Since the private sector is severely limited in its capacity to create economic opportunities for all, there is a need for the public sector to assume a greater role in creating the economy of the future. Moreover, unlike previous periods of economic expansion, the politics that determine the structure of the economy of the future must also be explicit about expanding opportunities to racially subjugated people. Based on these core tenets, the arguments presented by modern monetary theorists provide the most promising potential.

Modern Monetary Theory (MMT) traces its origins to the early 20th century but has gained more attention over the past two decades and challenges conventional arguments about US government budget deficits. Contrary to the widely accepted belief that the US government should run its budget like a household, where revenues have to equal expenses to maintain a balanced budget, MMT scholars argue that unlike households, where individuals "use" currency, the US government "issues" currency.[16] In other words, since the United States has a sovereign currency (it produces its own money), it cannot run out of money. As a result, the US government does not have to subscribe to the dominant thinking on federal spending which has relied on either raising taxes to fund government programs or cutting programs to balance the federal budget. According to MMT scholars, as long as the government can control inflation, it can continue to spend on government programs it deems necessary for the economy.[17]

One of the strongest arguments for the adoption of the MMT approach involves its ability to create public-sector jobs for the unemployed. Since the federal government can spend on programs without risking the possibility of bankruptcy, the federal government can create public-sector jobs to ensure full employment.[18] While this approach is helpful during times of economic downturns, like economic recessions or depressions, it can also be utilized to promote employment when the private sector has proven incapable of creating job opportunities to a significant number of Americans. The federal government can become the "employer of last resort" when the private sector has failed to produce employment to those willing to work.[19]

As has been demonstrated throughout this book, professional organizations restrict access to their respective professions through the process of occupational closure. As a result, many Americans, particularly students of color, have been prevented from entering professions like education, engineering, nursing, and business. While the private sector has proved feckless in its ability to create opportunities for these students, through MMT, government can invest in a public-sector economy that creates employment opportunities for these students. As Stephanie Kelton, one of the earliest economists to advance MMT has argued, "If we have the building materials to fix our infrastructure, if we have people who want to become doctors, nurses, and teachers, if we can grow all the food we need—then the money can always be made available to accomplish our goals."[20]

MMT offers an opportunity to work through enduring economic obstacles for communities of color. Young people of color have always aspired to be "doctors, nurses, and teachers." However, the obstacle has always been a lack of opportunity. More poignantly, the hospitals and schools, particularly after desegregation, have not needed people of color to fill the positions of doctors, nurses, and teachers. These positions have overwhelmingly been filled by Whites, even in cities and communities where people of color represent the majority of the population. Indeed, as this book has shown, the emergence of racially biased testing to measure "competency" was in part motivated to displace Black people from their profession. However, by creating a public-sector economy that generates new opportunities based on the needs of communities,[21] job opportunities that have been traditionally closed off to students of color can now be made available.

The ability to issue currency is limited to the federal government, not states and local governments, which have to operate balanced budgets. Therefore, in order for MMT to create public-sector employment opportunities for graduates of state colleges and universities, as I have argued in this book, the federal government has to create partnerships with state and local governments and state colleges and universities. Through MMT, the federal government can work with states to create economic opportunities that the private sector has not been able to create. Moreover, by creating public-sector jobs in areas of need to local communities, like health and education, communities and their local officials must demand that colleges and universities admit and train their students to fill these positions. By doing so, pipelines to the medical and educational fields, among others, which have been nonexistent for communities of color, can begin to be established.

Equally as important, the creation of new pipelines and professional opportunities for people of color, where they are indeed "needed," can have significant implications well beyond higher education. By creating pipelines and demonstrating a need to prepare and develop young people for genuine opportunities in the economy, K–12 education, particularly in urban, majority communities of color, may be significantly affected as well. For instance, MMT may create new opportunities for hiring public school teachers, particularly teachers of color, which is associated with improved school performance for students of color.

But just as important as improving education for students of color by creating more opportunities for teachers of color to teach them, the expansion of economic opportunities can alter education systems by offering legitimate pipelines to meaningful employment. For generations, public school systems in urban communities have had to educate young people and promise benefits of an education that would, for generations, prove hollow. Since the economy has been structured in a way that the positions of doctors, teachers, nurses, and engineers in marginalized communities are constantly filled by people outside their communities, the need to develop young people to fill these positions has not existed. In other words, part of what contributes to the political and economic marginalization of communities is that their young people are robbed of the opportunity to develop their talents because the economy has not needed their talent. Creating genuine pipelines from racially subjugated communities to meaningful economic opportunities will have profound effects on public education by unleashing the potential of people historically discarded by an exclusionary economy.

In short, MMT provides an opportunity to overcome the limitations of an economic structure that has relied on the exclusion and misery of many. Too often, those excluded have been people of color. A renewed philosophy of government intervention in the economy, with a novel approach of including historically marginalized people, particularly Black people, can unlock the restrictions that have prevented young college students of color from entering the professions that they choose and that their communities need them to occupy.

DISMANTLING ARTIFICIAL BARRIERS TO EDUCATIONAL AND ECONOMIC OPPORTUNITY

By demonstrating that government can create opportunities for full employment, MMT also exposes and challenges the accepted policy of necessary unemployment. According to long-standing US Federal Reserve policy, the economy must always have a certain level of unemployment to guard against inflation. That is, if everyone who is able to be employed is indeed employed, the economy runs the risk of "overheating," or having more individuals competing to purchase goods than there are goods available for them to buy. This logic of necessary unemployment has created artificial barriers to employment and those often left on the losing end have historically been marginalized people and people of color. Over the past six decades, the rate of Black unemployment has consistently remained double that of White unemployment.[22]

The logic of creating artificial barriers to opportunities extends to education as well. At the same time that many believe that education is a right for all, the reality is that for generations, artificial barriers have prevented

significant number of Americans, particularly Black Americans, from receiving an education. Standardized test scores, requiring students to demonstrate arbitrary forms of competency before entering training programs,
and certification and licensing requirements that measure privilege not
ability are all artificial barriers imposed upon the marginalized.

However, for generations, communities have also fought against these
artificial barriers that tried to convince them that their young people were
not capable or worthy of an education. In the pursuit of higher education,
these communities and their young people challenged barriers and conventional logic about who was worthy of a college education and exposed
the fictitious claims of worthiness and merit by demonstrating that with
access, support, and guidance, all students can develop their talents. The
persistence of these communities and the courage of young activists who
demanded a right to an education, not just for them but for future generations, affirm the promise of higher education, but that promise can only
be fulfilled with a transformation of an economy that is capable of creating
opportunities for all.

PROTEST AS POLICY FEEDBACK

In March of 2020, the COVID-19 pandemic, which began to spread rapidly throughout the early months of the year, caused shutdowns throughout the United States. Restaurants, movie theaters, and schools, from pre-kindergarten through higher education, all experienced some form of closing as a result of the pandemic. The University of Rhode Island, like many universities throughout the country, transitioned to virtual instruction, leaving the campus devoid of students.

Then, in May of 2020, another event would shake the nation. Videos of a White police officer in Minneapolis killing George Floyd by kneeling on his neck began to surface through social media. Immediately, protests began in Minneapolis and within days, protests spread throughout the country. By the first week of June, protests had occurred in more than 550 locations throughout the United States.[1] Estimates show that by mid-June, between 15 million and 26 million Americans had been involved in a protest.[2] The protests, which were ignited by the killing of George Floyd, but which also grew to include demands for justice for Breonna Taylor, who was killed by police officers in Louisville, Kentucky, were part of a broader Black Lives Matter movement.

While protests spread through cities and towns across the country, college campuses did not emerge as sites of vigorous protest. Although the protests occurred at a time when students traditionally leave campuses for the summer break, the pandemic had emptied college campuses.

However, at the University of Rhode Island, a campus without students did not mean that the campus was spared from protest.

For several years before the pandemic shut down the campus and the Black Lives Matter movement gained nationwide attention, staff members of color at the University of Rhode Island were demanding better conditions for students and staff of color at the university. The staff members, who worked as academic advisors, administrators of multicultural activities, and enrollment services, among other functions, had demanded that university officials increase its commitment to admitting, hiring, and supporting students and staff of color at the university.

On June 15, as the nation was engulfed in protests, Black staff members at the University issued a letter to the president, stating:

> We, as individual members of the Black staff at the University of Rhode Island, both present and past, and across various units, have come together to voice our frustration over the Administration's response to events that impact the Black community; to express our exhaustion over the systemic racism and widespread apathy that continues to be a hallmark of Black life at the institution.[3]

The letter, which included specific demands for better conditions for Black members of the campus community, also included the following:

> [We] ask that on June 19, 2020, known across Black America as "Juneteenth," a collective mass of Black Administrators, Faculty, Staff, and others join us in holding a University-wide day of exhaustion. . . . In observance of this unofficial holiday for Black people in America, we ask that our Black employees elect not to "come in" or telework from home on this day. We ask that there be no communication with URI in an effort to allow the institution to recognize the

necessity of Blackness in the same manner it constantly reinforces the priority of Whiteness.

The Black members of the staff who signed the letter were mostly Talent Development (TD) alums. Some, like Michelle Fontes, were part of the Black Student Leadership Group which organized the 1992 takeover of Taft Hall. Others, like John Carl Cruz, were part of the Brothers United for Action group who organized the protest on campus in 1998. Shirley Consuegra, a staff member who also signed the letter, was involved with the campus protest in 1998 and has an older sister, Norelys Consuegra, who was part of the Black Student Leadership Group in 1992. Bobby Britto-Oliveira, another staff member, had family members involved in the campus protests of the 1990s as well. All were politicized to utilize protest to improve conditions for Black members of the campus community.

In political science, scholars have used the concept of policy feedback to demonstrate how policies influence politics. As a result of policy feedback processes, policies can have the effect of increasing or decreasing the likelihood that citizens affected by those policies participate in politics.[4] Research has shown how the Social Security program, for instance, has produced a positive experience for recipients, which in turn, produces higher levels of political engagement among recipients.[5] On the other hand, "paternalistic" policies, which are intended as forms of social control, and are disproportionately targeted at Black and poor people, have the opposite effect. Citizens who are engaged with these policies, like those who encounter the criminal justice system and its many tentacles, and welfare policies like Medicaid which can be punitive toward its recipients, are less likely to feel government is trustworthy, which influences their political views and political participation.[6]

In higher education policy, Suzanne Mettler, showed how college attendance, largely as a result of the G.I. Bill, transformed the political views and participation of the World War II generation.[7] Mettler wrote that the "G.I. Bill's education and training provisions had an overwhelmingly positive effect on male veterans' civic involvement. Those veterans who utilized the provisions became more active citizens in public life in the postwar years than those who did not."[8] Similarly, Deondra Rose showed how the federal college access initiatives of the 1960s had profound positive effects on women's participation in American politics.[9]

Although this study did not examine the policy feedback effects of special college access programs on political participation, efficacy, or government trustworthiness, one can expect that these programs have a positive effect on those outcomes. Research has shown how attaining higher levels of education and income increase the likelihood of political participation.[10] The examination of the policy feedback effects of these college access programs on political participation and views of government among participants is an empirical question worthy of future examination.

At the same time, the findings discussed in this book and the example of former TD students engaging in protest as staff members at a time when the campus was hollowed-out of students, suggests that protest itself is a form of policy feedback, and it too is worthy of further examination. Unlike the "Greatest Generation" examined in Mettler's study of World War II veterans' political participation as a result of the G.I. Bill, the students in the TD Program have had to employ protest as means to maintain the program and ensure that its students, and staff, are supported on campus. Without their protest, it is likely, based on examples of other programs across the country, that the program would have been significantly diminished or cut altogether.

Therefore, a more complete examination of the potential policy feedback effects of these programs cannot be limited to simply understanding how college access programs affect voting, political efficacy, or trust in government. Since programs specifically designed for people of color are subject to cuts and elimination, and protest is an essential tool in the process of preventing the elimination of a program, the passing of knowledge from one generation to the next about the importance of protest to save the program, is itself, a policy feedback. Indeed, a more accurate analysis is that for these programs, protest produced policy and the maintenance of that policy requires protest. This is an area of policy feedback that merits further examination.

In many ways, it is unfair to put the burden of protest on students for the maintenance of a program, or programs, that offer opportunities to young people who otherwise would not have an opportunity to attend and graduate college. Political scientist Sally Nuamah has developed the concept of "collective participatory debt" to show how the burden of continued political mobilization for policy goals has negative consequences for Black and poor people.[11] Her research shows a decline in an interest in future political participation among citizens because of "mobilization fatigue that transpires when citizens engaged in policy processes are met with a lack of democratic transparency and responsiveness despite high levels of repeated participation."[12]

Indeed, in contemplating the burden of protest for policy maintenance I am reminded of the Malcolm X quote engraved on the front of the library at the University of Rhode Island which helped create the conditions for the campus protests in 1992. The complete quote, which was not engraved on the library wall, stated: "I told the Englishmen that my alma mater was books, a good library. Every time I catch a plane, I have with me a book that I want to read. And that's a lot of books. If I weren't out there every day battling the white man, I could spend the rest of my life reading, just satisfying my curiosity."

Unlike other college students, who enjoy the privilege of reading books, studying, and just being students, TD students have not had that privilege. Like other students of color across campuses and across generations, the ability to attend and graduate from college has involved significant political struggle. Reverend Arthur Hardge, who helped create the TD Program and served as its second director, was known to say, "We're in the business, to get out of business." In other words, in his view, the whole purpose of the program was to create opportunities so that one day, these programs would no longer be necessary. However, the history of the program he helped create and led suggests that policies for people of color are always politically vulnerable, and their maintenance demands constant political vigilance and struggle.

While collective participatory debt has been experienced by past and current TD students and staff, somehow the protests persist, despite their "exhaustion." Perhaps it is because the young people who continue to en-gage in protest, generation after generation, have no illusion that they have a secured place in this democracy. And yet, although their place is not se-cure, somehow, they believe that place can be fought for. It is perhaps why students like Georgia Machado, who had Lupus, and put her life at risk to save the program in 1971 by taking over the administration building, knew that she was protesting not only for herself and her place but for future students and our place, even if she never got a chance to know us. That burden of protest for the right to learn and exist is unjust and unfair, and yet, in America, still urgent.

ACKNOWLEDGMENTS

There are so many people to thank and acknowledge for the love, support, and guidance they provided as I wrote this book. The book was written during the COVID-19 pandemic and served as an anchor amid uncertainty, fear, and pain. I lost my younger brother Pedro during the pandemic and his life has been and continues to be a source of inspiration for me. To Lisa, Natalya, and Camila, I love you and thank you for everything. To the rest of my family and friends, I thank you for your love and support.

I want to thank Marion Orr and Susan Moffitt for your friendship and mentorship throughout the writing of this book. I also owe a great deal of gratitude to Patricia Strach who provided valuable feedback that helped improve the manuscript. Many thanks to Gwen Prowse, Lexi Brown, Ethan Morelion, Lorena Bueno, Chantel Ramos, and Ayesha Ali, the great team of research assistants who provided enormous support at every stage of this project.

Finally, I want to thank all the former and current students and staff of the Talent Development Program. I hope the book does justice to our story.

Special College Access Programs Created
between 1966–1968 at Public Institutions

State	Program Name	Year Created
California	Education Opportunity Program	1967
Connecticut	Education Opportunity Program	1968
Florida	Horizon Unlimited Program (Florida State University)	1968
Illinois	Experiment in Higher Education (Southern Illinois University)	1966
Indiana	Groups Scholars Program (Indiana University)	1968
Massachusetts	College Now	1968
Michigan	Detroit Project (Michigan State University)	1967
New Jersey	Education Opportunity Fund	1968
New York	Search for Education, Elevation, and Knowledge (SEEK) (City University of New York) Education Opportunity Program (State University of New York)	1966 1967
Oregon	Education Opportunity Program	1968
Pennsylvania*	Opportunity Program (Temple University)	1966
Rhode Island	Talent Development Program	1968
Washington	Education Opportunity Program	1968
Wisconsin	Five Year Program (University of Wisconsin)	1966

* In 1971, the Higher Education of the Disadvantaged (Act 101) Program was created in Pennsylvania.

Data Sources for GPA Statistical Analysis

Variable	Year	Variable Description and Coding	Sources
Instate Tuition	2019	Total In-State Tuition and Fees	National Center for Education Statistics. Integrated Postsecondary Education Data System. https://nces.ed.gov/ipeds/datacenter
% Admitted	2019	Percent of Applicants Admitted	National Center for Education Statistics. Integrated Postsecondary Education Data System. https://nces.ed.gov/ipeds/datacenter
% Black Students	2019	Percent of Undergraduate Enrollment Who Are Black or African American	National Center for Education Statistics. Integrated Postsecondary Education Data System. https://nces.ed.gov/ipeds/datacenter
% Latino Students	2019	Percent of Undergraduate Enrollment Who Are Hispanic/Latino	National Center for Education Statistics. Integrated Postsecondary Education Data System. https://nces.ed.gov/ipeds/datacenter

(cotinued)

Variable	Year	Variable Description and Coding	Sources
% White Students	2019	Percent of Undergraduate Enrollment Who Are White	National Center for Education Statistics. Integrated Postsecondary Education Data System. https://nces.ed.gov/ipeds/datacenter
% Women Enrollment	2019	Percent of Undergraduate Enrollment Who Are Women	National Center for Education Statistics. Integrated Postsecondary Education Data System. https://nces.ed.gov/ipeds/datacenter
Undergraduate Enrollment	2019	Total Undergraduate Enrollment	National Center for Education Statistics. Integrated Postsecondary Education Data System. https://nces.ed.gov/ipeds/datacenter
% Pell Grant Recipients	2019	Percent of Full-Time First-Time Undergraduates Receiving Pell Grants	National Center for Education Statistics. Integrated Postsecondary Education Data System. https://nces.ed.gov/ipeds/datacenter
State Net Public FTE Enrollment	2017	Full-Time Equivalent (FTE) Student Enrollment at State's Public Institutions	State Higher Education Executive Officers Association. (2018). State Higher Education Finance: FY 2017. Boulder, CO. https://shef.sheeo.org/data-downloads/
State Educational Appropriations per FTE	2017	Amount of State Funding Provided per FTE Student	State Higher Education Executive Officers Association. (2018). State Higher Education Finance: FY 2017. Boulder, CO. https://shef.sheeo.org/data-downloads/

Variable	Year	Variable Description and Coding	Sources
Special college access program	2019	1 = If College/ University has a special college access program for students of underrepresented populations as of 2019, 0 = Does not have a special college program.	Data collected by author. Data primarily gathered by visiting university websites and contacting admissions offices at state colleges and universities via email or telephone calls.
State population	2019	Total state population	US Census. 2019. Population Estimates. https://www. census.gov/quickfacts/fact/ table/
% White of state population	2019	White (non-Hispanic) percent of state population	US Census. 2019. Population Estimates. https://www. census.gov/quickfacts/fact/ table/
% Black of state population	2019	Black percent of state population	US Census. 2019. Population Estimates. https://www. census.gov/quickfacts/fact/ table/
% Latino of state population	2019	Latino percent of state population	US Census. 2019. Population Estimates. https://www. census.gov/quickfacts/fact/ table/
State Board of Higher Education Governing Power	2019	1 = Governing Power (Strong), 0=OnlyCoordinating Function (Weak);	Education Commission of the States. "50-State Comparison: State Postsecondary Governance Structures." March 5, 2019. Mary Fulton. https:// www.ecs.org/50-state-comparison-postsecondary-governance-structures/

(cotinued)

Variable	Year	Variable Description and Coding	Sources
# of members on State Board of Higher Education	2019	Number of members on State Board of Higher Education	Education Commission of the States. "50-State Comparison: State Postsecondary Governance Structures." March 5, 2019. Mary Fulton. https://www.ecs.org/50-state-comparison-postsecondary-governance-structures/
State Board of Higher Education Elected	2019	1 = Elected, 0 = Appointed	Education Commission of the States. "50-State Comparison: State Postsecondary Governance Structures." March 5, 2019. Mary Fulton. https://www.ecs.org/50-state-comparison-postsecondary-governance-structures/
# of education interest groups in state	2007	Number of education interest groups registered in the state. Includes groups such as: school districts, principals, unions	Jordan, Marty P., and Matt Grossmann. 2020. *The Correlates of State Policy Project v.2.1.* East Lansing, MI: Institute for Public Policy and Social Research (IPPSR); Gray, Virginia, and David Lowery, "Interest Group Politics and Economic Growth in the U.S. States." *The American Political Science Review* 82, no. 1 (1988): 109–31; Lowery, David, Virginia Gray, and John Cluverius. "Temporal Change in the Density of State Interest Communities 1980 to 2007." *State Politics & Policy Quarterly* 15, no. 2 (2015): 263–86.

Variable	Year	Variable Description and Coding	Sources
Union density	2011	Proportion of (nonagricultural) workforce represented by a union	Jordan, Marty P., and Matt Grossmann. 2020. *The Correlates of State Policy Project v.2.1.* East Lansing, MI: Institute for Public Policy and Social Research (IPPSR); Kelly, Nathan J., and Christopher Witko, "Government Ideology and Unemployment in the U.S. States." *State Politics & Policy Quarterly* 14, no. 4 (2014): 389–413.
Democratic control of state government	2010	Ranney Party control of state government: 4-yr. moving average. 0 = unified Republican control, 1 = unified Democratic control, 0.5 = neither.	Jordan, Marty P., and Matt Grossmann. 2020. The Correlates of State Policy Project v.2.1. East Lansing, MI: Institute for Public Policy and Social Research (IPPSR); Ranney, Austin. 1976. "Parties in State Politics." In *Politics in the American States*, 3rd ed. Edited by Herbert Jacob and Kenneth Vines. Boston: Little, Brown & Co. Klarner, Carl, 2013, "Other Scholars' Competitiveness Measures." https://doi.org/10.7910/DVN/QSDYLH, Harvard Dataverse, V1

INTRODUCTION

1. Gerald Carbone, "Cruel Fate Was No Match for a Determined URI Student," *Providence Journal*, May 17, 1998, A-1.
2. The average SAT (English Language Arts/Math) score at Central High School has remained around the 800. In 2017–2018 and 2018–2019, the average combined SAT score for Central High School students was 795. See Rhode Island Department of Education. Assessment Data Portal. https://www3.ride.ri.gov/ADP
3. Jamila Michener, Mallory SoRelle, and Chloe Thurston, "From the Margins to the Center: A Bottom-Up Approach to Welfare State Scholarship," *Perspectives on Politics* 20, no. 1 (2020): 154–69. https:doi.org/10.1017/S153759272000359X.
4. C. J. Libassi, "The Neglected College Race Gap: Racial Disparities Among College Completers," *Center for American Progress*, May 23, 2018. https://www.americanp rogress.org/issues/education-postsecondary/reports/2018/05/23/451186/neglected-college-race-gap-racial-disparities-among-college-completers/; Anthony Carnevale, Megan Fasules, Andrea Porter, and Jennifer Landis-Santos, *African Americans College Majors and Earnings* (Washington, DC: Center on Education and the Workforce, Georgetown University, 2016). https://cew.georgetown.edu/cew-reports/african-american-majors/#resources.
5. Eric Schickler, *Disjointed Pluralism: Institutional Innovation in the U.S. Congress* (Princeton, NJ: Princeton University Press, 2001); Jacob S. Hacker, "Privatizing Risk without Privatizing the Welfare State: The Hidden Politics of Social Policy Retrenchment in the United States," *American Political Science Review* 98, no. 2 (2004): 243–59.

CHAPTER 1

1. Christopher Loss, *Between Citizens and the State: The Politics of American Higher Education in the 20th Century* (Princeton, NJ: Princeton University Press, 2012), 55.
2. U.S. Department of Education. 2014. "Historical summary of faculty, enrollment, degrees conferred, and finances in degree-granting postsecondary

institutions: Selected years, 1869–70 through 2013–14." https://nces.ed.gov/progr
ams/digest/d15/tables/dt15_301.20.asp.

3. On the political and democratic consequences to the G.I. Bill, see Suzanne
   Mettler. *Soldiers to Citizens: The G.I. Bill and the Making of the Greatest Generation*
   (New York: Oxford University Press, 2007). Mettler shows how college attendance,
   largely as a result of the G.I. Bill, transformed the political views and participation
   of the World War II generation.

4. Deondra Rose, *Citizens by Degree: Higher Education Policy and the Changing Gender
   Dynamics of American Citizenship* (New York: Oxford University Press, 2018), 38.

5. Ibid.

6. David Onkst, "First a Negro . . . Incidentally a Veteran: Black World War Two
   Veterans and G.I. Bill of Rights in the Deep South, 1944–1948." *Journal of Social
   History* 31, no. 3 (1998): 517–43; Loss, *Between Citizens and the State*, 116.

7. Bridge T. Long, "Supporting College Access to Education," in *Legacies of the War
   on Poverty*, ed. Martha J. Bailey and Sheldon Danziger, 93–120 (New York: Russell
   Sage Foundation, 2013); Rose, *Citizens by Degree*.

8. Pell Institute, "The First Summer of Upward Bound, 1965." http://www.pellinstit
   ute.org/downloads/trio_clearinghouse-The_First_Summer_of_UB_1965.pdf.

9. Jerome Karabel, *The Chosen: The Hidden History of Admission and Exclusion at
   Harvard, Yale, and Princeton* (Boston: Mariner Books, 2006).

10. Nicholas Lemann, *The Big Test: The Secret History of the American Meritocracy*
    (New York: Farrar, Straus and Giroux, 1999).

11. See ibid., 33–34.

12. U.S. Department of Labor, Executive Order 11246—Equal Employment
    Opportunity. https://www.dol.gov/agencies/ofccp/executive-order-11246/ca-11246;
    In 1967, the order was amended to include gender discrimination.

13. Ibid.

14. Amaka Okechukwu, *To Fulfill These Rights: Political Struggle Over Affirmative
    Action and Open Admissions* (New York: Columbia University Press, 2019), 46.

15. Natasha Warikoo, *The Diversity Bargain: And Other Dilemmas of Race, Admissions,
    and Meritocracy at Elite Universities* (Chicago: University of Chicago Press, 2016).

16. Lemann, *Big Test*, 164.

17. Karabel, *The Chosen*.

18. See Ira Katznelson, *When Affirmative Action Was White: An Untold History of Racial
    Inequality in Twentieth-Century America* (New York: Norton, 2005); Okechukwu,
    To Fulfill These Rights.

19. See Katznelson, *When Affirmative Action Was White*, App.

20. Ibid, 143.

21. Ibid, 144.

22. Omar Wasow, "Agenda Seeding: How 1960s Black Protests Moved Elites, Public
    Opinion and Voting." *American Political Science Review* 114, no. 3 (2020): 638–59.

23. David O. Sears and John B. McConahay, *The Politics of Violence: The New Urban
    Blacks and the Watts Riot* (Boston: Houghton Mifflin, 1973); Martin Gilens,
    Affluence and Influence: Economic Inequality and Political Power in America
    (Princeton, NJ: Princeton University Press, 2012).

24. Elizabeth Hinton, *America on Fire: The Untold History of Police Violence and Black Rebellion since the 1960s* (New York: Liveright, 2021), 7.

25. Robert Lilley, Raymond Brown, John Dougherty, Alfred Driscoll, John Gibbons, Ben Leuchter, Oliver Lofton, Robert Meyner, Prince Taylor, and William Wachenfeld, *Governor's Select Commission on Civil Disorder* [Report for Action] (New York: Lemma, 1968).

26. Richard McCormick, *The Black Student Protest Movement at Rutgers* (New Brunswick, NJ: Rutgers University Press, 1990), 34.

27. Anthony Imperiale was a politician from the North Ward in Newark who organized the North Ward Citizens Committee, an armed White vigilante group who patrolled the city of Newark ostensibly as "White self-defense" following the 1967 rebellion. However, Black Newarkers and New Jersey Governor Richard Hughes viewed Imperiale and his organization as a racist, terrorizing force in Newark. See https://www.nytimes.com/1999/12/28/nyregion/anthony-imperiale-68-dies-polarizing-force-in-newark.html.

28. *Rise Up North Newark*, interview with Junius Williams. http://riseupnewark.com/chapters/chapter-3/part-3/black-organization-students/.

29. Press Release from Rutgers University—Newark on Black Organization of Students demands, March 3, 1969.

30. Following the Newark student and community protests, students at the New Brunswick and Camden campuses began making similar demands for increases in Black students, faculty, and staff on their campuses.

31. McCormick, *Black Student Protest Movement at Rutgers*, 69.

32. Ibid, 73.

33. See "Appendix A: Special College Access Programs Created between 1966–1971 at Public Institutions."

34. For a detailed history of the mobilization efforts at the City University of New York, see Okechukwu, *To Fulfill These Rights*.

35. Key among them was Shirley Chisholm from Brooklyn, who served in the New York State Assembly between 1965 and 1968. In 1968, Chisholm became the first Black woman to get elected to the US Congress. In addition to Chisholm, the prominent Black politicians from Harlem, Percy Sutton, Charles Rangel, Basil Paterson, and David Dinkens, who became known as the "Gang of Four," were instrumental in helping establish the SEEK Program. Percy Sutton, a civil rights activist and attorney who represented Malcolm X, represented Harlem in the New York State Assemblyman from 1965 to 1966. From the Bronx, Herman Badillo, the Puerto Rican politician who served as Bronx Borough President from 1965 to 1969, was also involved in helping establish the program.

36. John Egerton, "Higher Education for 'High Risk' Students": A Report from the Southern Education Foundation, Atlanta, Georgia. April 1968, 1.

37. Education Opportunity Fund Progress Report 2015. https://www.state.nj.us/highereducation/documents/pdf/index/EOFPROGRESSREPORTFINALMay12015.pdf.

38. SEEK Annual Report 2015. http://www2.cuny.edu/wp-content/uploads/sites/4/page-assets/academics/academic-programs/seek-college-discovery/news-eve

nts/publications/2015-2016-annual-report/SEEK-CD-2015-16-annual-rep ort_WEB.pdf.

39. See Robert O'Neill, "Young, Educated, and Upwardly Mobile: What Colleges Are Doing to Help Low-Income Students Climb the Economic Ladder," October 26, 2018. https://www.hks.harvard.edu/faculty-research/policy-topics/education-train ing-labor/young-educated-and-upwardly-mobile.

40. Ryan Enos, Aaron Kaufman, and Melissa Sands, "Can Violent Protest Change Local Policy Support? Evidence from the Aftermath of the 1992 Los Angeles Riot," *American Political Science Review* 113, no. 4 (2019): 1012–28.

41. See Martha Biondi, *The Black Revolution on Campus* (Berkeley: University of California Press, 2012); Ibram Kendi, *The Black Campus Movement: Black Students and the Racial Reconstitution of Higher Education, 1965–1972* (New York: Palgrave Macmillan, 2012); Fabio Rojas, "Social Movement Tactics, Organizational Change and the Spread of African-American Studies," *Social Forces* 84, no. 4 (2006): 2147–266.

42. Kendi, *Black Campus Movement*, 161–70.

43. See Paul Pierson, *Dismantling the Welfare State? Reagan, Thatcher and the Politics of Retrenchment* (New York: Cambridge University Press, 1995); Jacob S. Hacker, "Privatizing Risk without Privatizing the Welfare State: The Hidden Politics of Social Policy Retrenchment in the United States," *American Political Science Review* 98, no. 2 (2004): 243–60.

44. Vesla Weaver, "Frontlash: Race and the Development of Punitive Crime Policy," *Studies in American Political Development* 21, no. 2 (2007): 230–65; Elizabeth Hinton, *From the War on Poverty to the War on Crime: The Making of Mass Incarceration in America* (Cambridge, MA: Harvard University Press, 2015).

45. Frances F. Piven and Richard Cloward, *Regulating the Poor: The Functions of Public Welfare* (New York: Pantheon Books, 1993), xv. First published 1971.

46. Kim Phillips-Fein, *Fear City: New York's Fiscal Crisis and the Rise of Austerity Politics* (New York: Metropolitan Books, 2017).

47. See Hacker, "Privatizing Risk without Privatizing the Welfare State," 243–59; Eric Patashnik and Julian E. Zelizer, "The Struggle to Remake Politics: Liberal Reform and the Limits of Policy Feedback in the Contemporary American State," *Perspectives on Politics* 11, no. 4 (2013): 1071–87.

    For a critique of the elite-centered, "top-down" welfare policy scholarship in the United States, see Jamila Michener, Mallory SoRelle, and Chloe Thurston, "From the Margins to the Center: A Bottom-Up Approach to Welfare State Scholarship," *Perspectives on Politics* 20, no. 1 (2020): 154–69. https://doi.org/10.1017/S153759272 000359X.

48. Sara Goldrick-Rab, Jed Richardson, Joel Schneider, Anthony Hernandez, and Clare Cady, "Still Hungry and Homeless in College," *Wisconsin Hope Lab* (2018). https:// www.theotx.org/wp-content/uploads/2018/05/Wisconsin-HOPE-Lab-Still-Hun gry-and-Homeless.pdf.

49. See Hacker, "Privatizing Risk without Privatizing the Welfare State"; and Wolfgang Streeck and Kathleen Thelen, "Introduction: Institutional Change in Advanced Political Economies," in *Beyond Continuity: Institutional Change in*

Advanced Political Economies, ed. Wolfgang Streeck and Kathleen Thelen, 1–39 (New York: Oxford University Press, 2005), for detailed description of each mode of policy change.

50. Eric Schickler, *Disjointed Pluralism: Institutional Innovation in the U.S. Congress* (Princeton, NJ: Princeton University Press, 2001); Hacker, "Privatizing Risk without Privatizing the Welfare State," 248.

CHAPTER 2

1. City of Providence Human Relations Commission, 2018 Annual Report. http://www.providenceri.gov/wp-content/uploads/2016/08/PHRC-Annual-Report-2018.pdf.

2. *Providence Journal,* "Governor Plans to Set Up Civil Rights Task Force," June 27, 1963, 28.

3. Report of the Governor's Task Force on Civil Rights, January 3, 1964.

4. John Mathews, "Minority Programs Urged at Hearing," *Providence Journal,* November 5, 1963, 38.

5. Report of the Governor's Task Force on Civil Rights.

6. "Education in Rhode Island: A Plan for the Future," Final Report to the General Assembly, June 1968. Rhode Island Special Commission to Study the Entire Field of Education.

7. The Commission recommended that "A Board for the Education of Special Populations should be created and given the responsibility for special populations which can be dealt with best on a statewide basis. 'Special Populations' should be defined as including but not limited to the gifted, the talented, the handicapped, the culturally disadvantaged, the economically deprived, and members of racial and ethnic minorities." This recommendation did not address concerns with college admissions standards that prevented Black students from entering the state's colleges and university.

8. *Providence Journal,* "Four Colleges Accept Special Student Group," August 8, 1968, 45.

9. Office of Economic Opportunity, Poverty Program Information, Fiscal Year 1969.

10. Daniel Moynihan, *Maximum Feasible Misunderstanding: Community Action in the War on Poverty* (New York: Free Press, 1970).

11. David Greenstone and Paul Peterson, *Race and Authority in Urban Politics: Community Participation and the War on Poverty* (New York: Russell Sage, 1973); James Morone, *The Democratic Wish: Popular Participation and the Limits of American Government* (New Haven, CT: Yale University Press, 1990); Mark Krasovic, *The Newark Frontier: Community Action in the Great Society* (Chicago: University of Chicago Press, 2016).

12. *Providence Journal,* "Racism Is Topic of URI Panel: Antipoverty Official Urges Whites to Change Attitude," November 13, 1968, 5.

13. Christine Dunn, "Fox Point Neighborhood: A Walk on the Historic Side," *Providence Journal,* May 24, 2015. https://www.providencejournal.com/article/20150524/NEWS/150529698.

14. Fox Point Neighborhood Association, "Fox Point History." https://www.fpna.net/fox-point-history.

15. Mia God, "Forgotten Fox Point," Remembering Race at Brown, Brown University. November 12, 2014. https://blogs.brown.edu/ethn-0790d-s01/2014/11/12/forgotten-fox-point-an-examination-of-the-expansion-of-brown-university-and-the-development-of-the-cape-verdean-fox-point-community/.

16. In 1966, Rhode Island College created Upward Bound, a federal college preparatory initiative for high school students from underserved communities. The Upward Bound program at Rhode Island College was supported by a $67,777 grant from the US Office of Economic Opportunity and $7,532 from the College (see *Providence Journal*, "50 High School Students Will Taste College Life," June 12, 1966, N-35.

17. Peter Levy, *The Great Uprising: Race Riots in Urban American during the 1960s* (New York: Cambridge University Press, 2018).

18. Thomas Sugrue. *The Origins of the Urban Crisis: Race and Inequality in Postwar Detroit* (Princeton, NJ: Princeton University Press, 1996).

19. *Providence Journal*, "Disturbances Quelled in South Providence," August 1, 1967, 1.

20. *Providence Journal*, "Shots Mark S. Providence Disturbances," August 2, 1967, 1.

21. *Providence Journal*, "Watch Society Urged as a Riot Preventative," April 3, 1968, 31.

22. Wallace Roberts, "R.I. Colleges Trustees Act to Help Negroes," *Providence Journal*, April 10, 1968, 1.

23. Ibid.

24. Ibid.

25. Robert C. Spencer, #2—Interview and Memoir, 1983, The Oral History Collection of the University of Illinois at Springfield, Illinois Digital Archives. http://www.idaillinois.org/digital/collection/uis/id/4149.

26. Kerner Commission, *Report of the National Advisory Commission on Civil Disorders* (Washington, DC: U.S. Government Printing Office, 1968), 250.

27. *Providence Journal*, "College Board Getting Plan for Negroes," May 1, 1968, 1.

28. The Committee was chaired by Robert Spencer, Dean of the Graduate School at URI and included Prof. Mitchell Salomon (URI), Rev. John Hall (URI Chaplain), Louise Miller (Research Associate, URI), Prof. Maureen T. Lapan (RIC), Prof. Lawrence Sykes (RIC), Prof. Raymond W. Houghton (RIC), Prof. Louis or Lewis Davis (RIJC), Rabbi Jacob Handler (RIJC), Prof. John Fallon (RIJC). Carol Fuller of the Urban League of RI and Rev. Arthur Hardge, Executive Director of the RI Commission Against Discrimination worked with the committee as well.

29. *Providence Journal*, "College Board Getting Plan for Negroes," May 1, 1968, 1.

30. Wallace Roberts, "Urban Educational Plan Okayed." *Providence Journal*, May 2, 1968, 1, 12.

31. Ibid.

32. Ibid.

33. Interview with Harold Langlois, May 8, 2019.

34. Interview with Robert Spencer, 1983. http://www.idaillinois.org/digital/collection/uis/id/4149.

35. Carol Young, "Blacks on the Campus—How Much Progress?" *Providence Journal*, May 16, 1971, G-1.
36. Interview with Frank Santos, May 28, 2019.
37. Interview with Donna-jean Wosencroft, June 9, 2020.
38. Interview with Robert Spencer, 1983. http://www.idaillinois.org/digital/collection/uis/id/4149.
39. David Card and Thomas Lemieux, "Going to College to Avoid the Draft: The Unintended Legacy of the Vietnam War," *The American Economic Review* 91, no. 2 (2001): 97–102.
40. Letter from Lawrence Dennis, the Chancellor of the state college system to University of Rhode Island President, Werner Baum on July 30, 1968.
41. Ibid.
42. Letter from University of Rhode Island President Werner Baum to .University Vice President Jerome Pollack on July 31, 1968. University of Rhode Island Library Special Collections.
43. At least one student was later accepted to Bryant College in Rhode Island.
44. Richard Pierce, Robert Carkhuff, Bernard Berenson, Andrew Griffin, and Theodore Friel. 1972. Special Program for Talent Development: A Consultation Report on Current Effectiveness and Future Direction. Eastern Psychological, Educational and Community Services, Inc.

CHAPTER 3

1. Rhode Island Board of Trustees of State Colleges, Public Higher Education in Rhode Island: 1968–69 Annual Report of the Board of Trustees of State Colleges.
2. University of Rhode Island Faculty Senate, "Admission Policy," Faculty Senate Bills, Paper 22, 1968. http://digitalcommons.uri.edu/facsen_bills/22.
3. Sonya Gray, "Ala. Violence a Threat, R.I. Negro Pastor Says," *Providence Journal*, September 22, 1963, N-3.
4. *Providence Journal*, "Judge Reverses Own Edict, Frees 9 Clergy," August 7, 1964, 3.
5. *Providence Journal*, "O'Connor Integration Plan Endorsed by Three Groups," November 17, 1966, 28.
6. Wallace Roberts, "Racial Bias Discussion Bogs Down," *Providence Journal*. September 15, 1967, 1.
7. *Providence Journal*, "Minister Fills New State Post," July 26, 1968, 37.
8. *Providence Journal*, "New Vice President for RIC Is Approved," June 6, 1969, 3.
9. Ibid., 3.
10. Harold V. Langlois and Robert W. MacMillan, "Evaluation of Pre-Matriculation Program for Disadvantaged Students at the University of Rhode Island," November 1, 1969.
11. "New Vice President for RIC," 3.
12. Interview with Deborah Bush and Donna-jean Wosencroft, June 9, 2020.
    For further discussion and critiques of the "politics of respectability," see Evelyn Brooks Higginbotham, *Righteous Discontent: The Women's Movement in the Black Baptist Church, 1880–1920* (Cambridge, MA: Harvard University Press, 1993); Cathy

Cohen, *The Boundaries of Blackness: AIDS and the Breakdown of Black Politics* (Chicago: University of Chicago Press,1999); E. Frances White, *Dark Continent of Our Bodies: Black Feminism and the Politics of Respectability* (Philadelphia, PA: Temple University Press, 2001); Fredrick Harris, "The Rise of Respectability Politics." *Dissent Magazine,* 2014. https://www.dissentmagazine.org/article/the-rise-of-respectability-politics.

13. Talent Development Program, "TD Honors former director Leo F. DiMaio, Jr." https://web.uri.edu/talentdevelopment/2001/12/01/td-honors-former-director-leo-dimaio/.

14. *Providence Journal,* "Head of Center at URI Named," September 4, 1969, 11

15. *Providence Journal,* "URI Plan Salvages Students," October 6, 1969, 27.

16. Ibid.

17. Alan Sadovnik, *Equity and Excellence in Higher Education: The Decline of a Liberal Educational Reform* (New York: Peter Lang, 1994).

18. Ibid., 31.

19. Amaka Okechukwu, *To Fulfill These Rights: Political Struggle Over Affirmative Action and Open Admissions* (New York: Columbia University Press, 2019).

20. Ibid.

21. *Providence Journal,* "Tutoring Program Impresses Garrahy," August 7, 1969, 14.

22. "URI Plan Salvages Students," 27.
    A group of University of Rhode Island faculty and "townspeople," led by Louise Miller, its URI president, and Robert Weisbord, a history professor at URI, created an organization, Citizens to Advance Negro Education (C.A.N.E) to support "educational opportunities for disadvantaged black person in this area." Memo to Faculty, May 8, 1969. University of Rhode Island Special Collections.

23. Letter from University of Rhode Island President Werner A. Baum to University Vice President Pollack on April 9, 1969. University of Rhode Island Library Special Collections.

24. See Martha Biondi, *The Black Revolution on Campus* (Berkeley: University of California Press, 2012); Ibram Kendi, *The Black Campus Movement: Black Students and the Racial Reconstitution of Higher Education, 1965–1972* (New York: Palgrave Macmillan, 2012); Stefan Bradley, *Upending the Ivory Tower: Civil Rights, Black Power, and the Ivy League* (New York: New York University Press, 2018).

25. Bradley, *Upending the Ivory Tower,* 104.

26. "URI Afro-American Society," Letter to President Werner A. Baum. University of Rhode Island," May 5, 1969, University of Rhode Island Library Special Collections.

27. "Statement by Dr. Werner A. Baum, President, University of Rhode Island," May 11, 1969, University of Rhode Island Library Special Collections.

28. John Herbes, "Most States Plan Tax Increases Despite Efforts to Slash Costs," *New York Times,* February 9, 1971, 1. https://www.nytimes.com/1971/02/09/archives/most-states-plan-tax-increases-despite-efforts-to-slash-costs-most.html.

29. *Providence Journal,* "Licht Sworn In, Promises Task Force Study of State Education, Medical, Welfare Aid," January 6, 1971, 2.

30. The following details from the events on May 5, 1971, were gathered from accounts published in the *Providence Journal* and student and staff interviews.

31. See Grace Kelly, "The Fight for Justice: URI's History of Student-Led Civil Rights Activism," *University of Rhode Island Magazine*, Fall 2020. https://www.uri.edu/magazine/issues/fall-2020/the-fight-for-justice/.

32. *Providence Journal*, "Lawmen Wade Into Throng of Students; Clear URI Building," May 6, 1971, 1.

33. Talent Development Program. "Excerpts from Primary Source: Daniel Price, Jr. One of the Uhuru Sasa/Takeover Leaders," in *Talent Development: Opportunity and Activism* (8th ed.) (Providence: University of Rhode Island, 2020), 9.

34. Ibid.

35. Carol Young, "Black on Campus—How Much Progress?" *Providence Journal*, May 16, 1971, G-1.

36. Ibid.

37. Ibid.

38. See Domingo Morel, *Takeover: Race, Education, and American Democracy* (New York: Oxford University Press, 2018).

39. Young, "Black on Campus," G-4.

40. Richard Pierce, Robert Carkhuff, Bernard Berenson, Andrew Griffin, and Theodore Friel, 1972, Special Program for Talent Development: A Consultation Report on Current Effectiveness and Future Direction. Eastern Psychological, Educational and Community Services, Inc. "Abstract," 14.

CHAPTER 4

1. Interview with Sharon Forleo, June 11, 2020.

2. Carol Young, "Black on Campus—How Much Progress?," *Providence Journal*, May 16, 1971, G-1.

3. The mid-semester evaluation form was used, and is still used, by the program to assess student progress at the midpoint of the semester. The form is sent to each faculty member teaching a course with Talent Development students. Faculty members are asked to provide a brief assessment of how the student is doing in their class with the goal of addressing any concerns before it is too late for the student to address these concerns.

4. Interview with Frank Forleo, June 11, 2020.

5. Lisa Gordon, "Southeast Asian Refugee Migration to the United States," in *Pacific Bridges: The New Immigration from Asia and the Pacific Islands*, ed. James T. Fawcett and Benjamin V. Carino, 153–73 (Staten Island, NY: Center for Immigration Studies, 1987).

6. John Finck, "The Hmong Resettlement Study Site Report: Providence, Rhode Island," Report Prepared by the Office of Refugee Resettlement (Washington, DC: U.S. Department of Health and Human Services, 1984). https://files.eric.ed.gov/fulltext/ED267161.pdf.
Center for Southeast Asians, "Southeast Asian Data and Trends Analysis: Facts and Community Trends Report (Rhode Island. Spring 2014)." http://www.cseari.org/uploads/3/7/4/5/37456521/fact_book.pdf.

7. Nuestras Raíces: The Latino Oral History Project of Rhode Island, "Latinos in Rhode Island: Colombians/Los Colombianos." http://www.nuestrasraicesri.org/ColombiansinRhodeIsland.html.

8. Nuestras Raíces: The Latino Oral History Project of Rhode Island, "Latinos in Rhode Island: Dominicans/Los Dominicanos." http://www.nuestrasraicesri.org/ColombiansinRhodeIsland.html.

9. Waltraud Berger Coli and Richard Lobban, *Cape Verdeans in Rhode Island: A Brief History* (Providence: Rhode Island Heritage Commission and Rhode Island Publications Society, 1990).

10. P. Khalil Saucier, "Liberian Immigrants in Rhode Island: The Trauma, the Bliss, and the Dilemma," *Ìrìnkèrindò: A Journal of African Migration* 5 (December 2011): 29–54.

11. *Providence Journal*, "School Board OKs Tutoring Proposal," September 12, 1969, 25.

12. Prison Policy Initiative, Rhode Island Profile. https://www.prisonpolicy.org/profiles/RI.html.

13. Vera Institute of Justice, State Incarceration Trends: Rhode Island. https://www.vera.org/downloads/pdfdownloads/state-incarceration-trends-rhode-island.pdf; Prison Policy Initiative, Rhode Island Profile. https://www.prisonpolicy.org/profiles/RI.html.

14. Becky Pettit, Bryan Sykes, and Bruce Western, *Technical Report on Revised Population Estimates and NLSY79 Analysis Tables for the Pew Public Safety and Mobility Project* (Cambridge, MA: Harvard University, 2009).

15. Joan Biskupic, "On Race, a Court Transformed," *Washington Post*. December 15, 1997, A01. https://www.washingtonpost.com/wp-srv/politics/special/affirm/stories/aa121597.htm.

16. See Sara Goldrick-Rab, *Paying the Price: College Costs, Financial Aid, and the Betrayal of the American Dream* (Chicago: University of Chicago Press, 2016), 16, fig. 4.

17. Ibid., 17.

18. See Tressie McMillan Cottom, *Lower Ed: The Troubling Rise of For-Profit Colleges in the New Economy* (New York: New Press, 2017), 27.

19. Ibid., 21.

20. See Donald E. Heller, "The Policy Shift in State Financial Aid Programs," in *Higher Education: Handbook of Theory and Research* (Vol. 17), ed. J. C. Smart, 221–61 (New York: Agathon Press, 2002); Donald E. Heller, "State Funding for Higher Education: The Impact on College Access" (paper presented at the Symposium on Financing Higher Education, Illinois State University, Normal, 2004).

21. Suzanne Mettler, *Degrees of Inequality: How the Politics of Higher Education Sabotaged the American Dream* (New York: Basic Books, 2014), 11.

22. Roger Geiger and Donald Heller, "Financial Trends in Higher Education: The United States," *Educational Studies, Higher School of Economics* 3 (2012): 5–29.

23. Suzanne Mettler, *Degrees of Inequality: How the Politics of Higher Education Sabotaged the American Dream* (New York: Basic Books, 2014), 11.

24. D. Morgan McVicar, "Carothers Markets URI to Assembly as a Vital Cog," *Providence Journal*, January 30, 1992, A-03.

25. D. Morgan McVicar, "Out-of-Staters Still Lead URI Freshman Enrollments," *Providence Journal*, June 25, 1992, B-03.

26. OIC of Rhode Island, "Our History." http://oicrhodeisland.org/history-2/.

27. Gerald S. Goldstein, "In the Minority at URI," *Providence Journal*, May 1, 1994, M-08.

28. Stephen Heffner. "URI Reassigns Man in Charge of Campus Affirmative Action," *Providence Journal*, April 17, 1992, B-03.

29. Ibid.

30. Gerald Carbone, "Study of Attitudes at URI Accuses Police of Racism," *Providence Journal*, September 15, 1992, A-03.

31. Richard C. Dujardin and Gerald Carbone, "Hundreds at URI Protest Racism," *Providence Journal*, November 10, 1992, A-01.

32. https://web.uri.edu/quadangles/the-takeover-of-taft-hall/.

33. Gerald Carbone, "300 Students Hold Building at URI to Protest," *Providence Journal*, November 11, 1992, A-01.

34. Dujardin and Carbone, "Hundreds at URI Protest Racism," A-01.

35. Carbone. "300 Students Hold Building at URI to Protest," *Providence Journal*, A-01.

36. Gerald Carbone, "Racism Pervasive at URI, Adviser Asserts," *Providence Journal*, November 3, 1992, A-03.

37. Gerald Carbone, "URI Minority Group Gets Answers," *Providence Journal*, November 13, 1992, A-01.

38. Ibid.

39. Amaka Okechukwu, *To Fulfill These Rights: Political Struggle Over Affirmative Action and Open Admissions* (New York: Columbia University Press, 2019).

40. Interview with Gerald Williams, October 5, 2020.

41. I left the program in 2009 to work on my Ph.D. at Brown University.

42. The review committee consisted of Anna Cano Morales, '91, a Talent Development alumna and associate vice president for Community, Equity, and Diversity, Rhode Island College; Victor Capellan, '92, a Talent Development alumnus and superintendent of the Central Falls School District; Jeffrey Coleman, director of the Multicultural Center, Georgia State University; Kristen Renn, review team chair, professor of Higher, Adult, & Lifelong Education, Michigan State University; Debra Sanborn, president of the National Student Exchange; William Trezvant, '91, a Talent Development alumnus and special assistant attorney general for Rhode Island.

43. University of Rhode Island, "URI Completes Review of Talent Development Program," March 8, 2017. Communication from Kathy Collins, Vice President for Student Affairs.

44. Ibid.

CHAPTER 5

1. Rhode Island Office of the Postsecondary Commissioner, Term and completions 2012–2018 [Data files] (RIOPC Data Warehouse, 2022).

2. C. J. Libassi, *The Neglected College Race Gap: Racial Disparities among College Completers* (Washington, DC: Center for American Progress, May 23, 2018). https://

www.americanprogress.org/issues/education-postsecondary/reports/2018/05/23/ 451186/neglected-college-race-gap-racial-disparities-among-college-completers/.

3. Anthony Carnevale, Megan Fasules, Andrea Porter, and Jennifer Landis-Santos, "African Americans College Majors and Earnings" (Washington, DC: Center on Education and the Workforce. Georgetown University, 2016). https://cew.georget own.edu/cew-reports/african-american-majors/#resources.

4. U.S. Department of Education, National Center for Education Statistics, "Bachelor's Degrees Conferred by Postsecondary Institutions, by Race/Ethnicity and Field of Study: 2014–15 and 2015–16, Table 322.30" (2016). https://nces.ed.gov/programs/ digest/d17/tables/dt17_322.30.asp.

5. Beverly Cole, "The Black Educator: An Endangered Species," *The Journal of Negro Education* 55, no. 3 (1986): 326–34.

6. Charles Payne, "Introduction," in *Teach Freedom: Education for Liberation in the African-American Tradition*, ed. Charles M. Payne and Carol Sills Strickland (New York: Teachers College Press, 2008), 2.

7. Jarvis Givens, *Fugitive Pedagogy: Carter G. Woodson and the Art of Black Teaching* (Cambridge, MA: Harvard University Press, 2021), 3.

8. Adam Fairclough, *A Class of Their Own: Black Teachers in the Segregated South* (Cambridge, MA: Harvard University Press, 2007), 5.

9. Barbara Ransby, *Ella Baker and the Black Freedom Movement: A Radical Democratic Vision* (Chapel Hill: University of North Carolina Press, 2005), 7.

10. Alia Wong, "The U.S. Teaching Population Is Getting Bigger, and More Female Women Now Make Up a Larger Share of Educators Than They Have in Decades," *The Atlantic*, February 20, 2019. https://www.theatlantic.com/education/archive/ 2019/02/the-explosion-of-women-teachers/582622.

11. Susanna Loeb and Luke C. Miller, *A Review of State Teacher Policies: What Are They, What Are Their Effects, and What Are Their Implications for School Finance?* (Berkeley, CA: Institute for Research on Education Policy & Practice (IREPP) School of Education, Stanford University, 2007).

12. Daniel Aaronson and Katherine Meckel, "The Impact of Baby Boomer Retirements on Teacher Labor Markets," *The Federal Reserve Bank of Chicago*, no. 254 (September 2008). https://www.chicagofed.org/publications/chicago-fed-letter/2008/septem ber-254.

13. Michael Fultz, "The Displacement of Black Educators Post-*Brown*: An Overview and Analysis," *History of Education Quarterly* 44, no. 1 (2004): 11–45.
    Mildred Hudson and Barbara Holmes, "Missing Teachers, Impaired Communities: The Unanticipated Consequences of *Brown v. Board of Education* on the African American Teaching Force at the Precollegiate Level," *Journal of Negro Education* 63, no. 3 (1994): 388–93.
    Linda Tillman, "(Un)intended Consequences? The Impact of the *Brown v. Board of Education* Decision on the Employment Status of Black Educators," *Education and Urban Society* 36, no. 3 (2004): 280–303.

14. Deirdre Oakely, Jacob Stowell, and John Logan, "The Impact of Desegregation on Black Teachers in the Metropolis, 1970–2000," *Ethnic and Racial Studies* 39, no. 9 (2009): 1576–98.

15. Owen Thompson, "School Desegregation and Black Teacher Employment" (NBER working paper No. 25990, 2019).

16. Joseph Stewart, Kenneth Meier, and Robert England, "In Quest of Role Models: Change in Black Teacher Representation in Urban School Districts, 1968–1986," *The Journal of Negro Education* 58, no. 2 (1989): 140–52.

17. Diane Ravitch, *A Brief History of Teacher Professionalism: White House Conference on Preparing Tomorrow's Teachers* (Washington, DC: U.S. Department of Education, 2003). https://www2.ed.gov/admins/tchrqual/learn/preparingteachersconference/ravitch.html.

18. National Commission on Excellence in Education, *A Nation at Risk: The Imperative for Educational Reform: A Report to the Nation and the Secretary of Education* (Washington, DC: U.S. Department of Education, 1983); Diane Ravitch, "Education in the 1980's: A Concern for 'Quality,'" *Education Week*, January 10, 1990. https://www.edweek.org/ew/articles/1990/01/10/09200009.h09.html.

19. See "Teacher Testing and Assessment," *Journal of Negro Education* 55, no. 3 (Summer 1986).

20. Beverly Cole, "Testing Blacks Out of Education and Employment," *The Crisis* 92, no. 9 (1984): 8–11.

21. Cole, "Black Educator."

22. Edward Fiske, "Ranks of Minority Teachers Are Dwindling, Experts Fear," *New York Times*, February 9, 1986, 1 https://www.nytimes.com/1986/02/09/us/ranks-of-minority-teachers-are-dwindling-experts-fear.html.

23. Data for University of Rhode Island majors and admission requirements for majors (grade point average, standardized test scores, accreditation, and licensing) between 1972 and 2019, were gathered from the University of Rhode Island Archived Undergraduate Course Catalogs (https://web.uri.edu/catalog/archives/). For archived catalogs, 1972–1989, see https://digitalcommons.uri.edu/course-catalogs/3/.

24. Linda Tyler, Brooke Whiting, Sarah Ferguson, Segun Eubanks, Jonathan Steinberg, Linda Scatton, and Katherine Bassett, *Toward Increasing Teacher Diversity: Targeting Support and Intervention for Teacher Licensure Candidates* (Princeton, NJ: Education Testing Service and National Education Association, 2011).

25. The database does not include military institutions or historically Black colleges and universities (HBCUs).

26. See Appendix B for more information about the data collection and sources for each variable.

27. James Alt and Robert Lowry, "Divided Government, Fiscal Institutions, and Budget Deficits: Evidence from the States," *American Political Science Review* 94, no. 4 (1994): 811–28; Michael McLendon, Steven Deaton, and James Hearn, "The Enactment of Reforms State Governance of Higher Education: Testing the Political Instability Hypothesis," *The Journal of Higher Education* 78, no. 6 (2007): 645–75; Michael McLendon, James Hearn, and Christine Mokher, "Partisans, Professionals, and Power: The Role of Political Factors in State Higher Education Funding," *The Journal of Higher Education* 80, no. 6 (2009): 686–713; Michael Rizzo, "State Preferences for Higher Education Spending: A Panel Data Analysis, 1977–2001," in

What's Happening to Public Higher Education?: The Shifting Financial Burden, ed. Ronald Ehrenberg, 3–36 (Baltimore, MD: Johns Hopkins University Press, 2009); David Tandberg, "Politics, Interest Groups and State Funding of Public Higher Education," *Research in Higher Education* 51, no. 5 (2010): 416–50; Luciana Dar and Dong-Wook Lee, "Partisanship, Political Polarization, and State Higher Education Budget Outcomes," *The Journal of Higher Education* 85, no. 4 (2014): 469–98; Barrett Taylor, Brendan Cantwell, Kimberly Watts, and Olivia Wood, "Partisanship, White Racial Resentment, and State Support for Higher Education," *The Journal of Higher Education* 91, no. 6 (2019): 858–87.

28. Joel Thompson and Arthur Felts, "Politicians and Professionals: The Influence of State Agency Heads in Budgetary Success," *The Western Political Quarterly* 45, no. (1992): 153–68; Tandberg, "Politics, Interest Groups and State Funding of Public Higher Education."

29. Clive Thomas and Ronald Hrebenar, "Interest Groups in the States," in *Politics in the American States: A Comparative Analysis*, 8th ed., 100–28 (Washington, DC: CQ Press, 2004); Tandberg, "Politics, Interest Groups and State Funding of Public Higher Education."

Chapter 6

1. Diane Ravitch, *A Brief History of Teacher Professionalism: White House Conference on Preparing Tomorrow's Teachers* (Washington, DC: U.S. Department of Education, 2003). https://www2.ed.gov/admins/tchrqual/learn/preparingteachersconference/ravitch.html.

2. Gary T. Henry, Shanyce L. Campbell, Charles L. Thompson, Linda A. Patriarca, Kenneth J. Luterbach, Diana B. Lys, and Vivian Martin Covington, "The Predictive Validity of Measures of Teacher Candidate Programs and Performance: Toward an Evidence-Based Approach to Teacher Preparation," *Journal of Teacher Education* 64, no. 5 (2013): 439–53.

3. Dara Wakefield, "Screening Teacher Candidates: Problems with High-Stakes Testing," *The Educational Forum* 67, no. 4 (2003): 380–88; Christine Bennett, Lynn McWhorter, and John Kuykendall, "Will I Ever Teach? Latino and African American Students' Perspectives on PRAXIS I," *American Educational Research Journal* 43, no. 3 (2006): 531–75.

4. Dee, Thomas, "Teachers, Race and Student Achievement in a Randomized Experiment," *The Review of Economics and Statistics* 86, no. 1 (2004): 195–210; Travis Bristol and Javier Martin-Fernandez, "The Added Value of Latinx and Black Teachers for Latinx and Black Students: Implications for Policy," *Policy Insights from the Behavioral and Brain Sciences* 6, no. 2 (2019): 147–53.

5. Ann Jarvella Wilson, "Knowledge for Teachers: The Origin of the National Teacher Examination Program" (paper presented at the Annual Meeting of the American Education Research Association, March 31–April 4, 1982, Chicago, IL).

6. Ibid., 18.

7. Scott Baker, "Testing Equality: The National Teacher Examinations and the NAACP's Legal Campaign to Equalize Teachers' Salaries in the South, 1936–63," *History of Education Quarterly* 35, no. 1 (1995): 49–64.

8. Ibid.

9. Lawrence Dennis and William Eaton, "Equal Justice: The Alston Case," *The Negro Educational Review* 30, no. 1 (1979): 4–11.

10. Baker, "Testing Equality."

11. Ibid.

12. Johnny Butler, "Black Educators in Louisiana—A Question of Survival," *The Journal of Negro Education* 43, no. 1 (1974): 9–24.

13. Ibid., 18.

14. See Hanes Walton Jr., "The Politics of Negro Educational Associations," *The Negro Educational Review* 20, no. 1 (1969): 34–41; Jarvis Givens, *Fugitive Pedagogy: Carter G. Woodson and the Art of Black Teaching* (Cambridge, MA: Harvard University Press, 2021).

15. Wayne Urban, *Gender, Race and the National Education Association: Professionalism and Its Limitations* (New York: Routledge, 2000).

16. Donald Medley and Thomas Quirk, "The Application of a Factorial Design to the Study of Cultural Bias in General Culture Items on the National Teaching Examinations," *Journal of Educational Measurements* 4 (1974): 235–45.

17. Elaine Witty, *Prospects for Black Teachers: Preparation, Certification, and Employment* (Washington, DC: ERIC Clearinghouse on Teacher Education, 1982).

18. Ibid.

19. Beverly Cole, "Testing Blacks Out of Education and Employment," *The Crisis* 92, no. 9 (1984): 8–11.

20. Edward Fiske, "Teachers' Exam, Often Criticized, to Be Replaced," *New York Times*, October 28, 1988, § A, 1.

21. Education Testing Service, "About the Praxis Tests" (2021). https://www.ets.org/praxis/states_agencies.

22. Paul Starr, *The Social Transformation of American Medicine: The Rise of Sovereign Profession and the Making of a Vast Industry* (New York: Basic Books, 1982), 168.

23. Linda Dynan, "The Impact of Medical Education Reform on the Racial Health Status Gap, 1920–1930: A Difference-in-Difference Analysis," *The Review of Black Political Economy* 34, no. 3–4 (2007): 245–58.

24. Ibid.

25. Ibid., 251.

26. George Shepherd, "No African-American Lawyers Allowed: The Inefficient Racism of the ABA's Accreditation of Law Schools," *Journal of Legal Education* 53, no. 1 (2003): 103–56.

27. Ibid.

28. Ibid., 110.

29. Ibid.

30. Ibid.

31. Amy Slaton, *Race, Rigor, and Selectivity in U.S. Engineering: The History of an Occupational Color Line* (Cambridge, MA: Harvard University Press, 2010).

32. Max Weber, *Economy and Society: An Outline of Interpretive Sociology* (Berkeley: University of California Press, 1978). First published 1922.

33. Raymond Murphy, *Social Closure: The Theory of Monopolization and Exclusion* (New York: Clarendon Press, 1988), 8.

34. Randall Collins, *Conflict Sociology: Toward an Explanatory Science* (New York: Academic Press, 1975). Also see, Randall Collins, *The Credential Society: An Historical Sociology of Education and Stratification* (New York: Academic Press, 1979).

35. Murphy, *Social Closure*, 164.

36. Kim Weeden, "Why Do Some Occupations Pay More than Others? Social Closure and Earnings Inequality in the United States," *American Journal of Sociology* 108, no. 1 (2002): 55–101.

37. Binyamin Appelbaum, *The Economists' Hour: False Prophets, Free Markets, and the Fracture of Society* (New York: Little, Brown, 2019).

38. See Zachary Carter, *The Price of Peace: Money, Democracy, and the Life of John Maynard Keynes* (New York: Random House, 2020), for a historical analysis of Keynesian economics and the influence of the Keynesian approach of Roosevelt administration economic policies.

39. Juan G. Valdes, *Pinochet's Economists: The Chicago School in Chile* (New York: Cambridge University Press, 1995).

40. Quinn Slobodian, *Globalists: The End of Empire and the Birth of Neoliberalism* (Cambridge, MA: Harvard University Press, 2018).

41. Ibid., 151.

42. See James Alt and Robert Lowry, "Divided Government, Fiscal Institutions, and Budget Deficits: Evidence from the States," *American Political Science Review* 94, no. 4 (1994): 811–28; Michael McLendon, Steven Deaton, and James Hearn, "The Enactment of Reforms in State Governance of Higher education: Testing the Political Instability Hypothesis," *The Journal of Higher Education* 78, no. 6 (2007): 645–75; Michael McLendon, James Hearn, and Christine Mokher, "Partisans, Professionals, and Power: The role of Political factors in State Higher Education Funding," *The Journal of Higher Education* 80, no. 6 (2009): 686–713; Michael Rizzo, "State Preferences for Higher Education Spending: A Panel Data Analysis, 1977–2001," in *What's Happening to Public Higher Education?: The Shifting Financial Burden*, ed. Ronald Ehrenberg, 3–36 (Baltimore, MD: Johns Hopkins University Press, 2008); David Tandberg, "Politics, Interest Groups and State Funding of Public Higher Education," *Research in Higher Education* 51, no. 5 (2010): 416–50; Luciana Dar and Dong-Wook Lee, "Partisanship, Political Polarization, and State Higher Education Budget Outcomes," *The Journal of Higher Education* 85, no. 4 (2014): 469–98.

43. Barrett Taylor, Brendan Cantwell, Kimberly Watts, and Olivia Wood, "Partisanship, White Racial Resentment, and State Support for Higher Education," *The Journal of Higher Education* 91, no. 6 (2020): 858–87.

CHAPTER 7

1. W. E. B. Du Bois, "The Talented Tenth," in *The Negro Problem*, ed. Booker T. Washington (New York: James Pott, 1903), 33–34.
2. Ibid.
3. Ibid.
4. See Frances F. Piven and Richard Cloward, *Regulating the Poor: The Functions of Public Welfare* (New York: Pantheon Books, 1993) (first published 1971); Fabio Rojas, "Social Movement Tactics, Organizational Change and the Spread of African-American Studies," *Social Forces* 84, no. 4 (2006): 2147–66; Vesla Weaver, "Frontlash: Race and the Development of Punitive Crime Policy," *Studies in American Political Development* 21, no. 2 (2007): 230–65; Martha Biondi, *The Black Revolution on Campus* (Berkeley: University of California Press, 2012); Ibram Kendi, *The Black Campus Movement: Black Students and the Racial Reconstitution of Higher Education, 1965–1972* (New York: Palgrave Macmillan, 2012).
5. C. J. Libassi, "The Neglected College Race Gap: Racial Disparities Among College Completers," Center for American Progress (May 23, 2018). https://www.americanprogress.org/issues/education-postsecondary/reports/2018/05/23/451186/neglected-college-race-gap-racial-disparities-among-college-completers/; Anthony Carnevale, Megan Fasules, Andrea Porter, and Jennifer Landis-Santos, "African Americans College Majors and Earnings" (Washington, DC: Center on Education and the Workforce. Georgetown University, 2016). https://cew.georgetown.edu/cew-reports/african-american-majors/#resources.
6. Suzanne Mettler, *Degrees of Inequality: How the Politics of Higher Education Sabotaged the American Dream* (New York: Basic Books, 2014), 11.
7. Sara Goldrick-Rab, *Paying the Price: College Costs, Financial Aid, and the Betrayal of the American Dream* (Chicago: University of Chicago Press, 2016).
8. Emma Kerr, "See 10 Years of Average Total Student Loan Debt," *US News and World Report*, September 15, 2020. https://www.usnews.com/education/best-colleges/paying-for-college/articles/see-how-student-loan-borrowing-has-risen-in-10-years.
9. Julie M. Morgan and Steinbaum, Marshall, *The Student Debt Crisis, Labor Market Credentialization, and Racial Inequality: How the Current Debt Debate Gets the Economics Wrong* (New York: Roosevelt Institute, October 2018); Raphaël Charron-Chénier, Louise Seamster, Thomas M. Shapiro, and Laura Sullivan, "A Pathway to Racial Equity: Student Debt Cancellation Policy Designs," *Social Currents* 9, no. 5 (2021): Article no. 232949652110246. https://doi.org/10.1177/23294965211024671.
10. Julie M. Morgan and Steinbaum, Marshall, *The Student Debt Crisis, Labor Market Credentialization, and Racial Inequality: How the Current Debt Debate Gets the Economics Wrong* (New York: Roosevelt Institute, October 2018), 30.
11. For a review of scholarship on student loan debt, see Elizabeth Tandy Shermer, "The Student Debt Crisis and Its Deniers," *Public Books*, March 15, 2017. https://www.publicbooks.org/the-student-debt-crisis-and-its-deniers/.
12. Jessica Dickler, "Free College Could be a Reality under a Biden Administration," *CNBC*, November 10, 2020. https://www.cnbc.com/2020/11/10/free-college-could-be-a-reality-under-a-biden-administration.html.

13. Neil Vigdor and Johnny Diaz, "More Colleges Are Waiving SAT and ACT Requirements," *New York Times*, May 21, 2020. https://www.nytimes.com/article/sat-act-test-optional-colleges-coronavirus.html.

14. Kelly Ochs Rosinger, "If You Thought Colleges Making the SAT Optional Would Level the Playing Field, Think Again," *The Conversation*, January 19, 2018. https://theconversation.com/if-you-thought-colleges-making-the-sat-optional-would-level-the-playing-field-think-again-89896.

15. Sam Baker, "Affirmative Action is at Death's Door at the Supreme Court," *Axios*, October 31, 2022. https://www.axios.com/2022/10/30/affirmative-action-supreme-court-harvard-unc

16. Stephanie Kelton, *The Deficit Myth: Modern Monetary Theory and the Birth of the People's Economy* (New York: Public Affairs, 2020).

17. MMT scholars caution that inflation must be taken seriously. A major argument among MMT scholars is that as long as government spending on creating jobs leads to the production of goods and services, inflation can be controlled. Additionally, MMT scholars have proposed a series of measures to curb inflation that include the government setting a nominal wage for the employees hired by the government, the use of taxation particularly for the highest earners to control the circulation of currency, and "tightening financial and credit regulations to reduce bank lending, market finance, speculation and fraud." See Scott Fullwiler, Rohan Grey, and Nathan Tankus, "An MMT Response on What Causes Inflation," *Financial Times*, March 1, 2019. https://www.ft.com/content/539618f8-b88c-3125-8031-cf46ca197c64; Dylan Matthews, "Modern Monetary Theory, Explained: A Very Detailed Walkthrough of the Big New Left Economic Idea," *Vox*, April 16, 2019. https://www.vox.com/future-perfect/2019/4/16/18251646/modern-monetary-theory-new-moment-explained; L. Randall Wray, *Understanding Modern Money: The Key to Full Employment and Price Stability* (Northampton, MA: Edward Elgar, 1998); Kelton, *Deficit Myth*.

18. L. Randall Wray, Flavia Dantas, Scott Fullwiler, Pavlina Tcherneva, and Stephanie Kelton, "Public Sector Employment: A Path to Full Employment," Levy Economics Institute of Bard College (April 2018).

19. Wray, *Understanding Modern Money*

20. Kelton, *Deficit Myth*, 255.

21. See Pavlina Tcherneva, *The Case for a Job Guarantee* (Cambridge, UK: Polity Press, 2020).

22. Drew Desilver, "Black Unemployment Rate Is Consistently Twice That of Whites," *Pew Research Center*, August 21, 2013. https://www.pewresearch.org/fact-tank/2013/08/21/through-good-times-and-bad-black-unemployment-is-consistently-double-that-of-whites/.

EPILOGUE

1. Larry Buchanan, Quoctrung Bui, and Jugal K. Patel, "Black Lives Matter May Be the Largest Movement in U.S. History," *New York Times*, July 3, 2020. https://www.nytimes.com/interactive/2020/07/03/us/george-floyd-protests-crowd-size.html.

2. Ibid.

3. "Are You Exhausted Yet?: A Message to Administration." Letter from Black staff members at the University of Rhode Island to President David Dooley, June 15, 2020.

4. Elmer E. Schattschneider, *Politics, Pressures and the Tariff: A Study of Free Private Enterprise in Pressure Politics, as Shown in the 1929–1930 Revision of the Tariff* (New York: Prentice-Hall, 1935); Paul Pierson, "When Effect Becomes Cause: Policy Feedback and Political Change," *World Politics* 45, no. 4 (1993): 595–628; Andrea Campbell, "Self-Interest, Social Security, and the Distinctive Participation Patterns of Senior Citizens," *American Political Science Review* 96, no. 3 (2002): 565–74; Suzanne Mettler, "Bringing the State back in to Civic Engagement: Policy Feedback Effects of the GI Bill for World War II Veterans," *American Political Science Review* 96, no. 2 (2002): 351–65; Suzanne Mettler and Joe Soss, "The Consequences of Public Policy for Democratic Citizenship: Bridging Policy Studies and Mass Politics," *Perspectives on Politics* 2, no. 1 (2004): 55–73.

5. Campbell, "Self-Interest, Social Security, and the Distinctive Participation Patterns of Senior Citizens."

6. Joe Soss, "Lessons of Welfare: Policy Design, Political Learning, and Political Action," *American Political Science Review* 93, no. 2 (1999): 363–80; Amy Lerman and Vesla Weaver, *Arresting Citizenship: The Democratic Consequences of American Crime Control* (Chicago: University of Chicago Press, 2014); Jamila Michener, *Fragmented Democracy: Medicaid, Federalism, and Unequal Politics* (New York: Cambridge University Press, 2018).

7. Suzanne Mettler, *Soldiers to Citizens: The G.I. Bill and the Making of the Greatest Generation* (New York: Oxford University Press, 2007).

8. Ibid., 9.

9. Deondra Rose, *Citizens by Degree: Higher Education Policy and the Changing Gender Dynamics of American Citizenship* (New York: Oxford University Press, 2018).

10. Sidney Verba, Kay Lehman Schlozman, and Henry Brady, *Voice and Equality: Civic Voluntarism in American Politics* (Cambridge, MA: Harvard University Press, 1995).

11. Sally Nuamah, "The Cost of Participating while Poor and Black: Toward a Theory of Collective Participatory Debt," *Perspectives on Politics* 19, no. 4 (2021): 1115–30.

12. Ibid., 1115.

Aaronson, Daniel and Katherine Meckel. "The Impact of Baby Boomer Retirements on Teacher Labor Markets." *The Federal Reserve Bank of Chicago* No. 254 (September 2008). https://www.chicagofed.org/publications/chicago-fed-letter/2008/september-254.

Alt, James, and Robert Lowry. 1994. "Divided Government, Fiscal Institutions, and Budget Deficits: Evidence from the States." *American Political Science Review* 94, no. 4: 811–28.

Appelbaum, Binyamin. 2019. *The Economists' Hour: False Prophets, Free Markets, and the Fracture of Society*. New York: Little Brown.

Baker, Sam. 2022. "Affirmative Action is at Death's Door at the Supreme Court." *Axios*, October 31. https://www.axios.com/2022/10/30/affirmative-action-supreme-court-harvard-unc.

Baker, Scott. 1995. "Testing Equality: The National Teacher Examinations and the NAACP's Legal Campaign to Equalize Teachers' Salaries in the South, 1936–63." *History of Education Quarterly* 35, no. 1: 49–64.

Bennett, Christine, Lynn McWhorter, and John Kuykendall. 2006. "Will I Ever Teach? Latino and African American Students' Perspectives on PRAXIS I." *American Educational Research Journal* 43, no. 3: 531–75.

Berger Coli, Waltraud, and Richard Lobban. 1990. *Cape Verdeans in Rhode Island: A Brief History.* Providence: Rhode Island Heritage Commission and Rhode Island Publications Society.

Biondi, Martha. 2012. *The Black Revolution on Campus.* Berkeley: University of California Press.

Biskupic, Joan. 1997. "On Race, a Court Transformed." *Washington Post*, December 15, A01. https://www.washingtonpost.com/wp-srv/politics/special/affirm/stories/aa121597.htm.

Bradley, Stefan. 2018. *Upending the Ivory Tower: Civil Rights, Black Power, and the Ivy League.* New York: New York University Press.

Bristol, Travis, and Javier Martin-Fernandez. 2019. "The Added Value of Latinx and Black Teachers for Latinx and Black Students: Implications for Policy." *Policy Insights from the Behavioral and Brain Sciences* 6, no. 2: 147–53.

Buchanan, Larry, Quoctrung Bui, and Jugal K. Patel. 2020. "Black Lives Matter May Be the Largest Movement in U.S. History." *New York Times*, July 3. https://www.nytimes.com/interactive/2020/07/03/us/george-floyd-protests-crowd-size.html.

Butler, Johnny. 1974. "Black Educators in Louisiana-A Question of Survival." *The Journal of Negro Education* 43, no. 1: 9–24.

Campbell, Andrea. 2002. "Self-Interest, Social Security, and the Distinctive Participation Patterns of Senior Citizens." *American Political Science Review* 96, no. 3: 565–74.

Carbone, Gerald. 1992. "300 Students Hold Building at URI to Protest." *Providence Journal*, November 11, 1992, A–01.

Carbone, Gerald. 1992. "Racism Pervasive at URI, Adviser Asserts." *Providence Journal*, November 3, 1992, A–03.

Carbone, Gerald. 1992. "Study of Attitudes at URI Accuses Police of Racism." *Providence Journal*, September 15, 1992, A–03.

Carbone, Gerald. 1992. "URI Minority Group Gets Answers." *Providence Journal*, November 13, 1992, A–01.

Carbone, Gerald. 1998. "Cruel Fate Was No Match for a Determined URI Student." *Providence Journal*, May 17, 1998, A-1.

Card, David, and Thomas Lemieux. 2001. "Going to College to Avoid the Draft: The Unintended Legacy of the Vietnam War." *The American Economic Review* 91, no. 2: 97–102.

Carnevale, Anthony, Megan Fasules, Andrea Porter, and Jennifer Landis-Santos. 2016. "African Americans College Majors and Earnings, 1–12." Washington, DC: Center on Education and the Workforce, Georgetown University. https://cew.georgetown.edu/cew-reports/african-american-majors/#resources.

Carter, Zachary. 2020. *The Price of Peace: Money, Democracy, and the Life of John Maynard Keynes.* New York: Random House.

Charron-Chénier, Raphaël, Louise Seamster, Thomas M. Shapiro, and Laura Sullivan. 2021. "A Pathway to Racial Equity: Student Debt Cancellation Policy Designs." *Social Currents* 9, no. 5: Article no. 232949652110246.https://doi.org/10.1177/2329496521 1024671.

City of Providence Human Relations Commission. 2018 Annual Report. http://www.providenceri.gov/wp-content/uploads/2016/08/PHRC-Annual-Report-2018.pdf.

Cohen, Cathy. 1999. *The Boundaries of Blackness: AIDS and the Breakdown of Black Politics.* Chicago: University of Chicago Press.

Cole, Beverly. 1984. "Testing Blacks Out of Education and Employment." *The Crisis* 92, no. 9. 8–11.

Cole, Beverly. 1986. "The Black Educator: An Endangered Species." *The Journal of Negro Education* 55, no. 3: 326–34.

Collins, Randall. 1975. *Conflict Sociology: Toward an Explanatory Science.* New York: Academic Press.

Collins, Randall. 1979. The Credential Society: An Historical Sociology of Education and Stratification. New York: Academic Press.

Dar, Luciana, and Dong-Wook Lee. 2014. "Partisanship, Political Polarization, and State Higher Education Budget Outcomes." *The Journal of Higher Education* 85, no. 4: 469–98.

Dee, Thomas. 2004. "Teachers, Race and Student Achievement in a Randomized Experiment." *The Review of Economics and Statistics* 86, no. 1, 195–210.

Dennis, Lawrence, and William Eaton. 1979. "Equal Justice: The Alston Case." *The Negro Educational Review* 30, no. 1: 4–11.

Desilver, Drew. 2013. "Black Unemployment Rate Is Consistently Twice that of Whites." *Pew Research Center.* August 21. https://www.pewresearch.org/fact-tank/2013/08/21/through-good-times-and-bad-black-unemployment-is-consistently-double-that-of-whites/.

Dickler, Jessica. 2020. "Free College Could Be a Reality under a Biden Administration." *CNBC*, November 10. https://www.cnbc.com/2020/11/10/free-college-could-be-a-reality-under-a-biden-administration.html.

Du Bois, W. E. B. 1903. "The Talented Tenth." In *The Negro Problem*. Edited by Booker T. Washington, 31–75. New York: James Pott.

Dujardin, Richard C., and Gerald Carbone. 1992. "Hundreds at URI Protest Racism." *Providence Journal*, November 10, 1992, A–01.

Dunn, Christine. 2015. "Fox Point Neighborhood: A Walk on the Historic Side." *Providence Journal*, May 24, 2015. https://www.providencejournal.com/article/20150524/NEWS/150529698.

Dynan, Linda. 2007. "The Impact of Medical Education Reform on the Racial Health Status Gap, 1920–1930: A Difference-in-Difference Analysis." *The Review of Black Political Economy* 34, no. 3–4: 245–58.

Egerton, John. 1968, April. "Higher Education for 'High Risk' Students": A Report from the Southern Education Foundation. Atlanta, Georgia.

Enos, Ryan, Aaron Kaufman, and Melissa Sands. 2019. "Can Violent Protest Change Local Policy Support? Evidence from the Aftermath of the 1992 Los Angeles Riot." *American Political Science Review* 113, no. 4: 1012–28.

Fairclough, Adam. 2007. *A Class of Their Own: Black Teachers in the Segregated South.* Cambridge, MA: Harvard University Press.

Finck, John. 1984. "The Hmong Resettlement Study Site Report: Providence, Rhode Island": Report Prepared by the Office of Refugee Resettlement. Washington, DC: U.S. Department of Health and Human Services. https://files.eric.ed.gov/fulltext/ED267161.pdf.

Fiske, Edward. 1986. "Ranks of Minority Teachers Are Dwindling, Experts Fear." *New York Times*, February 9, 1986, 1. https://www.nytimes.com/1986/02/09/us/ranks-of-minority-teachers-are-dwindling-experts-fear.html.

Fiske, Edward. 1988. "Teachers' Exam, Often Criticized, To Be Replaced." *New York Times*, October 28, 1988, sec. A, 1.

Fullwiler, Scott, Rohan Grey, and Nathan Tankus. 2019. "An MMT Response on What Causes Inflation." *Financial Times*, March 1, 2019. https://www.ft.com/content/539618f8-b88c-3125-8031-cf46ca197c64.

Fultz, Michael. 2004. "The Displacement of Black Educators Post-*Brown*: An Overview and Analysis." *History of Education Quarterly*, 44, no. 1: 11–45.

Geiger, Roger, and Donald Heller. 2012. "Financial Trends in Higher Education: The United States," *Educational Studies, Higher School of Economics* 3: 5–29.

Gilens, Martin. 2012. *Affluence and Influence: Economic Inequality and Political Power in America.* Princeton, NJ: Princeton University Press.

Givens, Jarvis. 2021. *Fugitive Pedagogy: Carter G. Woodson and the Art of Black Teaching.* Cambridge, MA: Harvard University Press.

Goldrick-Rab, Sara. 2016. *Paying the Price: College Costs, Financial Aid, and the Betrayal of the American Dream.* Chicago: University of Chicago Press.

Goldrick-Rab, Sara, Jed Richardson, Joel Schneider, Anthony Hernandez, and Clare Cady. 2018. "Still Hungry and Homeless in College." *Wisconsin Hope Lab.* https://www.theotx.org/wp-content/uploads/2018/05/Wisconsin-HOPE-Lab-Still-Hungry-and-Homeless.pdf.

Goldstein, Gerald S. 1994. "In the Minority at URI." *Providence Journal,* May 1, 1994, M–08.

Gordon, Lisa. 1987. "Southeast Asian Refugee Migration to the United States." In *Pacific Bridges: The New Immigration from Asia and the Pacific Islands.* Edited by James T. Fawcett and Benjamin V. Carino, 153–73. Staten Island, NY: Center for Immigration Studies.

Gray, Sonya. 1963. "Ala. Violence a Threat, R.I. Negro Pastor Says." *Providence Journal,* September 22, 1963, N-3.

Greenstone, David, and Paul Peterson. 1973. *Race and Authority in Urban Politics: Community Participation and the War on Poverty.* New York: Russell Sage.

Hacker, Jacob S. 2004. "Privatizing Risk without Privatizing the Welfare State: The Hidden Politics of Social Policy Retrenchment in the United States." *American Political Science Review* 98, no. 2: 243–59.

Harris, Fredrick. 2014. "The Rise of Respectability Politics." *Dissent Magazine.* https://www.dissentmagazine.org/article/the-rise-of-respectability-politics.

Heffner, Stephen. 1992. "URI Reassigns Man in Charge of Campus Affirmative Action." *Providence Journal,* April 17, 1992, B-03.

Heller, Donald E. 2004. "State Funding for Higher education: The Impact on College Access." Paper presented at the Symposium on Financing Higher Education, Illinois State University, Normal.

Heller, Donald E. 2002. "The Policy Shift in State Financial Aid Programs." In *Higher Education: Handbook of Theory and Research.* Vol. 17. Edited by J. C. Smart, 221–61. New York: Agathon Press.

Henry, Gary T., Shanyce L. Campbell, Charles L. Thompson, Linda A. Patriarca, Kenneth J. Luterbach, Diana B. Lys, and Vivian Martin Covington. 2013. "The Predictive Validity of Measures of Teacher Candidate Programs and Performance: Toward an Evidence-Based Approach to Teacher Preparation." *Journal of Teacher Education* 64, no. 5: 439–53.

Herbes, John. 1971. "Most States Plan Tax Increases Despite Efforts to Slash Costs." *New York Times,* February 9, 1971, 1. https://www.nytimes.com/1971/02/09/archives/most-states-plan-tax-increases-despite-efforts-to-slash-costs-most.html.

Higginbotham, Evelyn Brooks. 1993. *Righteous Discontent: The Women's Movement in the Black Baptist Church, 1880–1920.* Cambridge, MA: Harvard University Press.

Hinton, Elizabeth. 2015. *From the War on Poverty to the War on Crime: The Making of Mass Incarceration in America*. Cambridge, MA: Harvard University Press.

Hinton, Elizabeth. 2021. *America on Fire: The Untold History of Police Violence and Black Rebellion since the 1960s*. New York: Liveright.

Hudson, Mildred and Barbara Holmes. 1994. "Missing Teachers, Impaired Communities: The Unanticipated Consequences of *Brown v. Board of Education* on the African American Teaching Force at the Precollegiate Level." *Journal of Negro Education* 63, no. 3: 388–93.

Karabel, Jerome. 2006. *The Chosen: The Hidden History of Admission and Exclusion at Harvard, Yale, and Princeton*. Boston: Mariner Books.

Katznelson, Ira. 2005. *When Affirmative Action Was White: An Untold History of Racial Inequality in Twentieth-Century America*. New York: Norton.

Kelly, Grace. 2020, Fall. "The Fight for Justice: URI's History of Student-Led Civil Rights Activism." *University of Rhode Island Magazine*. https://www.uri.edu/magazine/iss ues/fall-2020/the-fight-for-justice/.

Kelton, Stephanie. 2020. *The Deficit Myth: Modern Monetary Theory and the Birth of the People's Economy*. New York: Public Affairs.

Kendi, Ibram. 2012. *The Black Campus Movement: Black Students and the Racial Reconstitution of Higher Education, 1965–1972*. New York: Palgrave Macmillan.

Kerner Commission. 1968. *Report of the National Advisory Commission on Civil Disorders*. Washington, DC: U.S. Government Printing Office.

Kerr, Emma. 2020. "See 10 Years of Average Total Student Loan Debt." *US News and World Report*, September 15, 2020. https://www.usnews.com/education/best-colleges/ paying-for-college/articles/see-how-student-loan-borrowing-has-risen-in-10-years.

Krasovic, Mark. 2016. *The Newark Frontier: Community Action in the Great Society*. Chicago: University of Chicago Press.

Langlois, Harold V., and Robert W. MacMillan. 1969, November 1. "Evaluation of Pre-Matriculation Program for Disadvantaged Students at the University of Rhode Island."

Lemann, Nicholas. 1999. *The Big Test: The Secret History of the American Meritocracy*. New York: Farrar, Straus and Giroux.

Lerman, Amy, and Vesla Weaver. 2014. *Arresting Citizenship: The Democratic Consequences of American Crime Control*. Chicago: University of Chicago Press.

Levy, Peter. 2018. *The Great Uprising: Race Riots in Urban American During the 1960s*. New York: Cambridge University Press.

Libassi, C. J. 2018, May 23. *The Neglected College Race Gap: Racial Disparities among College Completers*. Washington, DC: Center for American Progress. https://www. americanprogress.org/issues/education-postsecondary/reports/2018/05/23/451186/ neglected-college-race-gap-racial-disparities-among-college-completers/.

Lilley, Robert, Raymond Brown, John Dougherty, Alfred Driscoll, John Gibbons, Ben Leuchter, Oliver Lofton, Robert Meyner, Prince Taylor, and William Wachenfeld. 1968. *Governor's Select Commission on Civil Disorder*. Report for Action. New York: Lemma.

Loeb, Susanna, and Luke C. Miller. 2007. *A Review of State Teacher Policies: What Are They, What Are Their Effects, and What Are Their Implications for School Finance?*

Berkeley, CA: Institute for Research on Education Policy & Practice (IREPP) School of Education, Stanford University.

Long, Bridge T. 2013. "Supporting College Access to Education." In *Legacies of the War on Poverty*. Edited by Martha J. Bailey and Sheldon Danziger, 93–120. New York: Russell Sage Foundation.

Loss, Christopher. 2012. *Between Citizens and the State: The Politics of American Higher Education in the 20th Century*. Princeton, NJ: Princeton University Press.

Mathews, John. 1963. "Minority Programs Urged at Hearing." *Providence Journal*, November 5, 1963.

Matthews, Dylan. "Modern Monetary Theory, Explained: A Very Detailed Walkthrough of the Big New Left Economic Idea." *Vox*, April 16, 2019. https://www.vox.com/future-perfect/2019/4/16/18251646/modern-monetary-theory-new-moment-explained.

McCormick, Richard. 1990. *The Black Student Protest Movement at Rutgers*. New Brunswick, NJ: Rutgers University Press.

McLendon, Michael, Steven Deaton, and James Hearn. 2007. "The Enactment of Reforms in State Governance of Higher education: Testing the Political Instability Hypothesis." *The Journal of Higher Education* 78, no. 6: 645–75.

McLendon, Michael, James Hearn, and Christine Mokher. 2009. "Partisans, Professionals, and Power: The Role of Political Factors in State Higher Education Funding." *The Journal of Higher Education* 80, no. 6: 686–713.

McMillan Cottom, Tressie. 2017. *Lower Ed: The Troubling Rise of For-Profit Colleges in the New Economy*. New York: New Press.

McVicar, D. Morgan. 1992. "Carothers Markets URI to Assembly as a Vital Cog." *Providence Journal*, January 30, 1992, A–03.

Medley, Donald, and Thomas Quirk. 1974. "The Application of a Factorial Design to the Study of Cultural Bias in General Culture Items on the National Teaching Examinations." *Journal of Educational Measurements* 4: 235–45.

Mettler, Suzanne. 2002. "Bringing the State back in to Civic Engagement: Policy Feedback Effects of the GI Bill for World War II Veterans." *American Political Science Review* 96, no. 2: 351–65.

Mettler, Suzanne. 2007. *Soldiers to Citizens: The G.I. Bill and the Making of the Greatest Generation*. New York: Oxford University Press.

Mettler, Suzanne. 2014. *Degrees of Inequality: How the Politics of Higher Education Sabotaged the American Dream*. New York: Basic Books.

Mettler, Suzanne, and Joe Soss. 2004. "The Consequences of Public Policy for Democratic Citizenship: Bridging Policy Studies and Mass Politics." *Perspectives on Politics* 2, no. 1: 55–73.

Michener, Jamila. 2018. *Fragmented Democracy: Medicaid, Federalism, and Unequal Politics*. New York: Cambridge University Press.

Michener, Jamila, Mallory SoRelle, and Chloe Thurston. 2020. "From the Margins to the Center: A Bottom-Up Approach to Welfare State Scholarship." *Perspectives on Politics* 20, no. 1: 154–69. https://doi.org/10.1017/S153759272000359X.

Morel, Domingo. 2018. *Takeover: Race, Education, and American Democracy*. New York: Oxford University Press.

Morgan, Julie M., and Steinbaum, Marshall. 2018, October. *The Student Debt Crisis, Labor Market Credentialization, and Racial Inequality: How the Current Debt Debate Gets the Economics Wrong.* New York: Roosevelt Institute.

Morone, James. 1990. *The Democratic Wish: Popular Participation and the Limits of American Government.* New Haven, CT: Yale University Press.

Moynihan, Daniel. 1970. *Maximum Feasible Misunderstanding: Community Action in the War on Poverty.* New York: Free Press.

Murphy, Raymond. 1988. *Social Closure: The theory of Monopolization and Exclusion.* New York: Clarendon Press.

National Commission on Excellence in Education. 1983. *A Nation at Risk: The Imperative for Educational Reform: A Report to the Nation and the Secretary of Education.* Washington, DC: United States Department of Education.

Nuamah, Sally. 2021. "The Cost of Participating while Poor and Black: Toward a Theory of Collective Participatory Debt." *Perspectives on Politics* 19, no. 4: 1115–30.

O'Neill, Robert. 2018. "Young, Educated, and Upwardly Mobile: What Colleges Are Doing to Help Low-Income Students Climb the Economic Ladder." October 26. https://www.hks.harvard.edu/faculty-research/policy-topics/education-training-labor/young-educated-and-upwardly-mobile

Oakely, Deirdre, Jacob Stowell, and John Logan. 2009. "The Impact of Desegregation on Black Teachers in the Metropolis, 1970–2000." *Ethnic and Racial Studies* 39, no. 9: 1576–98.

Okechukwu, Amaka. 2019. *To Fulfill These Rights: Political Struggle Over Affirmative Action and Open Admissions.* New York: Columbia University Press.

Onkst, David. 1998. "First a Negro . . . Incidentally a Veteran: Black World War Two Veterans and G.I. Bill of Rights in the Deep South, 1944–1948." *Journal of Social History* 31, no. 3: 517–43.

Patashnik, Eric, and Julian E. Zelizer. 2013. "The Struggle to Remake Politics: Liberal Reform and the Limits of Policy Feedback in the Contemporary American State." *Perspectives on Politics* 11, no. 4: 1071–87.

Payne, Charles. 2008. "Introduction." In *Teach Freedom: Education for Liberation in the African-American Tradition.* Edited by Charles M. Payne and Carol Sills Strickland, 1–11. New York: Teachers College Press.

Pettit, Becky, Bryan Sykes, and Bruce Western. 2009. "Technical Report on Revised Population Estimates and NLSY79 Analysis Tables for the Pew Public Safety and Mobility Project." Cambridge, MA: Harvard University.

Phillips-Fein, Kim. 2017. *Fear City: New York's Fiscal Crisis and the Rise of Austerity Politics.* New York: Metropolitan Books.

Pierce, Richard, Robert Carkhuff, Bernard Berenson, Andrew Griffin, and Theodore Friel. 1972. *Special Program for Talent Development: A Consultation Report on Current Effectiveness and Future Direction.* Amherst, Massachusetts: Eastern Psychological, Educational and Community Services.

Pierson, Paul. 1993. "When Effect Becomes Cause: Policy Feedback and Political Change." *World Politics* 45, no. 4: 595–628.

Pierson, Paul. 1995. *Dismantling the Welfare State? Reagan, Thatcher and the Politics of Retrenchment.* New York: Cambridge University Press.

Piven, Frances F., and Cloward, Richard. 1993. *Regulating the Poor: The Functions of Public Welfare*. New York, NY: Pantheon Books. First published 1971.

Prison Policy Initiative. Rhode Island Profile. https://www.prisonpolicy.org/profiles/RI.html

Providence Journal. 1963. "Governor Plans to Set Up Civil Rights Task Force," June 27, 1963.

Providence Journal. 1964. "Judge Reverses Own Edict, Frees 9 Clergy." August 7, 1964, 3.

Providence Journal. 1966. "O'Connor Integration Plan Endorsed by Three Groups." November 17, 1966, 28.

Providence Journal. 1967. "Disturbances Quelled in South Providence." August 1, 1967, 1.

Providence Journal. 1967. "Shots Mark S. Providence Disturbances." August 2, 1967, 1.

Providence Journal. 1968. "Watch Society Urged as a Riot Preventative." April 3, 1968, 31.

Providence Journal. 1968. "College Board Getting Plan for Negroes." May 1, 1968, 1.

Providence Journal. 1968. "Minister Fills New State Post." July 26, 1968, 37.

Providence Journal. 1968. "Four Colleges Accept Special Student Group." August 8, 1968, 45.

Providence Journal. 1968. "Racism Is Topic of URI Panel: Antipoverty Official Urges Whites to Change Attitude." November 13, 1968, 5.

Providence Journal. 1969. "New Vice President for RIC Is Approved." June 6, 1969, 3.

Providence Journal. 1969. "Tutoring Program Impresses Garrahy." August 7, 1969, 14.

Providence Journal. 1969. "Head of Center at URI Named." September 4, 1969, 11

Providence Journal. 1969. "School Board Oks Tutoring Proposal." September 12, 1969, 25.

Providence Journal. 1969. "URI Plan Salvages Students." October 6, 1969, 27.

Providence Journal. 1971. "Lawmen Wade into Throng of Students; Clear URI Building." May 6, 1971, 1.

Providence Journal. 1971. "Licht Sworn In, Promises Task Force Study of State Education, Medical, Welfare Aid." January 6, 1971, 2.

Ransby, Barbara. 2005. *Ella Baker and the Black Freedom Movement: A Radical Democratic Vision*. Chapel Hill: University of North Carolina Press.

Ravitch, Diane. 1990. "Education in the 1980's: A Concern for 'Quality.'" *Education Week*, January 10, 1990. https://www.edweek.org/ew/articles/1990/01/10/09200009.h09.html.

Ravitch, Diane. 2003. *A Brief History of Teacher Professionalism: White House Conference on Preparing Tomorrow's Teachers*. Washington DC: U.S. Department of Education. https://www2.ed.gov/admins/tchrqual/learn/preparingteachersconference/ravitch.html.

Rhode Island Board of Trustees of State Colleges. *Public Higher Education in Rhode Island: 1968-69 Annual Report of the Board of Trustees of State Colleges*. Providence, Rhode Island: Rhode Island Board of Trustees of State Colleges.

Rizzo, Michael. 2008. "State Preferences for Higher Education Spending: A Panel Data Analysis, 1977-2001." In *What's Happening to Public Higher Education? The Shifting Financial Burden*. Edited by Ronald Ehrenberg, 3-36. Baltimore, MD: Johns Hopkins University Press.

Roberts, Wallace. 1967. "Racial Bias Discussion Bogs Down." *Providence Journal*, September 15, 1967, 1.

Roberts. Wallace. 1968. "R.I. Colleges Trustees Act to Help Negroes." *Providence Journal*, April 10, 1968, 1.

Roberts, Wallace. 1968. "Urban Educational Plan Okayed." *Providence Journal*. May 2, 1968.

Rojas, Fabio. 2006. "Social Movement Tactics, Organizational Change and the Spread of African-American Studies." *Social Forces* 84, 4: 2147–66.

Rose, Deondra. 2018. *Citizens by Degree: Higher Education Policy and the Changing Gender Dynamics of American Citizenship*. New York: Oxford University Press.

Rosinger, Kelly Ochs. 2018. "If You Thought Colleges Making the SAT Optional Would Level the Playing Field, Think Again." *The Conversation*, January 19, 2018. https://thec onversation.com/if-you-thought-colleges-making-the-sat-optional-would-level-the-playing-field-think-again-89896.

Sadovnik, Alan. 1994. *Equity and Excellence in Higher Education: The Decline of a Liberal Educational Reform*. New York: Peter Lang.

Saucier, P. Khalil. 2011. "Liberian Immigrants in Rhode Island: The Trauma, the Bliss, and the Dilemma." *Ìrìnkèrindò: A Journal of African Migration* 5(December): 29–54.

Schattschneider, Elmer E. 1935. *Politics, Pressures and the Tariff: A Study of Free Private Enterprise in Pressure Politics, as Shown in the 1929–1930 Revision of the Tariff*. New York: Prentice-Hall.

Schickler, Eric. 2001. *Disjointed Pluralism: Institutional Innovation in the U.S. Congress*. Princeton, NJ: Princeton University Press.

Sears, David O., and John B. McConahay. 1973. *The Politics of Violence: The New Urban Blacks and the Watts Riot*. Boston: Houghton Mifflin.

Shepherd, George. 2003. "No African-American Lawyers Allowed: The Inefficient Racism of the ABA's Accreditation of Law Schools." *Journal of Legal Education 53*, no. 1: 103–56.

Shermer, Elizabeth Tandy. 2017. "The Student Debt Crisis and Its Deniers." *Public Books*, March 15, 2017. https://www.publicbooks.org/the-student-debt-crisis-and-its-deniers/.

Slabodian, Quinn. 2018. *Globalists: The End of Empire and the Birth of Neoliberalism*. Cambridge, MA: Harvard University Press.

Slaton, Amy. 2010. *Race, Rigor, and Selectivity in U.S. Engineering: The History of an Occupational Color Line*. Cambridge, MA: Harvard University Press.

Soss, Joe. 1999. "Lessons of Welfare: Policy Design, Political Learning, and Political Action." *American Political Science Review* 93, no. 2: 363–80.

Spencer, Robert C. #2—Interview and Memoir. 1983. The Oral History Collection of the University of Illinois at Springfield. Illinois Digital Archives. http://www.idaillinois. org/digital/collection/uis/id/4149

Starr, Paul. 1982. *The Social Transformation of American Medicine: The Rise of Sovereign Profession and the Making of a Vast Industry*. New York: Basic Books.

Stewart, Joseph, Kenneth Meier, and Robert England. 1989. "In Quest of Role Models: Change in Black Teacher Representation in Urban School Districts, 1968–1986." *The Journal of Negro Education* 58, no. 2: 140–52.

Streeck, Wolfgang, and Kathleen Thelen. 2005. "Introduction: Institutional Change in Advanced Political economies." In *Beyond Continuity: Institutional Change in*

Advanced Political Economies. Edited by Wolfgang Streeck and Kathleen Thelen, pp. 1–39. New York: Oxford University Press.

Sugrue, Thomas. 1996. *The Origins of the Urban Crisis: Race and Inequality in Postwar Detroit.* Princeton, NJ: Princeton University Press

Tandberg, David. 2010. "Politics, Interest Groups and State Funding of Public Higher Education." *Research in Higher Education* 51, no. 5: 416–50.

Taylor, Barrett, Brendan Cantwell, Kimberly Watts, and Olivia Wood. 2020. "Partisanship, White Racial Resentment, and State Support for Higher Education." *The Journal of Higher Education* 91, no. 6: 858–87.

Tcherneva, Pavlina. 2020. *The Case for a Job Guarantee.* Cambridge, UK: Polity Press.

Thomas, Clive, and Ronald Hrebenar. 2004. "Interest Groups in the States." In *Politics in the American States: A Comparative Analysis*, 8th ed. Edited by Virgina Gray and Russell Hanson, 100–128. Washington, DC: CQ Press.

Thompson, Joel, and Arthur Felts. 1992. "Politicians and Professionals: The Influence of State Agency Heads in Budgetary Success." *The Western Political Quarterly* 45, no. 1: 153–68.

Thompson, Owen. 2019. "School Desegregation and Black Teacher Employment." NBER Working Paper No. 25990.

Tillman, Linda. 2004. "(Un)intended Consequences? The Impact of the *Brown v. Board of Education* Decision on the Employment Status of Black Educators." *Education and Urban Society* 36, no. 3: 280–303.

Tyler, Linda, Brooke Whiting, Sarah Ferguson, Segun Eubanks, Jonathan Steinberg, Linda Scatton, and Katherine Bassett. 2011. *Toward Increasing Teacher Diversity: Targeting Support and Intervention for Teacher Licensure Candidates.* Princeton, NJ: Education Testing Service and the National Education Association.

U.S. Department of Education. 2014. "Historical Summary of Faculty, Enrollment, Degrees Conferred, and Finances in Degree-Granting Postsecondary Institutions: Selected years, 1869–70 through 2013–14." https://nces.ed.gov/programs/digest/d15/tables/dt15_301.20.asp.

U.S. Department of Education. National Center for Education Statistics. 2016. "Bachelor's Degrees Conferred by Postsecondary Institutions, by Race/Ethnicity and Field of Study: 2014–15 and 2015–16, Table 322.30." https://nces.ed.gov/programs/digest/d17/tables/dt17_322.30.asp.

U.S. Department of Labor. Executive Order 11246—Equal Employment Opportunity. https://www.dol.gov/agencies/ofccp/executive-order-11246/ca-11246.

University of Rhode Island Faculty Senate. 1968. "Admission Policy." Faculty Senate Bills. Paper 22. http://digitalcommons.uri.edu/facsen_bills/22.

Urban, Wayne. 2000. *Gender, Race and the National Education Association: Professionalism and its Limitations.* New York: Routledge.

Valdes, Juan G. 1995. *Pinochet's Economists: The Chicago School in Chile.* New York: Cambridge University Press.

Vera Institute of Justice. State Incarceration Trends: Rhode Island. https://www.vera.org/downloads/pdfdownloads/state-incarceration-trends-rhode-island.pdf.

Verba, Sidney, Kay Lehman Schlozman, Henry Brady. 1995. *Voice and Equality: Civic Voluntarism in American Politics.* Cambridge, MA: Harvard University Press.

Vigdor, Neil, and Johnny Diaz. 2020. "More Colleges Are Waiving SAT and ACT Requirements." *New York Times*, May 21, 2020. https://www.nytimes.com/article/sat-act-test-optional-colleges-coronavirus.html.

Wakefield, Dara. 2003. "Screening Teacher Candidates: Problems with High-Stakes Testing." *The Educational Forum*, 67, no. 4: 380–88.

Walton Jr., Hanes. 1969. "The Politics of Negro Educational Associations." *The Negro Educational Review* 20, no. 1: 34–41.

Warikoo, Natasha. 2016. *The Diversity Bargain: And Other Dilemmas of Race, Admissions, and Meritocracy at Elite Universities*. Chicago: University of Chicago Press.

Wasow, Omar. 2020. "Agenda Seeding: How 1960s Black Protests Moved Elites, Public Opinion and Voting." *American Political Science Review* 114, no. 3 638–59.

Weaver, Vesla. 2007. "Frontlash: Race and the Development of Punitive Crime Policy." *Studies in American Political Development* 21, no. 2: 230–65.

Weber, Max. 1978. *Economy and Society: An Outline of Interpretive Sociology*. Berkeley: University of California Press. First published 1922.

Weeden, Kim. 2002. "Why Do Some Occupations Pay More than Others? Social Closure and Earnings Inequality in the United States." *American Journal of Sociology* 108, no. 1: 55–101.

White, E. Frances. 2001. *Dark Continent of Our Bodies: Black Feminism and the Politics of Respectability*. Philadelphia, PA: Temple University Press.

Wilson, Ann Jarvella. 1982. "Knowledge for Teachers: The Origin of the National Teacher Examination Program." Paper presented at the Annual Meeting of the American Education Research Association, March 31–April 4, Chicago, IL.

Witty, Elaine. 1982. *Prospects for Black teachers: Preparation, Certification, and Employment*. Washington, DC. ERIC Clearinghouse on teacher education.

Wong, Alia. 2019. "The U.S. Teaching Population Is Getting Bigger, and More Female Women now make up a larger share of educators than they have in decades." *The Atlantic*, February 20, 2019. https://www.theatlantic.com/education/archive/2019/02/the-explosion-of-women-teachers/582622/.

Wray, L. Randall. 1998. *Understanding Modern Money: The Key to Full Employment and Price Stability*. Northampton, MA: Edward Elgar.

Wray, L. Randall, Flavia Dantas, Scott Fullwiler, Pavlina Tcherneva, and Stephanie Kelton. 2018, April. "Public Sector Employment: A Path to Full Employment." New York: Levy Economics Institute of Bard College.

Young, Carol. 1971. "Black on Campus—How Much Progress?" *Providence Journal*, May 16, 1971, G-1.

For the benefit of digital users, indexed terms that span two pages (e.g., 52–53) may, on occasion, appear on only one of those pages.

Tables and figures are indicated by *t* and *f* following the page number